T0355147

Ways to be Blameworthy

There must be some connection between our deontic notions, rightness and wrongness, and our responsibility notions, praise- and blameworthiness. Yet traditional approaches to each set of concepts tend to take the other set for granted. This book takes an integrated approach to these questions, drawing on both ethics and responsibility theory, and thereby illuminating both sets of concepts. Elinor Mason describes this as 'normative responsibility theory': the primary aim is not to give an account of the conditions of agency, but to give an account of what sort of wrong action makes blame fitting. She presents a pluralistic view of both obligation and blameworthiness, identifying three different ways to be blameworthy, corresponding to different ways of acting wrongly.

First, ordinary blameworthiness is essentially connected to subjective wrongness, to acting wrongly by one's own lights. Subjective obligation, and ordinary praise and blame, apply only to those who are within our moral community, who understand and share our value system. By contrast, detached blame can apply even when the agent is outside our moral community, and has no sense that her act is morally wrong. In detached blame, the blame rather than the blameworthiness is fundamental. Finally, agents can take responsibility for some inadvertent wrongs, and thus become responsible. This third sort of blameworthiness, 'extended blameworthiness', applies when the agent understands the objective wrongness of her act, but has no bad will. In such cases, the social context may be such that the agent should take responsibility, and accept ordinary blame from the wronged party.

Elinor Mason is Professor of Philosophy at The University of California, Santa Barbara. She works on a wide range of issues in ethics, moral responsibility, and feminist philosophy.

Ways to be Blameworthy

Rightness, Wrongness, and Responsibility

Elinor Mason

OXFORD
UNIVERSITY PRESS

OXFORD
UNIVERSITY PRESS

Great Clarendon Street, Oxford, OX2 6DP,
United Kingdom

Oxford University Press is a department of the University of Oxford.
It furthers the University's objective of excellence in research, scholarship,
and education by publishing worldwide. Oxford is a registered trade mark of
Oxford University Press in the UK and in certain other countries

First published 2019
First published in paperback 2021

Published in the United States of America by Oxford University Press
198 Madison Avenue, New York, NY 10016, United States of America

British Library Cataloguing in Publication Data
Data available

Library of Congress Cataloging in Publication Data
Data available

ISBN 978-0-19-883360-4 (Hbk.)
ISBN 978-0-19-284354-8 (Pbk.)

Contents

Preface and Acknowledgements

I completed the first draft of this book while on research leave from Edinburgh University, on a Laurence S. Rockefeller Visiting Fellowship at the Center for Human Values at Princeton University. I am extremely grateful for the opportunity.

I am heavily indebted to many people, but a few stand out as being heroically helpful. Michael McKenna read several drafts and was unfailingly generous: this book has benefited enormously from his astute comments and suggestions. Gunnar Björnsson has not only discussed these ideas with me on numerous occasions, and read various sections at various points, but also arranged a workshop on the final draft in Gothenburg. I am incredibly grateful to him and to the other commentators on that occasion for their careful and insightful criticisms (Krister Bykvist, Andreas Brekke Carlsson, Ragnar Francén, Robert Hartman, Kristin Mickelson, and András Szigeti). I am also immensely grateful to Guy Fletcher for organizing a reading group on an early draft at the University of Edinburgh, and to the other participants (Matthew Chrisman, Guy Fletcher, Kieran Oberman, Euan MacDonald, Mike Ridge, Debbie Roberts, Simon Rosenqvist, and Patrick Todd). Both of these reading groups transformed my own understanding of what I wanted to say in various ways, and I feel very privileged to have had the chance to benefit from such impressive and willing interlocutors. I would also like to specially thank Matthew Talbert for extensive and constructive comments in his role as a reader for Oxford University Press, almost all of which I have gratefully incorporated into the final version.

There are many others who have helped me in various ways, reading and commenting on chapters, discussing the ideas at various stages, and providing general intellectual support and stimulation. I would particularly like to thank Luc Bovens, Ruth Chang, Stewart Cohen, Ben Colburn, Julia Driver, David Enoch, Fred Feldman, Alex Guerrero, Elizabeth Harman, Matt King, Tori McGeer, Jennifer Morton, Rik Peels, Doug Portmore, David Shoemaker, Holly Smith, Jonathan Spelman, and Monique Wonderly. I would also like to thank Peter Momtchiloff at Oxford University Press for advice and encouragement.

I have been fortunate in being invited to present sections of this work in various contexts, and I have learned a lot from comments and questions on those occasions. I would especially like to thank my colleagues in philosophy at Edinburgh, who have heard several iterations of these ideas and have tirelessly provided helpful feedback. I would also like to give special thanks to my fellow fellows and faculty at the University Center for Human Values at Princeton, for a wonderful sabbatical year in 2015–16. Additionally, I am very grateful to organizers and audiences at the University of West Virginia, University of Pennsylvania Law School, Fordham Law School, Glasgow University, University of York, Warwick University (CELPA), The Arizona Workshop on Normative Ethics, The New Orleans Workshop on Agency and Responsibility, University of Colorado, Boulder, The Responsibility Project at the University of Gothenburg, University of Oslo, and the St Andrews Workshop on Blame.

Some parts of this book draw on previously published work. My overall argument draws on my 2015 *Philosophical Studies* paper, where I originally sketched my account of different kinds of blameworthiness ('Moral Ignorance and Blameworthiness', *Philosophical Studies* 172 (11) (2015): 3037–57). Section 3 of Chapter 2 summarizes some arguments that I originally presented in my 'Do the Right Thing: An Account of Subjective Obligation' in Mark Timmons (ed.), *Oxford Studies in Normative Ethics*, Oxford University Press (2017): 117–37. The arguments of Chapter 6 draw on the arguments I presented in 'Moral Incapacity and Moral Ignorance' in Rik Peels (ed.), *Perspectives on Ignorance from Moral and Social Philosophy*, Routledge (2016): 30–51. The argument about taking responsibility that I present in Chapter 8 appears in 'Respecting Each Other and Taking Responsibility for our Biases' in earlier versions in Marina Oshana, Katrina Hutchison, and Catriona Mackenzie (eds.), *Social Dimensions of Moral Responsibility*, Oxford University Press (2018): 163–84. I am grateful to the publishers for granting permission to reuse material here.

Finally, I would like to thank my family. First, thank you to my father, Donald Mason, who introduced me to philosophy, and has been a constant source of encouragement, not to mention a careful reader and editor. I am very grateful and appreciative. Most of all, I thank my husband, Eric Freund, for endless love and support, and my children, Inez and Leon, for inspiration and joy.

1
Introduction

On a very simplistic view of blameworthiness, a view that nobody holds, we are always blameworthy when we act wrongly and always praise-worthy when we act rightly. Of course the relationship between rightness and wrongness on the one hand, and praise- and blameworthiness on the other, is more complex than that. Wrongness and blameworthiness must come apart to some extent, although perhaps not completely. It seems undeniable that it is possible to act wrongly without being blameworthy. Similarly, it seems obvious that one can act rightly without being praise-worthy, and not just because the bar for praiseworthiness seems higher than the bar for blameworthiness: clearly one can act rightly without deserving any credit at all.

On the other hand, there is surely some essential relationship between our moral concepts, rightness and wrongness, and our responsibility related concepts, like praiseworthiness and blameworthiness. To be praiseworthy must involve the idea that the agent has done something right—has acted rightly *in some sense*. And likewise, an agent who is blameworthy must have acted wrongly in some sense. My overall aim in this book is to shed light on our notions of praise- and blameworthiness. Clearly, moral praise- and blameworthiness must have something to do with the agent's relationship to right or wrong action. But what, exactly? We need to know what 'rightness' and 'wrongness' mean in this context. We should not take for granted that there is an independent account of rightness and wrongness that we can simply help ourselves to.

In this book I defend a pluralistic view of both our deontic concepts and our responsibility concepts. I argue that there are three different ways to be blameworthy: ordinary blameworthiness, detached blame-worthiness, and extended blameworthiness. The first way is closest to the way that we ordinarily think of praise- and blameworthiness, and so I call it 'ordinary praiseworthiness and blameworthiness', and refer correspondingly to 'ordinary praise and blame'. I argue that ordinary praise- and blameworthiness are essentially connected to a particular conception of rightness and wrongness, that which is used in subjective obligation.[1] Agents are blameworthy in the ordinary way when they have acted wrongly by their own lights. Subjective obligation and ordinary blameworthiness apply only to those who are within our moral community, that is to say, those who understand and share our value system. By contrast, the second sort of blameworthiness, detached blameworthiness, can apply even when the agent is outside our moral community, and has no sense that her act is morally wrong. We blame agents for acting objectively wrongly, even if we do not have any view about their state of mind in so doing. Finally, I argue for a third sort of blameworthiness, extended blameworthiness, which applies in some contexts where the agent has acted wrongly, and understands the wrongness, but has acted wrongly entirely inadvertently. In such cases the agent is not personally at fault in the ordinary sense, but, I argue, the social context may be such that she should take responsibility.

1. Methodology

The methodology I use in coming to this account of how we should use our concepts is a sort of reflective equilibrium. We need to think both about the way we actually use these concepts and about what we want from them. We want our concepts to be clear and well defined, we want as many as we need, we want to be able to make some fairly fine-grained distinctions, and of course we want them to serve the purpose that we have them for. We might end up doing some conceptual engineering: adjusting our concepts to better suit our needs. On one common view, a view I share, both our moral concepts and our responsibility concepts are there to regulate and make sense of our interpersonal engagement. We should decide on which concepts to use, and how to use them, on the basis of how those concepts function in our relationships.

[1] Throughout the book I assume that 'rightness', 'obligation', and 'ought' are corollaries, and likewise for the converses, 'wrongness', 'prohibition', and 'ought-not'. I am aware that, pragmatically, 'ought' seems less strong than 'obligation', and similarly, 'ought-not' seems less strong than 'prohibition', but I set that complication aside here.

The project that I am engaged in straddles ethics and moral responsibility. Insofar as it is ethics, what I am doing might be described as falling into the field known as 'normative ethics', to be contrasted with 'meta-ethics'. By that I mean that I am not primarily concerned with the ultimate truthmakers for claims about rightness or wrongness. I am not arguing about relativism and realism. Rather, I am interested in what limits our deontic concepts and makes them proper deontic concepts: how the concepts of rightness and wrongness function, what the conditions are for ascribing them, and how they relate to other normative concepts. Likewise, though we do not tend to talk about 'meta-responsibility theory' and 'normative responsibility theory', I am doing normative responsibility theory. I am not concerned with questions about free will and determinism, but with *when* responsibility concepts are correctly attributed. My aim is to investigate how responsibility attributions interact with other responsibility concepts, and with normative concepts.[2]

Both normative ethics and meta-ethics are well developed as sub-disciplines and (although it is sometimes controversial) function independently. Normative ethicists ask questions about the subject matter of rightness and wrongness (Is lying wrong? Is harming wrong? Does animal suffering matter morally? What about the environment?) and also (the questions I am interested in) about the structural conditions that apply to the normative concepts (e.g. Can an agent act rightly or wrongly accidentally? Can non-agents act rightly or wrongly? Is rightness a maximizing notion?). In normative ethics it is common to take these questions seriously independently of any commitment to any of the various possible meta-ethical positions.

By contrast, the literature on free will and responsibility has focused much more on the meta issues, on whether we have free will and whether we might have moral responsibility even if we don't have free will.

---

[2] Much of the literature on moral responsibility is focused on the 'meta' debate—the debate about whether we can account for moral responsibility in the absence of free will. That includes the work of R. J. Wallace, who gives us an account of responsibility according to which an agent is responsible when it is appropriate to hold her responsible, and it is appropriate to hold her responsible when she has violated an obligation that we accept (1994). Wallace is arguing that this is what makes responsibility attributions true. Wallace's terminology is different to mine here: he has a normative account of responsibility in the sense that he thinks we should use normative considerations rather than factual ones to determine when someone is responsible.

Normative responsibility theory is in its infancy.[3] I am engaged in the project of normative theorizing about responsibility, which I take to be analogous to normative theorizing in ethics. I examine our deontic concepts, and explore their relationship to responsibility concepts, praise- and blameworthiness. I ask what the relationship is between these two sets of notions, how they limit each other, and what else shapes them.

I start with rightness and wrongness. Standards of right action are sensible—of interest to us—only if it is sometimes possible for us to meet the standard. No account of rightness would claim that it can be right to do things that are always impossible for us, such as teletransport. However, there is a further condition on a sensible account of right action: it must be reasonably easy to act rightly on purpose, at least under the right conditions. As I put it in this book, there is a 'responsibility constraint' that applies to all conceptions of rightness. That is just to say that useful deontic concepts must, to some degree (I will be giving an account of the various appropriate degrees) be related to what we could be responsible for.

There are different concepts of rightness and wrongness, and they differ in the extent to which they correlate with praise- and blameworthiness. I suspect that we most often use the concepts of rightness and wrongness in a moderately objective sense. I start by elucidating a useful objective concept of rightness that does not correlate exactly with praiseworthiness, but is not entirely independent of it. In other words, it meets a weak version of the responsibility constraint. It is not hyper-objective, but it is nonetheless an objective account of rightness, in that it is independent of the agent who is acting on that occasion.

---

[3] Gary Watson and Michael Zimmerman have, in different ways, done a lot of work on normative responsibility, though neither describes it as such. Michael McKenna (2012), Manuel Vargas (2013), and David Shoemaker (2015) all have recent books that seem to me to be clear examples of work on normative responsibility in my sense. McKenna focuses on the overall shape of our responsibility concepts, arguing that they must be seen as part of a communicative practice; Vargas likewise focuses on the overall shape, arguing that the background justification for particular practices is consequentialist. Shoemaker focuses on the correctness conditions for blame, giving a pluralist account of what sort of quality of will is relevant to responsibility. I contrast my account with Shoemaker's at various points, but the main difference is that whereas Shoemaker's is a sentimentalist account, arguing that there are various reactive attitudes that are fitting in response to various qualities of will in the blamee, mine is more radically pluralist. On my view there can be more to blameworthiness than quality of will, and more to blame than sentiment, and the fundamental sorting issue is the way in which the agent acted wrongly.

This leads to the important question, what is it that fundamentally makes agents praiseworthy or blameworthy? If an agent can act wrongly without being blameworthy, what is it that makes her blameworthy when she is blameworthy? This has historically been a question in the literature on free will and responsibility, and is associated with the notion of desert. The thought has been that we need to find something in virtue of which the agent deserves to be blamed, where the challenge is made harder if we think that to blame is to impose suffering. If determinism is true, if we are all at the mercy of causal forces, and not the source of our own actions in any deeply meaningful sense, it is notoriously hard to say how we could deserve blame.[4]

In this book I do not frame the issue in terms of desert. I provide an account of the conditions under which it is fitting to blame people. The account I give is consistent with various different views about desert, and about compatibilism and incompatibilism. My aim is to give a convincing story about the connections between acting wrongly in a certain way and being blameworthy. My story is not supposed to transcend or justify the normative realm: I am interested in the normative conditions of blame, the question of when it is appropriate to blame people within the terms of our practices, not the metaphysical conditions that might make blame appropriate.

I develop the idea that there is one special sense of wrongness, subjective wrongness, that correlates with ordinary blameworthiness. This is not the way we always use the term 'wrongness'. I think we usually use the terms 'rightness' and 'wrongness' in a moderately objective sense. But we do sometimes use deontic concepts in a way that suggests that to act wrongly is pretty much automatically to be blameworthy. For example, we might say that a doctor who randomly picks a medicine off the shelf acted wrongly, even if what she did turned out very well. What we mean is that, by her own lights, what she did was bad, and blameworthy. This is subjective wrongness. There has not been a huge amount of interest in or analysis of subjective rightness and wrongness.[5]

---

[4] See, for example Pereboom (2001) and elsewhere. Pereboom doubts that we can give an account of the normative conditions for blame that are anything but consequentialist. I do not address that head on in this book, but I give a non-consequentialist account.

[5] Holly Smith is an exception; I discuss her work in what follows. I refer to her views as presented in her published papers, but her arguments are developed in more detail in her book, *Making Morality Work*, in press as I write this.

I argue for an account of subjective rightness and wrongness, and I show that it does correlate with, and illuminate, our concepts of praise- and blameworthiness.

Our account of subjective rightness should capture our sense that what an agent does, from their own point of view, is what makes them praiseworthy. In a nutshell, I argue that to act subjectively rightly is to try to do well by morality. I show that trying to do well by morality relates to praise- and blameworthiness in the appropriate way. An agent who sincerely tries to do well by morality is praiseworthy (even if she goes astray in various ways), and an agent who fails to try to do well by morality is blameworthy. The equivalence between acting subjectively wrongly and being blameworthy is mutually explanatory. In understanding each in terms of the other, we make better sense of these ideas.

This picture is harmonious with a bigger picture, according to which our blaming practices are essentially interpersonal, and inextricably linked with the fact that we exist in a moral community with others.[6] We blame others in our moral community in an ordinary way when they knowingly do something that violates our moral standards. On my account ordinary blame makes sense because it attaches to subjective wrongdoing. In blaming in the ordinary way, we are appealing to the agent's own sense of what they ought to have done, by the light of the values we share. Those outside our moral community can be blamed, but in a very different way: they can be blamed with detached blame, which is not communicative.

In thinking about the conditions that make blame fitting, I look at both individual cases and the bigger picture. In ethics there are simpler and more complex accounts of the shape of our concepts, and the same is true in thinking about moral responsibility. In ethics, a wonderfully neat and simple account of the overall shape of our normative concepts is consequentialism. Notoriously, consequentialism clashes with our

---

[6] The idea that we should understand moral responsibility practices in terms of interpersonal interactions is of course due to P. F. Strawson (1962). See Shabo (2012) for a defence of the Strawsonian view that responsibility practices and relationships are deeply intertwined. Recent commentators have pointed out and developed Strawson's emphasis on the moral community, and the communicative aspects of our moral responsibility practices—see Watson (2004 and elsewhere), Hieronymi (2004), Darwall (2006), Scanlon (2008), McKenna (2012), and Macnamara (2015a). I draw on much of this work in what follows.

intuitions about particular cases. The price for theoretical neatness is intuitive implausibility in many situations. At the other extreme is Ross-style pluralism, which gives us plausible answers a lot of the time, but no pleasing theoretical neatness.

This same structure appears in thinking about responsibility, though as writers on responsibility do not usually think of things in this framework it is not as easy to characterize their views in these terms. Take debates about quality of will. One very neat sort of view says that all responsibility depends on quality of will. The justification for thinking about quality of will might be understood as a way of answering worries about metaphysical free will.[7] But we might also understand it as a contribution to normative theorizing: thinking about the justifying and unifying account of the substance of our responsibility practices—why do we hold P responsible but not Q? How do excuses work? And so on. Neater theories, that attempt to reduce all responsibility practice to one sort of quality of will are less able to match up with our pre-theoretical intuitions about cases. Messier, pluralistic theories do better at accommodating our messy intuitions, but of course must be marked down for lack of theoretical neatness.

I end up with a pluralistic view of both normative ethical concepts and responsibility concepts. I argue that reflecting on what we need from our responsibility practices allows some cases of blaming that are not based on quality of will. Sometimes we need to blame people for things that they have done with no bad quality of will at all. Here I am following Bernard Williams into the deep end of a pluralistic view. As Williams puts it:

Everywhere, human beings act, and their actions cause things to happen, and sometimes they intend those things, and sometimes they do not; everywhere, what is brought about is sometimes to be regretted or deplored, by the agent or by others who suffer from it or by both; and when that is so, there may be a demand made by himself, by others, or by both. Wherever all this is possible, there must be some interest in the agent's intentions, if only to understand what has

---

[7] Strawson is often interpreted as arguing that our reactions to quality of will in others are what make sense of our moral responsibility practices. Bennett (1980) certainly takes Strawson to be a projectivist, as do later commentators who take themselves to be improving on Strawson's projectivism by giving an account of when it is appropriate to have the reactive attitudes—Wallace (1994), Fischer and Ravizza (1998). My own view is that Strawson's most interesting contributions here should not be read as a contribution to the compatibilism/incompatibilism debate at all; rather, they are a contribution to normative responsibility theorizing.

happened . . . it must be a possible question how the intentions and actions of an agent at a given time fit in with, or fail to fit in with, his intentions and actions at other times . . .

These really are universal materials. What we must not suppose is that they are always related to one another in the same way or, indeed, that there is one ideal way in which they should be related to one another.   (1993, 55–6)

I think Williams is right about this. In the end, we cannot expect the four elements he speaks of, cause, intention, state of mind, and appropriate response, to relate in exactly the same way in every circumstance. I argue, in a Williams-esque vein, that we can be blameworthy for more than just what we intend, and for more than just what comes from our deep motivations. I argue that sometimes people should take responsibility for what they do through glitches or automated psychological processes.

2. The Arguments

In Chapter 2 I introduce the responsibility constraint, which is a way to put the claim that our normative concepts, rightness and wrongness, are essentially related to responsibility concepts. The responsibility constraint is vague as it stands, and in this chapter I explore various ways to cash out the fundamental thought.

I argue that there is a sensible objective account of rightness and wrongness that meets a fairly weak version of the responsibility constraint. The point of an objective account of rightness is to provide a general benchmark for behaviour, a standard that we should strive to meet. The account of objective rightness I favour, prospective rightness, does not abstract away from all uncertainty, but takes into account reasonable factual ignorance. Thus, when we look at what is prospectively right, we are thinking about what it would be reasonable to do in the circumstances. We are not just thinking about what would be best, but about what agents like us might be expected to do.

I then turn to the concept of rightness that I am really interested in, subjective rightness. I argue that the point of an account of subjective obligation is to give us a story about what makes the agent praise- or blameworthy. Objective obligation specifies a target, which the agent may or may not hit. Hitting the target would be good, but sometimes agents miss through no fault of their own. So even if we know that an agent fulfilled (or failed to fulfil) her objective obligation, we do not necessarily know how to appraise her. By contrast, the notion of subjective obligation identifies what it is in the agent's own psychology that renders her praise- or blameworthy.

There are two ideas that are associated with the notion of subjective obligation: that it should be action guiding, and that it should be accessible to the agent. I show that there are various complexities here. Subjective obligation can be neither fully action guiding, nor fully accessible. However, it is important that an account of subjective obligation is able to explain the plausibility and element of truth in these two ideas. The account I develop explains the limited sense in which subjective obligation is action guiding (I argue that the subjectively right thing to do genuinely ought to be done, there is a genuine imperative there, even if this is not always immediately helpful), and I argue that the accessibility requirement is limited in some ways, but that there is a general reflexivity requirement that is met, the agent must know what she is doing in that she must have background knowledge of her aim. This account makes sense of praise- and blameworthiness.

The standard way to formulate subjective rightness is in terms of the agent's beliefs: something like, 'an agent acts subjectively rightly when she does what she believes is the most morally suitable thing to do'. I argue that the belief formulation cannot make sense of a crucial element of our subjective obligation: our ongoing and continuous obligation to improve our beliefs, and to be alert to new evidence. If we base subjective obligation on belief, we cannot criticize an agent who acts on her current beliefs, even if those beliefs are faulty. I argue that in order to make sense of our duty to improve our beliefs we need a practical aim, and that is exactly what is involved in the concept of 'trying'. Thus our subjective obligation is not to do what we believe is morally suitable, but to try to do well by morality.

For both the belief formulation and the trying formulation of subjective obligation, there arises a question about whether we are talking about the value system that the agent happens to have, or the correct value system. I argue that for subjective rightness to align with praiseworthiness in the right sense, we need some sort of anchor in the correct moral view. (I initially defend this idea in Chapter 2 and develop the argument in Chapter 4). I argue that an agent acts subjectively rightly when she tries to do well by the standards of what *really is* morally appropriate. In other words, she has to get morality right. My account of subjective obligation thus depends on an agent having a grasp of the correct morality.

In the book I use a capital letter to denote that I am talking about the one true Morality, 'The True and the Good', as Susan Wolf calls it (1990).

I talk of this as if it is an objective meta-ethical fact, but that is just a way of talking. The view is not that this must be metaphysically real, rather the view is that we need to refer to our shared understanding of the moral facts. I leave it open to fill in the meta-ethical account of the status of these facts. All I need here is that it makes sense to us to talk about getting morality right and getting it wrong—and it clearly does, in sharp contrast to our views about the tastiness of Marmite, for example, which we obviously take to be a non-factive issue.

It is important to point out that my account of Morality is broad, and allows for reasonable error. One can 'have a grasp of Morality' in my sense without getting everything right. There is room for reasonable disagreement (I defend that in Chapter 2). Also, although I think that most people do have a grasp of Morality, I do not want to imply that people have all the answers at their fingertips. The claim is rather that people would assent to the main tenets of Morality if they thought through their most seriously held convictions and commitments, and that they can use their knowledge of Morality to figure out what to do on particular occasions.

In Chapter 3 I give an intuitive account of the sense of trying that I am interested in here. Acting subjectively rightly and trying are both subject to some sort of accessibility requirement. I argue that in the case of trying, this is best understood as a reflexivity requirement: the agent must know what she is doing. Trying to do something involves having the goal as a conscious aim. A flower is not trying to turn towards the sun and similarly, I argue, human behaviour may be causally affected by an aim without its being the case that the agent is trying to achieve that aim. At the same time, we can be trying to do things that we are not aware, *at the time*, of trying to do. Thus, surprisingly, it may sometimes be the case that we are acting subjectively rightly and do not know it, or believe that we are acting subjectively right but are not. I defend this consequence of my view by arguing that there is no theory that can fully meet an accessibility requirement, and so the accessibility requirement must be relaxed.

I use the concept of trying in a broad sense, so that it applies to doings as well as 'setting oneself'. When an agent is trying to do well by Morality, she must seek more information when necessary, including about the nature of Morality. It is essential that she has a good grasp of

Morality in the broad sense: her basic understanding of Morality gives her a framework for resolving uncertainties within Morality.

I conclude with an account of failing to try, which correlates with ordinary blameworthiness. It is important to be able to distinguish between failing to try and merely not trying. A lazy agent might not try to save a trapped kitten in a situation where she knows that there is a trapped kitten, and that counts as failing to try. But if the agent had no idea that the kitten was there, her *not* trying is not *failing* to try. Again, the crucial factor is knowledge. Someone who grasps Morality, and has it as an aim, can fail to try. Someone who does not grasp Morality may 'not try', but they do not count as failing to try. The reflexivity requirement, the idea that the agent must be able to recognize what she is doing, is essential to my account of the connection between subjective obligation and praise- and blameworthiness.

In Chapter 4, I give an account of ordinary praise- and blameworthiness, and show how these link up with subjective obligation. On my account, an agent is praiseworthy if she tries to do well by Morality. Praiseworthiness requires that the agent has Morality (at least broadly) correct. An agent is praiseworthy when she acts according to the true value system, not merely when she acts on her conscience. Correspondingly, an agent acts subjectively wrongly when she fails to try to do well by Morality.

I contrast my account with rival views of what is necessary and sufficient for praiseworthiness. On the one hand, there is a common view that being motivated in the right direction is sufficient for praiseworthiness. This is a view often held by attributionists, those who argue that choice and control are less important to moral responsibility than the deep motivations that drive an agent, or the agent's 'deep self' as it is often put.[8] On this sort of account, moral concern, or being motivation esteemworthy (in my terminology), is all that is needed for praiseworthiness: the agent might not know that her motivations are good, and might even think her motivations are leading her astray.

---

[8] The terminology is contested, but I will use the term 'attributionist' to refer to views that base moral responsibility for acts on the agent's deep character and motivations rather than on what she does knowingly. I am referring here to Arpaly and Schroeder's work on praise- and blameworthiness—see Arpaly and Schroeder (1999) and Arpaly (2003) in particular. As well as Arpaly and Schroeder's work, attributionism is developed (in various different ways) by Watson (1996, reprinted in 2004), Angela Smith (2005 and elsewhere), Scanlon (1998 and elsewhere), Sher (2009 and elsewhere), and Talbert (2008 and elsewhere).

I argue that this account fails to do justice to our ordinary account of praise- and blameworthiness. We do think that there is something to admire in people who have good motivations, but we do not think them fully praiseworthy. And so why not make a distinction here? We should agree that motivation esteemworthiness is a necessary component of praiseworthiness, but it is not the whole story: moral knowledge is also necessary. I argue that that is a better account of praiseworthiness and, in particular, it makes sense of the reflexivity requirement: the requirement that an agent be able to recognize the moral status of her own behaviour and judge her action as something she should or should not have done.

I also address a rival from the other end of the spectrum, the 'Searchlight' theorist, to use George Sher's term (2009), who argues that the only way to be blameworthy is to have full awareness of the wrongness of one's action, either at the time of action or at some earlier time from which the current action was predictable.[9] I argue that this takes the reflexivity requirement *too* seriously. On the best understanding of the reflexivity requirement, agents can be blameworthy just so long as it makes sense to say that they *should have known* what they were doing at the time. All this requires is a good grasp of Morality in general.

In Chapter 5 I discuss the nature of praise and blame. I argue that my account of ordinary praise- and blameworthiness meshes with an account of praise and blame as essentially communicative. I argue, using Michael McKenna's phrase (2012), that we should see praise and blame (though not necessarily the whole responsibility system) as being part of a conversation. Agents who are praise- or blameworthy in the ordinary way have the right background knowledge and background aim to engage in a meaningful conversation about their behaviour. Blame is a response to a certain sort of fault, and can involve a demand for acceptance of the blame, apology, remorse, reparation, and so on. The blamee who engages in the conversation should accept the blame, and be willing to move through the various steps of the conversation, to apologize, to make reparations, and eventually, in some but not all cases, to ask for and accept forgiveness. Praise is, perhaps surprisingly, roughly symmetrical. To praise someone is to open a sort of conversation with them,

[9] This sort of view is defended by Levy (2013 and elsewhere), Rosen (2002 and elsewhere), and Zimmerman (1997 and elsewhere).

and to make certain demands: chiefly the demand that the praise be accepted. What makes these exchanges possible is the shared moral community, the shared value system.

This leads to a discussion of another sort of praise and blame, which I call 'detached praise and blame'. These are reactive attitudes that we take to those who act wrongly, but without acting subjectively wrongly. Detached blame is not communicative. It is closer to what Strawson calls the 'objective attitude'. It does not demand an answer, it is an assessment of the agent's behaviour more than a demand that she behave better. Yet it is genuine blame, it is an emotional reaction to the agent that goes beyond a mere judgment of blameworthiness. Disdain and contempt are good examples of reactions that are often involved in detached blame. Furthermore, drawing on Scanlon's account of blame (2008), I argue that detached blame may involve a modification of the relationship: the blamer sees, not so much that something has been damaged in her relationship, but rather, that something that she might have hoped was possible is not in fact possible. The blamee does not have the attitudes that qualify her for proper interpersonal engagement.

As with ordinary blame and ordinary praise, detached blame and detached praise are symmetrical. We might see that someone has very good attitudes, or is deeply motivated towards good things, but if that person lacks a grasp of Morality; if they lack an awareness of the right-making features of their actions *qua* right-making features, then we cannot praise them in the ordinary way. However, we can think well of them, we can approve of them, we can admire them: we find them to be praiseworthy in the detached way.

In Chapter 6 I argue that the sorts of factor that count as excusing differ between the two sorts of blameworthiness. In the case of ordinary blameworthiness, the usual sort of excuse is a simple excuse: something that shows that the agent was not acting subjectively wrongly after all. There may also be partial excuses and mitigating circumstances, but, I argue, in the end they are also ways of showing that the agent was not acting as subjectively wrongly as it first appeared. In the case of detached blameworthiness, various factors that explain *why* the agent has a bad will can also function as an excuse. Thus, bad upbringing, bad social or epistemic environment, and so on, can be excuses, in the sense that they should undermine our detached blame responses. We come to see the agent as less of an agent when we reflect on the facts that explain their bad will, and retreat to an even more objective stance than that implied in detached blaming.

I have still not covered all of the terrain of wrongdoing and blameworthiness. There are mixed cases, cases where an agent has tried very hard, but still does badly. Someties, of course, the explanation for doing badly constitutes an excuse. If an agent is pushed, or is non-culpably ignorant, her efforts may not result in success, but it is clear that she is not blameworthy. Other cases are not so clear. An agent may have mixed motives: imagine an agent tries very hard to do well, and the explanation for her failure is that her own deep motivations are very poor. For example, an agent may try very hard to be calm and polite, but her deeply misanthropic character and vile temper get the better of her: she says mean things in an explosion of rage.

In mixed cases like that, we can say that the appropriate stance to take is complex. An agent can be in our moral community, and yet have a character trait, or tendency, that is not properly under her agential control. I argue that that doesn't mean that she has an excuse, the trait is still part of her agency, and thus we are bound to have some sort of blaming reaction. It is appropriate to think the agent praiseworthy in the ordinary way for trying hard, and even to praise her, but also to think that a local detached blameworthiness applies. This makes sense of the real complexity in our reactions: we would naturally disdain such agents for their bad traits, and modify our relationships accordingly, while still acknowledging that they are praiseworthy in the ordinary way for trying hard to do well by the right values.

This picture of the two sorts of blame takes very seriously the idea that moral community is an essential notion in understanding blame. Like Strawson, I think that relationships, both our fairly impersonal relationship with others in our moral community and our personal relationships, are essential to understanding how responsibility attributions and blameworthiness work. If someone is not in our moral community, the way in which we blame them changes, and rightly so. We cannot expect a response from someone who is outside our moral community.

In Chapter 7 I discuss exemptions from ordinary blameworthiness, and consider what exactly determines the boundaries of the realm of detached blame. In Chapter 4 I argued that moral knowledge is essential to ordinary blameworthiness. Here I focus on arguing that deep moral ignorance is sufficient for being outside our moral community, and in the realm of detached blame. Someone like Susan Wolf's JoJo (1987) may not lack any general capacities, or even any general moral capacities, but if he is deeply morally ignorant, he is not in our moral community, and communicative blame would be infelicitous.

I also address cases where the agent seems to have moral knowledge, but lacks a capacity to act well. I use Wolf's asymmetry thesis as a counterpoint, to argue that incapacity does not undermine either praise- or blameworthiness. So long as the agent is not acting in a compulsive or pathological way (in which case they would not be responsible at all for the act), an incapacity to act well, just like an incapacity to act badly, is consistent with being responsible and praise- or blameworthy. George Washington is said to have been unable to tell a lie. I argue that so long as he fully understood that lying was wrong, that fact that he had no option but to tell the truth does not undermine his praiseworthiness. Similarly, so long as someone understands Morality, and they are acting on their own volitions, they can be blameworthy, even if in a sense parallel to Washington's incapacity, they are incapable of acting well.

Finally, I consider what we might mean we talk about psychopaths, and I argue that one way to understand psychopathology is in terms of a lack of moral understanding, which would render psychopaths outside our moral community, and thus exempt from ordinary blame. It is conceivable that there are people who understand which things are right and wrong without understanding the way in which Morality is reason giving. If there are people like that, they are morally ignorant.

In Chapter 8 I argue for a third sort of blameworthiness, 'extended blameworthiness'. Sometimes an agent seems blameworthy even though she has not manifested bad will at all. To borrow an example from Randolph Clarke (2014, 165), imagine that I have promised my spouse that I will get milk on the way home. Imagine that there is nothing that I have failed to do that I should have done in order to remember. Thus, it seems that I am not blameworthy for the ignorance. However, it also seems plausible to Clarke, and to me, that I am blameworthy for there being no milk.

One might simply deny this. But it seems to many, including myself, that there must be a way of making sense of some sort of blameworthi- ness here. However, neither ordinary blame nor detached blame seems appropriate. I argue that in this sort of case, agents should *take* respon- sibility. This is not simply liability (which obviously is taken on or imposed in negligence type cases). It is more than that, it is a real blameworthiness, a licence for the offended party to feel something approaching resentment, and for the offender herself to feel remorse.

I give an account of the appropriate reactions of the offender here, and suggest that we should recognize that there are shades of agent regret, and that at one end, when an agent is willing to take ownership of the action, agent regret shades into remorse. The amount of blame that is appropriate does not always correspond with the amount of remorse that is appropriate, and one important feature of extended blameworthiness is that the sort of blame conversation that is appropriate has different norms to the sort that is appropriate when the agent has a clearly bad will.

I argue that what licenses a blame conversation at all are the requirements of our personal relationships. Sometimes, when an agent fails to meet standards that apply to her, and her own agential involvement is ambiguous, her relationships require that she take responsibility, that she accept extended blameworthiness. Relationships require a degree of emotional investment, not just in doing the relevant duties, but in the attitudes surrounding them. I argue that having a disposition to feel remorse for inadvertent fault can be an important sign of investment. It is not always necessary, and it is usually not necessary at all in impersonal relationships.

When it is necessary, it does not license the full blame part of the conversation. Rather, extended blameworthiness correlates with a truncated blame conversation, where the blamer should usually be satisfied with apology and remorse from the blamee as the end of the conversation. At that point, the blamer can let go—the person at fault has shown that she is invested in the relationship, that she cares more about the wrongdoing than about being a stickler about the limits of her own agency.

The underlying rationale for extended blameworthiness is no different to the rationale for any other kind of blameworthiness. Our responsibility practice has a function, the very same function as our morality practice, of course, of regulating and rationalizing our relationships. This is why there are such different ways of blaming those who are in our moral community and those who are outside it. This is how we can make sense of responsibility even without bad will. And this is why we care so much about the conditions of rightness and wrongness, and of praise and blame.

2

Subjective Obligation

In this chapter, I defend an account of subjective obligation. I start with the question, 'how should we define right and wrong?' I am not concerned with which things are right and wrong, such as whether lying is wrong, or whether we ought to act so as produce the greatest happiness of the greatest number. Rather, I am concerned with the conditions that limit when we can appropriately say that an agent's behaviour is *wrong*, as opposed to merely bad. An avalanche might be bad, but it is not wrong. Avalanches are not agents, and assuming an avalanche is not caused by agents, the concept of wrongness is simply not applicable. But even agents sometimes behave in ways that, although definitely bad, do not seem wrong. If a doctor prescribes a drug that entirely unpredictably ends up killing the patient, we do not usually say that the doctor has acted wrongly. This is because we are not responsible for all the bad things we cause. In other words, there is a 'responsibility constraint' on our concepts of rightness and wrongness.[1] My aim in this chapter is to elucidate that constraint. I will argue that we have different notions of rightness that correspond to different understandings of the responsibility constraint.

Here is a rough formulation:

The Responsibility Constraint: A normative theory must give an account of right and wrong action such that an agent could reasonably be deemed responsible for her action.

There are at least two ideas associated with the responsibility constraint. One is the idea that deontic concepts should make sense of assessment of the agent, the other is that deontic concepts should be able to guide

---

[1] As I said in footnote 1 in the Introduction, I assume that 'rightness', 'obligation', and 'ought' are corollaries, and likewise for the converses.

action. In order to make sense as assessment and guidance, deontic concepts must have some essential connection to human agency and capacities. But what is the connection? The responsibility constraint obviously rules out an account of rightness that instructs the agent to do things that are not possible for the agent, such as teletransport. As consequentialists have argued, it may also rule out accounts of rightness that allow all causal consequences to be relevant to rightness.[2] Plausibly, rightness could not depend on consequences that I (non-culpably) do not know about or are not up to me. Beyond that, however, it is not easy to see how our deontic concepts are limited.

We must think about what we need from our concepts of rightness and wrongness (and their corollaries, ought and obligation), what we are doing with them, and what makes them useful. I argue that we should be pluralists here: there are different ways to think about rightness and wrongness, and they are useful for different things. We can think of accounts of rightness on a scale, from hyper-objective rightness, which meets only a very weak version of the responsibility constraint, to subjective rightness, which meets a much stronger version of the responsibility constraint.[3] In this chapter I argue that we need both a moderately objective account of rightness, such that rightness is defined independently of particular agents' capacities and knowledge, and also a subjective account of rightness, that correlates with praise- and blameworthiness.

Even objective accounts of rightness need to meet some version of the responsibility constraint. For an account of objective rightness to be useful, it must have at least some connection to the abilities of ordinary agents. A conception of rightness that said that the right action is the one

[2] See e.g. Frances Howard-Snyder (1997).

[3] Unfortunately, the terminology is not completely standardized. Michael Zimmerman talks about objectivism, prospectivism, and subjectivism. I follow him in using the term prospectivism, but whereas he contrasts objectivism and subjectivism, I prefer to use 'objectivism' as an umbrella term, and distinguish between hyper-objectivism and prospectivism. Frank Jackson (1991) contrasts objective consequentialism with the 'decision-theoretic' approach (which is what I am calling prospectivism); Graham Oddie and Peter Menzies (1992) distinguish between actual-outcome consequentialism, objectivism (which is what I am calling prospectivism), and subjectivism. Bart Gruzalski (1981) talks about 'actual-consequence consequentialism' and 'foreseeable consequence consequentialism'. Julia Driver (2011) discusses a distinction between 'evaluational externalism', which bases rightness on factors that are external to agency, and 'evaluational internalism', which bases rightness on factors internal to agency.

that an omniscient and omnipotent being would identify is not of interest to us. It serves none of our purposes. Objective rightness gives us an independent standard to aim for, and a measure of achievement, so it must be at least possible to do what counts as objectively right, and to do it non-accidentally.

On objective accounts of rightness and wrongness, it is possible that an agent could act wrongly without being blameworthy, or act rightly without being praiseworthy.[4] It is possible, in other words, that an agent could stumble on a wrong action *by accident*, without any bad intent. She could act wrongly, but have an excuse. It seems important to leave room for that, to be able to say that this action is wrong, but that the agent herself is not at fault.

More subjective accounts of rightness, that is, accounts that meet a stronger version of the responsibility constraint, tie rightness and wrongness more closely to the agent's own point of view. As a result, it is plausible that subjective rightness is correlated with praise- and blameworthiness, and possibly, though I will explain this in a way that partly debunks it, action guidance. That is to say, an agent who acts subjectively rightly is thereby praiseworthy, and an agent who acts subject-ively wrongly, is thereby blameworthy. Roughly speaking (I will elaborate on this in what follows), on the subjective account of obligation, the agent's point of view is supreme, and so the agent cannot act subjectively wrongly by accident. To act subjectively wrongly is to act wrongly by one's own lights.

My main purpose in this chapter is to defend an account of subjective obligation. I start my account of subjective obligation with the common idea that it needs to be accessible. I argue that subjective obligation does not in fact need to be fully accessible. Rather, subjective obligation should be anchored in the true Morality. I argue that it should be action guiding, but not in the rich sense that people often intend when they say that subjective obligation should be action guiding. Subjective obligation is a genuine imperative, but if an agent cannot identify the right action, it does not necessarily help her to identify the right action.

---

[4] G. E. Moore argues that objections to the objectivist accounts of moral obligations confuse blameworthiness with 'having violated an obligation'. Moore argues that the two things are distinct, that one can be blameworthy without having violated an obligation (1912, 192–3). Peter Graham (2010, 93–4) argues along similar lines.

Finally, I argue that we cannot formulate subjective obligation in terms of the agent's beliefs about what ought to be done. Rather, we need to formulate subjective obligation in terms of trying: an agent is fulfilling her subjective obligation when she is trying to do well by Morality.

1. Objective Rightness: Hyper-objectivism and Prospectivism

In this section I give a brief overview of the objectivist position. I think there is a place for many different objectivist notions, so long as we are clear about what we are talking about, though, as I explain below, I favour prospectivism for the main objectivist role. Objectivist accounts of our deontic concepts are useful as a standard to aim for, and as a way to assess past performance and learn from it. These purposes give us a way to assess different contenders for the primary objectivist sense of rightness.

Objective rightness has been discussed fairly thoroughly in the literature, especially with reference to consequentialism (which, of course, seems particularly vulnerable to worries about the definition of rightness overreaching itself and including things that the agent could not possibly be responsible for), but also more generally. The debate has polarized around two accounts of the objective sense of rightness, which I will refer to as 'hyper-objectivism' and 'prospectivism'.[5]

The difference between different sorts of account of objective rightness can be brought out by considering an example, forms of which appear in various places in the literature (see Jackson, 1991, 462–3 and Regan, 1980, 264–5).[6] Imagine a doctor has a choice between three drugs she

---

[5] Defenders of hyper-objectivism (not necessarily consequentialist accounts) include Henry Sidgwick (1874), G. E. Moore (1912), W. D. Ross (1930), David Lyons (1965), Lars Bergstrom (1996), Fred Feldman (1986; 2003), Julia Driver (2001; 2012), and Peter Graham (2010). Defenders of prospectivism include Jeremy Bentham (1789), John Stuart Mill (1863), J. J. C. Smart (1973), Bart Gruzalski (1981), Frank Jackson (1991), Graham Oddie and Peter Menzies (1992), Brad Hooker (2000), Mark Timmons (2012), Frances Howard-Snyder (1997), Michael Zimmerman (2006; 2008), Elinor Mason (2013), and Errol Lord (2015). In my 'Consequentialism and Moral Responsibility' (2019a) I examine the way in which the responsibility constraint applies to consequentialism.

[6] Fred Feldman discusses a version of this example in Feldman (1986, 46–7), but Feldman's conclusion remains that what you ought to do is to prescribe the drug that would actually be best. More recently Parfit gives a version of the example (2011, 159). Parfit's overall conclusion is that there are many senses of right and wrong and that they are all useful.

could prescribe. The first drug will ameliorate the symptoms, but will not cure the patient. The doctor knows that one of the other two drugs will cure the patient completely, and the other one will kill the agent. Unfortunately, she doesn't know which is which. According to hyper-objectivism, the right one to prescribe is the one that will actually cure the patient. According to prospectivism, the right one to prescribe is the safe drug, even though the doctor knows that that would not be the best possible option.

The most common argument for prospectivism over hyper-objectivism can be characterized in terms of the responsibility constraint. Prospectivism does a better job of meeting the responsibility constraint than the hyper-objectivist account of rightness. The thought is something like this: 'what we really ought to do, cannot be what an omniscient agent would do. Rather, it must be based on a more realistic agent. We couldn't reliably do what an omniscient agent would do, and so we couldn't possibly be blameworthy for not doing what an omniscient agent would do.' Agents are not usually responsible for doing or failing to do the hyper-objectivism-right act because, although it is available in some sense, it is not sufficiently accessible to them.[7] Or, to put the same point a different way, on a hyper-objectivist account of rightness we will have excuses too often. Excuses will be the norm, not the exception.

As P. F. Strawson points out, the standard way to have an excuse is to have done something bad, but without having intended it that way. In Strawson's terms, the relevant bad quality of will is absent, and so the agent is not, after all, responsible for the injury (Strawson, 1962, in Watson, 2003, 77). This is consistent with J. L. Austin's distinction between a justification and an excuse. Austin avoids the terms 'right' and 'wrong', and instead uses non-deontic terms: "In the one defence, [justification] . . . we accept responsibility but deny that it was bad: in the other, [excuse] we admit that it was bad but don't accept full, or even any, responsibility" (1956, 2). We could put Austin's point in deontic terms: a justification involves admitting that you did the act but denying that it was wrong, whereas an excuse involves admitting that the act was wrong, but denying responsibility for it. An excuse here is a release from blameworthiness. Denying responsibility is not denying causal responsibility, it is denying blameworthiness.

---

[7] This is Howard-Snyder's argument (1997).

When we talk about excuses in everyday life we can be talking about a host of different things. There are different kinds of excusing condition, some of which are better described as exempting conditions, and there are also partial excuses, and mitigating circumstances.[8] What I am interested in here is relatively simple. The kind of excuse that would proliferate on the hyper-objective account of rightness is the kind that applies when an ordinary agent is not responsible for a particular act. I will call this a 'simple excuse'. Here is a useful way to characterize simple excuses: an agent has a simple excuse when her agency is not impaired, but it is blocked.[9] It could be blocked by someone else (who thwarts her in some way), or by circumstances (which cause unavoidable ignorance, or cause some physical impairment, e.g. sudden paralysis). This is the simplest form for an excuse: it looks as though I did it, but in fact, my agency was blocked, my motives were not flawed after all.

On a hyper-objectivist account of rightness, agents will often be non-culpably ignorant of the right action. Take Jackson's doctor. There is no way she can know which drug will cure the patient. So if she fails to do the right action, she will have a simple excuse: she didn't know which action the right action was.

On a prospectivist account of rightness it is possible to have a simple excuse, but for most people, prospectively wrong action will be blameworthy most of the time. The prospectively right action is (roughly) the one a reasonable agent would do. Most of the time we can strive towards being reasonable, and manage it. However, sometimes we do not identify what it would be prospectively right to do, even when we are sincerely trying our best.[10]

So the question is, which account should we prefer? The underlying issue here concerns what we want from an account of objective rightness. Being able to point to the very best possible action is interesting, but it does not capture anything that is particularly useful to us.

---

[8] I come back to exemptions, partial excuses, and mitigating circumstances in more detail in Chapter 6.

[9] This is the idea that Michael Tooley uses to defend his view that capacities are what determine rights: Tooley distinguishes between capacities that are immediately exercisable, and capacities that are blocked, and contrasts both with mere potentialities (1972, 149).

[10] Zimmerman is quite explicit about this (2008, 71). How common excuses will be depends on how demanding the standard for prospectively right action is: if it demands full rationality it will be much more common to have an excuse than if it only demands being reasonable.

We are interested in praise- and blameworthiness, which clearly the hyper-objective account is unable to capture. But more moderate object-ivist accounts do not perfectly capture praise- and blameworthiness either. It is always possible that an agent acts prospectively wrongly without being blameworthy.

Another thing we are very interested in is moral education, in teaching other people how to do better, and in learning how to do better ourselves. Objective standards for right action are good for that: we want to be able to point to what an agent should have done, and say, 'that's the right action in this case'. However, if we point to the very best possible action in a Jackson style case, we will not learn anything about what we should have done, or what we should encourage our children to do. The very best action is not one that we can genuinely recommend under that description—it is so often inaccessible.

Thus an account of objective rightness that is roughly an account of what the reasonable agent would do, seems about right. It is pitched at a level that is not unattainable, and is genuinely something to aspire to and aim for. You need an excuse for not doing what is prospectively right, and it will not be easy to point to one. The prospectivist account gives us a standard to aim for, something that we should usually be able to achieve. Usually, doing something that is prospectively wrong will be blameworthy, usually, prospective rightness is accessible to us.

Of course, in the end, all this is just another way of saying that prospectivism is more intuitive, that it fits better with our other concepts and ideas. Prospectivism meets the responsibility constraint in a way that seems particularly important and relevant.[11]

2. Subjective Obligation and Praise- and Blameworthiness

We might think that what we want from subjective obligation is simply that it captures what an agent ought to do from their own point of view. But, as I shall argue here and will continue to argue in Chapter 4, that is not a good way to characterize our ambitions for an account of subjective

[11] In my 2013 I give an argument for prospectivism that aims to show that prospectivism is superior to hyper-objectivism because it builds uncertainty into rightness. Again, that is a way of cashing out the basic intuitive attractiveness of prospectivism.

obligation. Rather, what we want is an account of what an agent ought to do, such that if they do it, they will be praiseworthy, and if they do not do it, they will be blameworthy. I will start by motivating that aim, explaining why it is important to give an account of subjective obligation that correlates with praise- and blameworthiness.

What are we trying to latch on to when we talk about praise- and blameworthiness? As I argued above, not simply acting rightly or wrongly, as clearly, on a standard moderately objective sense of rightness and wrongness, there is no necessary connection between acting wrongly and being blameworthy. According to an objective account of obligation, such as prospectivism, there are various ways that an agent can act wrongly and nonetheless have an excuse. She may be non-culpably ignorant of some relevant fact, or she may have tripped, or have been pushed. In those cases, an agent is not blameworthy, and she may even be praiseworthy. So my question here is, what is it that she is doing in such a case that renders her praiseworthy? And conversely, when an agent is blameworthy despite her act having good results, what is it that makes her blameworthy?

I should stress here that my question is not a question about 'desert' in anything but a very deflationary sense.[12] I am not claiming that when an agent acts subjectively wrongly she deserves blame, in the sense that that is what justifies the suffering that goes with being blamed. Rather, we want to give an explanation of what is going on when it is fitting to praise

---

[12] Derk Pereboom contrasts basic desert (which he is sceptical about) with consequentialist reasons that one might have for blaming someone. Pereboom argues that basic desert cannot be justified because we do not have free will (2001. The argument is further developed in his 2014). As Michael McKenna points out, there is no reason to think that any account of blameworthiness *must* be committed to a basic desert thesis. "... contrary to Pereboom's approach to a theory of moral responsibility which is tied to desert, *if* some other way of cashing out the propriety of the reactive attitudes is defensible, say, along the lines of fittingness within a conversation , as I have suggested, and *if* this allows us to make good sense of our moral responsibility practices, then *perhaps* one need not commit to fairly taxing views about the suffering of others merely by committing to a proper theory of moral responsibility..." (McKenna, 2012, 118). As the italics indicate, McKenna himself is not sure that we can talk about blameworthiness without talking about desert. My own view is that we can: what I offer can be read as a defence of blameworthiness as a relation of fittingness between certain behaviour (violating subjective obligation) and blame. However, my view is compatible with a more ambitious account of desert. In fact, I do not think that imposing suffering is an essential part of blame, so the burden on me to justify blame is lighter than on those who think that hostile attitudes are essential. I come back to this in Chapter 5.

or blame an agent. Obviously, we have to say something that adverts to the agent's actual engagement in the situation. Joel Feinberg calls this the 'aboutness principle' in his discussion of desert (1970): we must be able to say something about the agent. My aim is to defend an account of what activity of an agent makes blame fitting. I focus on what the relevant agential activity is, rather than on exactly how the condition of fittingness works, or what that means for theories about desert, or what desert requires. This is the sense in which my work is in normative responsibility theory rather than in the meta-level theory, the debate between compatibilists and incompatibilists.

Of course, it is very controversial what, exactly, we should say about the conditions that make blame fitting. The thought I start with here is that it is very plausible that we should say something about what the agent is doing; about her activity. It seems *prima facie* plausible to say that when an agent is praiseworthy despite her act having turned out badly, it is because of what she was up to, her agential contribution. Further, it seems plausible that we should be able to describe the fittingness conditions for moral praise or blame in terms of right or wrong action. For an agent to be morally blameworthy it seems, there must be *some* sense in which she acted wrongly. My argument in this book is that it is natural to think of the relevant thing that the agent was doing as *violating her subjective obligation*. I have not yet given an account of subjective obligation, so this claim is hard to assess. Roughly, I think that to act subjectively wrongly is to act badly by one's own lights. More precisely, acting subjectively wrongly means knowingly failing to try to do well by Morality.

Of course, that is very controversial. First, it will be rejected by those who think that praiseworthiness does not require any self-aware morally good action. Rather, such people argue, what makes an agent praiseworthy is just that she is in fact motivated in a good way, and this cannot be characterized as acting subjectively rightly. Nomy Arpaly uses the case of Huckleberry Finn to make the point vivid: Huck is not acting morally from his own point of view, in fact he thinks he is doing the wrong thing, and yet, Arpaly argues, he is praiseworthy (2003). I address that challenge in Chapter 4.

Second, there are those who will object that although one may be praiseworthy when one acts subjectively rightly, it is not the only way to be praiseworthy (and conversely, acting subjectively wrongly is only one way to be blameworthy), surely there are also other ways. I agree with that, and in what follows I argue for pluralism about praise- and blame-worthiness. However, I think that acting subjectively wrongly is a central and important way to be blameworthy, and understanding it properly sheds light on our overall understanding of blameworthiness. In what follows, in saying that an agent who acts subjectively wrongly is blame-worthy, I mean that she is blameworthy in the 'ordinary' way. I say more about what ordinary blameworthiness and ordinary blame are in Chapter 4.

Finally, my suggestion that acting subjectively wrongly is automatic-ally to be blameworthy will invite the objection that it is possible to have an excuse, even when one is acting subjectively wrongly.[13] An agent may be under enormous stress, or she may be in the grip of some sort of temporary glitch, or fugue. I will answer that briefly here, and I explore the issue more fully in Chapter 6. As I say, the view I defend is that when an agent is praiseworthy, it is because she was trying to do well by Morality; in a case where she is blameworthy, she was failing to try to do well by Morality.

The first thing to say is that an agent who appears to act subjectively wrongly will often appeal to an excuse. But, and here is the crucial point, the excuse has the form, 'it looks as though I am acting subjectively wrongly, but actually I am not'. She might say for example, "I did push him down, but I thought he was attacking me". Simple excuses aim to convince the would-be blamer that things were not quite as they appeared. The plea is that the agent didn't really do the thing it looked as though she did: she did not do it under the relevant description.

Here is another way to put it: the agent may have acted objectively wrongly, but she did not act subjectively wrongly, and so she is not blameworthy. An agent can have a simple excuse for acting prospectively wrongly, but she cannot have a simple excuse for acting subjectively wrongly. If you are acting subjectively wrongly, then, by definition, you know what you are doing under the relevant description.

Of course, an agent may be so impaired that she is not responsible at all. It seems possible someone could be acting subjectively wrongly, but not qualify as a responsible agent in the most basic sense. In that case, we do not think of the agent as blameworthy because we do not think of her

---

[13] Thanks to Michael McKenna and Doug Portmore for pressing me on this.

as responsible at all. But there is another worry here, which is that a competent agent could genuinely be acting subjectively wrongly, and yet have a *complex* excuse. Circumstances may be such that she is less blameworthy than she otherwise would have been. I address various ways to understand this thought in Chapter 6, where I suggest that there may be mitigating circumstances and complex partial excuses, but their role is to show that the agent was not acting as subjectively wrongly as it first appeared. Insofar as the agent is acting subjectively wrongly, she is blameworthy.

In the rest of this chapter I will expand and defend my account of subjective rightness and wrongness. My aim in giving an account of subjective obligation is to give an account of the agent's action in moral terms—an account of the way in which the agent is acting morally wrongly by her own lights—which specifies the conditions under which agents are blameworthy in the ordinary way.

3. Subjective Obligation and Action Guidance

I have just argued that what we are looking for from an account of subjective obligation is an account of rightness and wrongness that is reliably correlated with praise- and blameworthiness. But there is another aspect of our hopes for a notion of subjective obligation. It seems to many that action guidance is an important part of what we want from a normative theory. Even without a clear account of what 'action guidance' is, it seems obvious that neither the hyper-objectivist nor the prospective conceptions of rightness can reliably deliver action guidance. Rightness in those senses will often be inaccessible to actual agents.[14]

The notion of accessibility is very important here. Both praise- and blameworthiness and action guidance are somehow connected to it: it is the possible inaccessibility of hyper-objective and prospective obligations that means that an agent may not be responsible for not complying, and means that they are not action guiding. Subjective obligation, by contrast, should be accessible, and should be able to deliver on both

---

[14] Some of the material in this section originally appeared in Elinor Mason, 'Do the Right Thing: An Account of Subjective Obligation', in Mark Timmons (ed.), *Oxford Studies in Normative Ethics*, vol. 7. Oxford: Oxford University Press (2017): 117–37. Reprinted by permission from Oxford University Press.

praiseworthiness and action guidance. Or so it might seem. So perhaps the responsibility constraint that we are hoping to meet should be expressed as follows:

> **The Strong Responsibility Constraint (Accessibility)**: rightness will be accessible to the agent, so she is praise- or blameworthy for right or wrong action, *and* rightness is action guiding.

The idea that a moral theory should be action guiding is widely espoused.[15] But it is not completely clear what qualifies a theory as action guiding. Frank Jackson says: "the fact that a course of action would have the best results is not in itself a guide to action, for a guide to action must in some appropriate sense be present to the agent's mind. We need, if you like, a story from the inside of an agent to be part of any theory which is properly a theory in ethics" (1991, 466–7). It seems that we somehow have to shift the focus of the moral instruction from hitting the target to something that the agent is more in control of, something that the agent is able to do. We might simply translate the objectivist instruction, which mentions a target that is external to the agent, into an instruction that mentions only the agent's *beliefs* about that target. Instead of saying, 'do the right thing', we should say, perhaps, 'do what *you believe* the right thing to do is'.[16]

However, on one construal of action guidance, this will not do. An instruction that simply shifts focus from the target to the agent's beliefs regarding the target may not be helpful. If an agent has no clue what is right, an instruction to do what she believes is right will not help. Moving from talking about the world to talking about beliefs about the world does not increase the action guidingness of an instruction.

Consider Ross's proposal, that the (subjectively) right thing for someone to set himself to do is what "he thinks to be morally most suitable in the circumstances as he takes them to be" (1939, 61). Imagine someone sincerely asking for advice in a difficult moral situation. Such a person might say, "I don't know how things will turn out, though I have a good

---

[15] For arguments that theories should be action guiding see Bart Gruzalski (1981), James Hudson (1989), Frank Jackson (1991), Elinor Mason (2003), Andrew Sepielli (2009; 2012), Holly Smith (2010; 2011b; 2012), Fred Feldman (2012), and Mark Timmons (2012).

[16] See Prichard (1932) and Ross (1939). (Ross changed his view from an objectivist view to a subjectivist one after being convinced by Prichard.) Doug Portmore notes that pure subjectivism is not action guiding (2011, 22), as does Andrew Sepielli (2012, 60).

guess. But more worryingly, I am not sure whether keeping a promise is more important than producing good consequences—what should I do?" On Ross's view, this person ought to do what they think is most morally suitable. But they don't know what's most morally suitable—that's the whole problem. A fully subjective view like Ross's is action guiding only in a very weak sense. It tells us to obey our conscience, but no more than that.

The lesson here is that there are two ways to think about action guidance. We can think about it primarily in terms of helpfulness, so that what we are looking for is a set of instructions that helps an agent who lacks information. There is no point is saying to someone who is learning to ride a bicycle, 'don't fall off'. The point is to teach them *how* not to fall off. A good teacher will say useful things like, 'keep your knees and feet close to the bike'. They will give instructions that will result in the aim being achieved. Call this the 'helpfulness interpretation' of action guidance. On the other hand, we can think of action guidance in a different way, such that moving from an instruction about a target to an instruction about beliefs about a target is a relevant difference. The point of such a change is to move from something the agent cannot necessarily do to something they can do. Let's call this the 'accessibility interpretation' of action guidance, so that for a theory to be action guiding is just for it to give an instruction that is always going to be accessible to the agent.

Writers who argue that normative theories must be action guiding usually have the helpfulness interpretation in mind (e.g. Feldman, 2012; Holly Smith, 2010; 2012). They point out that instructions to 'do the right thing' are not helpful, we need to know what to do—we need something more usable. But should we be looking for action guidance in the helpfulness sense? The prospects for an immediately helpful instruction that always applies are bleak.[17] There is simply too much variation in the circumstances in which action guidance is needed. Different people in different contexts need hugely varying amounts of information to make an instruction usable. Take a simple example: a cake recipe. A recipe aimed at advanced chefs can take all sorts of knowledge for granted. A cake recipe aimed at children must spell out

---

[17] I argue this in more detail in Mason (2017), where I discuss Holly Smith's account of a hierarchy of secondary decision principles (Smith 2012). See also Michael Zimmerman's argument in chapter 4 of his 2014.

each stage. Furthermore, when mistakes are made, as they inevitably will be in the moral realm, we still have subjective obligations, and what we ought to do depends on what wrong turns we took.

This is enormously complex, and not something that we cannot expect our moral theory itself lay out in advance. Moral theories cannot always provide an immediately helpful instruction that we can use as a subjective guide to action. Subjective obligation is not the same as a decision procedure. It is not a demand for particular contextually sensitive advice. We need that, of course, but we must get that from each other, from past experience, from self-help books and so on, not from our moral principle. We should let go of the idea that the subjective 'ought' can be action guiding in a substantive sense, that it can give immediately helpful advice.[18]

Let's return to the accessibility sense of action guidance. On Ross and Prichard's view, we should do what we take to be most morally suitable. As I pointed out, that may not be very helpful, we may not have enough of a clue about what is morally suitable. But in that case, they would insist, we should nonetheless do the best we can, and we really should do that. We just have to rely on a weak sense of what it is to choose an option that is 'the most x' within a range of options. In a weak sense, we pick the option we take to be most x even in the case when we plump between a number of options that appear equally x, or which we cannot rank. Compare an instruction to pick the numbers you think most likely to win the lottery. In a weak sense, following that instruction simply involves writing down any set of numbers, as all sets are, from the point of view of the agent, equally likely to win the lottery. So Prichard and Ross's pure subjectivism is action guiding in the accessibility sense.

The crucial point about action guidance in the accessibility sense is that it involves a direct instruction. The subjective 'ought' says, 'you ought to do φ!', and that is more than just a way of saying, 'φ would be good'. Compare that to hyper-objective and prospective rightness, which are ways of talking about the *ideal* thing to do. It is very useful (for moral

---

[18] I think this is what Fred Feldman concludes in the end too, though he does not put it quite like that. Feldman starts by looking for secondary principles to make sense of subjective obligation, but ends up saying that all we can do is "identify the acts in this particular case that seem most nearly consistent with the general policy of maximizing utility where possible while avoiding things that put people at excessive risk of serious harm . . . perform one of them" (2012, 167).

learning, for advice, and so on) to have senses like that. But these senses of rightness are essentially *subjunctive*. They are not actually instructions. Morality does not say, 'do what is hyper-objectively right!', or 'do what is prospectively right!' Rather, it says something subjunctive: 'this is what it would be best to do', or 'this is what a reasonable person would do'.

So it is true that an account of subjective obligation should be action guiding, that it should meet the accessibility version of the strong responsibility constraint, properly understood. And this explains the way in which action guidingness is connected to praise- and blame-worthiness: an agent who does not do what she subjectively ought is defying a genuine instruction. What she subjectively ought to do is what she really should no, no matter what. She may lack information, but there is nonetheless something that is accessible to her, something that she ought to do.

Different accounts of subjective obligation vary on what they take to be accessible (it is usually beliefs, but I will argue that we should focus on the agent's trying). They also vary on how to understand the moral outlook that is relevant to subjective obligation. Ross and Prichard's account is subjective all the way down, they think that you act subjectively rightly when you act according to your own sense of what is morally appropriate, whatever that is. On my view, by contrast, we ought to try to do well by the standards of the true Morality. I defend that in the next section.

4. Anchoring Subjective Obligation: The True Morality

I have argued that subjective obligation is not action guiding in the sense of giving us advice we can follow. Rather, subjective obligation is action guiding in a different sense, it is accessible, and so it issues a genuine imperative. I now turn to the other general idea that seems to be motivating the need for an account of subjective obligation: the idea that subjective obligation will correlate with praise- and blameworthiness. The version of the responsibility constraint that we are now working with says:

> **The Strong Responsibility Constraint (Accessibility):** rightness will be accessible to the agent, hence she is praise- or blameworthy for right or wrong action, and she should genuinely do what her subject-ive obligation tells her to do.

The accessibility requirement directs us to the agent's own view of things. An agent may not have fully rational credences, but there is an important sense (the subjective sense of obligation) in which she should base her action on her own best credences. So long as she is sincerely doing her best, *trying*, as I shall argue, an agent seems praiseworthy for acting on her own best assessment of a situation. However, though this seems right for an agent's assessment of the non-moral aspects of the situation, I do not think that the same applies to the agent's assessment of the moral facts. I argue that subjective obligation is the obligation to try to do well by the standards of the correct value system, where I do not mean anything hugely ambitious by 'correct'.

Insisting on a particular value system might seem counterintuitive. If we introduce an objective element into subjective obligation, something that is not necessarily accessible to the agent, like a particular value system, then it seems we have undermined the point of subjective obligation. I will defuse the force of that worry in what follows. The main point is that, for those to whom the notion of subjective obligation applies, subjective obligation *is* accessible. Only those who have a grasp of Morality (as I designate the relevant value system) count as acting subjectively rightly when they try to do well by their value system. Those outside our moral community are in a different category, and different concepts of rightness and blameworthiness are relevant. I defend this in more detail in the next few chapters. Here I focus on defending the objective element in subjective rightness.

It is uncontroversial that objective accounts of rightness, even moderately objective accounts, such as prospectivism, are permitted to use the correct value system to anchor the theory.[19] After all, such accounts do not aim to be fully accessible to the agent in any case. The justification for using the correct account of value is that we are interested in a

---

[19] Jackson bases his prospectivism on the true value system. He describes the values that figure in the expected utility calculation in terms of idealized desires, "We can think of consequentialism's value function as telling us what, according to consequentialism, we ought to desire. For a person's desires can be represented—with, of course, a fair degree of idealization—by a preference function which ranks state of affairs in terms of how much the person would like the state of affairs to obtain, and we can think of consequentialism as saying that the desires a person ought to have are those which would be represented by a preference function which coincided with consequentialism's value function" (1991, 464; see also Jackson, 1986, 352). Zimmerman, by contrast, uses the values that it would be reasonable to have (2014, 36).

standard that we should aim for, that can be pointed out as worth attaining, independently of the limitations of particular agents. We can say, 'Amin should have chosen the other charity to give money to, this one is not efficient', even when Amin was not in a position to know that. And, when using an objective notion of rightness, if we think of someone who is giving their money to a morally horrible organization, even if they carefully choose which morally horrible organization they want to give it to, we can say that what they did was objectively wrong.

However, it might seem that accounts of subjective rightness should base subjective rightness on the agent's actual value system, whatever that happens to be. This has the advantage of ensuring that acting subjectively rightly is fully accessible, and that is the rationale that is implicit in both Prichard's and Ross's fully subjective accounts of obligation (Prichard, 1932; Ross, 1939). Both Prichard and Ross take it that an agent must always be able to know what is subjectively required of her: obligation is based on what the agent believes, not what is actually the case, and that includes her value system.

But there are various disadvantages to defining subjective obligation this way. First, it seems that there is unacceptable bootstrapping. As Michael Zimmerman points out, on this account of subjective rightness, agents who don't believe that they have any obligations don't have any, and those who have horrendous moral beliefs are acting rightly just so long as they believe that they are acting rightly (2008, 13–14).

Ross and Prichard both anticipate this objection. Prichard attempts to resolve it by saying that we should not understand rightness as something that belongs to actions, rather it belongs to the agent: " . . . when we make an assertion containing the term 'ought' or 'ought not', that to which we are attributing a certain character is not a certain activity, but a certain man" (1932, 99). Ross says something similar—the idea is that the point of subjective rightness is not to pick out an *independent* characteristic that the act has because of the fact that the agent takes it to be right. Rather, the agent's taking it to be right means that it is right *for the agent.*

We can accept that, and still worry that the account of subjective rightness presented by Ross and Prichard is uninteresting. A fully subjective account of rightness picks out something, but it is something that we might not think central to our responsibility practices. What one subjectively ought to do in this sense is, basically, to follow one's conscience. Anyone can follow their conscience, there is no external target in that at all. However, as I shall argue in more detail in Chapter 4, following one's conscience does not seem sufficient for praiseworthiness. When we say that someone is praiseworthy, we are saying more than that they followed their conscience.

The full subjectivist could defend their account by arguing that accessibility is crucial, and that subjective rightness in this sense would not be the whole story about the agent's action. The full subjectivist could point out that once we have a firm grip on a moderately objective account of rightness, we have the resources to show how someone whose values are badly misguided has gone wrong. We can say that they are acting subjectively rightly insofar as they are doing what they see as morally appropriate, but they are acting wrongly in the prospective sense of rightness. Arguably, this gives up on the idea that subjective obligation might capture praise- and blameworthiness, instead all it captures is acting on conscience, but perhaps that is the best we can do. Perhaps subjective obligation is not a very interesting notion.

However, I think there is another way to go here. We should say that acting subjectively rightly is indexed to a specific value system. On this picture, subjective obligation is always accessible, but not to everyone. Only those who accept the relevant value system can act subjectively rightly by that value system, and of course, for those people, the value system is accessible. This has the possible disadvantage that it leaves out a group of people who do not accept that value system, and we have to say something about them and the ways they might be blameworthy. I return to that in later chapters, and defend a different sort of blameworthiness for those outside our moral community. I argue that this is not a disadvantage but, rather, fits with our practices, which are essentially interpersonal.

Crucially, my way of thinking about subjective obligation leaves the potential for a correlation between subjective obligation and praise- or blameworthiness in a rich sense. To act subjectively rightly is to act rightly by one's own lights, but if subjective rightness is indexed to a particular value system, we have built in that those lights are beamed in the right direction, at least, given the value system in question. So acting subjectively rightly is not merely acting on conscience, it is also having the right sort of motivations. I shall argue in Chapter 4 that acting on conscience plus being motivated the right way (with some added subtleties) are together sufficient for our ordinary sense of praiseworthiness.

The question then is, what value system should we anchor subjective obligation in? We could say that subjective obligation is always relative to a particular moral theory—call this 'theory-relative subjectivism'. On this sort of view, a utilitarian acts U-subjectively rightly, and is U-praiseworthy when she does what she believes she ought to do by utilitarian standards.[20] On this picture, we would never be giving an overall assessment of subjectively right action or praiseworthiness, but rather, a very narrow theory-relative assessment.

Such narrowness is undesirable. Ordinary people do not usually think in terms of philosophical moral theories, and yet we want to assess their actions by something like a subjective standard, and we want to praise and blame them. But if an action is subjectively right only by the standards of a moral theory, then only self-identified utilitarians can act subjectively rightly in the 'U-sense', and only self-identified Kantians can act subjectively rightly in the 'K-sense', and so on. There are very few such people. Even philosophers are not usually certain about moral theories. And yet, it seems that philosophers have subjective obligations, which are partly obligations to figure out what they should actually do, in the real world. Ideally, an account of subjective obligation applies to ordinary people, who are trying to figure out what to do given their ordinary value system.

This brings us to the issue of obligations in the face of uncertainty. Subjective obligation, I argued, is a genuine imperative, the agent really ought to do what is subjectively right. And whereas she may simply fail to know what her objective obligation is, what she ought to do *subjectively* is to figure out the best course of action in the face of uncertainty about the situation. So, for example, Amin must decide which charity to give money to, even though he does not know all the relevant facts. He must use the information he has, and deal with uncertainty as best he can. It is important to notice that Amin must be using moral information as well

---

[20] James Hudson (1989) argues that we should see subjective obligation as relative to theories in this way, arguing that a theory cannot be expected to say anything about what ought to be done by anything other than the lights of the theory. This is also how both Holly Smith and Fred Feldman understand subjective obligation. I don't think there is anything incoherent about this (in fact it has the same structure as my own view). I just think that because it is so narrow, it is a less interesting way to use the various concepts. The theory-relative sense of subjective rightness is not incompatible with my sense, and could be used alongside Morality-relative subjective rightness if there was some pay-off for doing that.

as non-moral information: he is not just thinking about probabilities, but thinking about values, about which values are in play, and which are most relevant here. It seems very plausible that an account of subjective obligation should deliver the verdict that in going through this process, Amin is doing what he subjectively ought to do by the lights of his own value system. This is a version of the accessibility point: our objective obligations are not always accessible to us, but our subjective obligations can be worked out by looking at the available information.

So, what should we say about *moral* uncertainty? It is perfectly possible that someone is uncertain between two opposing value systems, but of course, they cannot look to the value systems themselves for guidance on how to decide between the two. Each view can only provide reasons that come from within that view. Any reasons that transcend the two views must be reasons of some other sort.[21] The right thing to do by Utilitarianism is one thing, the right thing to do by Kantian Deontology is another thing. If Utilitarianism and Kantian Deontology are, in some sense, part of a larger value system, then we can choose between them on the basis of that. However, if Utilitarianism and Kantian Deontology are simply divergent competing theories of morality, a choice between them cannot be based on either account of rightness and cannot be based on a larger moral theory to which they both belong. An agent who is hedging their bets between white supremacism and egalitarianism is not making a *moral* choice, they are (if anything) making a rational choice between two opposing moral views.

Thus there is no requirement that subjective obligation should cover *radical* normative uncertainty. There may be better or worse ways of deciding in the face of radical normative uncertainty, but that would

---

[21] James Hudson makes this point in defending an account of subjective obligation, but it applies equally to prospective obligation. Hudson says, "The purpose of a moral theory (subjective utilitarianism, for example) is to tell the agent how she should use whatever information she has available at the moment of decision. . . . Any moral theory, in telling the agent what to do, will ignore the agent's possible commitment to other moral theories" (1989, 224). See also Andrew Sepielli (2009). Ted Lockhart has produced a detailed account of what we should do when faced with normative uncertainty, and his account deals with all and any normative uncertainty. Lockhart's conclusion is that we should maximize expected moral rightness. Lockhart argues that it is possible to compare different accounts of value, and thus to hedge our bets between different moral theories (Lockhart, 2000). On my view we must be comparing the different accounts by reference to some higher standard, and the best way to think of that higher standard is as Morality as I define it here: the broad view we all more or less agree on.

be an evaluation of rationality, not of morality. However, given the desideratum that subjective obligation applies to ordinary people, it seems that subjective obligations should apply when the agent is in the grip of non-radical normative uncertainty. Non-radical normative uncertainty is uncertainty within a larger value system, where comparisons and compromises can be made on the basis of the larger value system, the 'covering value' as Ruth Chang calls it (1997).[22]

Again, then, the question is, what value system is subjective obligation indexed to? The foregoing considerations point us to a broad value system that covers a spectrum of philosophical and non-philosophical views about rules, principles, and intrinsic goods. I refer to this view as Morality, with a capital 'M'. For the purposes of this book, I take 'Morality' or 'M' as a placeholder for a fully worked out theory of a broad and plausible value system. A full defence would be another book. But I will assume that this is the *correct* value system in a broad sense. By 'M' I mean the best version of our current value system, a cleaned-up version of common sense morality, the highest common denominator rather than the lowest. We might be radically mistaken about this, but we have to work on the assumption that we are on the right track, that our value system is, at least roughly, correct.

5. Grasping Morality

Morality contains a mixture of general principles for action, accounts of what is valuable or intrinsically good, and rules for deciding what to do. However, M does not tell us what to do. An agent could count as having a good grasp of M, and yet in a particular case not be able to see what she should do. General principles sometimes conflict, with each other or with other sorts of value, and it can be hard to see how different values are relevant. But these uncertainties take place under a wide umbrella. For example, Kantians and Utilitarians disagreeing about trolley cases do not (usually) think their opponent is a moral monster, they take themselves to be disagreeing within a larger framework on which they basically agree.

---

[22] Chang points out that we do not always need to compare two options in terms of a value they have in common. All that we need is a covering value, something that the two compared items contribute to. We can ask, which is better with respect to the covering value? (1997).

Grasping M does not entail grasping every facet of M, it is a matter of being in the game, of having the right general outlook. Compare an ability to play chess: having a grasp of the game of chess does not mean playing every move perfectly, or spotting every possible combination of moves that one's opponent may make. It means grasping the basic shape of the game, the moves that may make sense, the plays that tend to work, and so on. One can make mistakes and yet still have played well. Or to take another example, think of the activity of 'doing philosophy'. Philosophy is hard, getting it right in the broad sense does not mean getting it right in every respect. In these cases we think that someone can be working in the right framework, and yet still be in the grip of reasonable uncertainty within that framework. The same is true for Morality. We can have things roughly correct, and yet face reasonable uncertainty. Morality is a broad enough framework that it can accommodate reasonable disagreement and, further, can provide resources for resolving that disagreement. When we worry about the trolley problem, we are really asking, 'which answer to the trolley problem is better with respect to Morality?' Diverting the trolley and letting it go could both be subjectively right on this account of subjective rightness.

Grasping Morality in my sense does not necessarily involve grasping every facet of Morality. So there is vagueness at the boundaries, it is not always clear when someone is 'in' and when they are 'out' of our moral community. It is a bit like the question of the point at which someone counts as an expert on Aphra Behn. Must they know all her plays and poems by heart? Clearly not. They must be familiar with a sufficient proportion and have some related general theoretical and historical knowledge. There is a threshold, and above that threshold one is an expert. The same applies to knowledge of Morality: to be in our moral community is to meet the threshold.

But there are two very important differences between the question of what counts as being an expert on Aphra Behn and what counts as having a good grasp on Morality. First, it is usually the case that the question of whether someone is an expert is not terribly important, and the answer may well be contextually variable. Whereas here it seems that I am looking for an answer that marks an important distinction: if you have moral knowledge you are *in* (the category of subjective obligation) and if you lack it you are *out*. So, it seems important that I have a good answer to the question of what counts as moral knowledge.

In fact, I think that vagueness at the boundaries of grasping Morality is just echoed in vagueness at the boundaries of whether you are in or out of subjective obligation, and that this sort of vagueness is familiar and expected, not something we should hope to eliminate. Take the case of Huckleberry Finn.[23] Nomy Arpaly's view is that Huck is reasons-responsive and praiseworthy when he acts akratically. I agree that he is reasons responsive, and esteemworthy for his motivations, but he is not praiseworthy in the ordinary sense. My argument, which I develop in Chapter 4, is that his quality of will is very different to the quality of will of someone who does understand Morality, and he is not praiseworthy in the same way that someone who understands Morality is. Huck believes that it is morally permissible to enslave some people. That false belief is probably not one that we can think of as part of the reasonable uncertainty that is allowed within having a grasp of Morality. So it seems that Huck does not have a grasp of Morality. On the other hand, Huck's actions betray a deeper level of moral reactivity in him, one that does align with Morality. Perhaps Huck does subconsciously recognize that slavery is impermissible. So is Huck in or out? I think it is unclear.[24]

There are many unclear cases. Historical and transitional cases, such as Huck's are one sort of case. A person, or a whole community, can transition from being outside of Morality to being in it. During the transitional phase they are neither out nor in, it is just unclear whether we can think of them as having subjective obligations, and whether we can praise or blame them in the ordinary way. Imagine a different version of the Huck story, in which Huck wrestles with his conscience in the way that Twain describes, and then, despite feeling a strong temptation to help Jim escape, turns him in. In such a case, we feel at least some pull to blaming Huck on the grounds that he *did* know that he should not turn Jim in. In other words, that he had enough of a grasp on Morality, and was failing to try to do well by Morality in this situation.

Another sort of unclear case involves blind spots: cases where agents have a grasp on most of Morality, but not some local part. We may often

---

[23] Mark Twain, *The Adventures of Huckleberry Finn*. Huck's first appearance in philosophy might be Jonathan Bennett (1974), and the case is discussed by Nomy Arpaly (2003).

[24] Paulina Sliwa's discussion of Huck Finn brings out the complexities of the case nicely. Sliwa is defending the idea that moral knowledge is essential to praiseworthiness (2016).

just have to admit that it is indeterminate whether such an agent counts as having a grasp on Morality. Did Woodrow Wilson have a grasp on Morality? What about Fidel Castro? Margaret Thatcher? These are agents with huge and problematic blind spots, and yet there are lots of things they get right. Again, I think there is vagueness at the boundaries here, but that reflects reality, it is not a problem from the view.

The second very important difference between questions like the question of whether someone is an expert on Aphra Behn and whether someone has a good grasp of Morality, is that Morality is directive. It is possible for an agent to have a good grasp of Morality and yet not know what to do in a particular situation. Moving from a grasp of all the general principles that may apply to a good decision in a particular circumstance is not easy, and part of trying to do well by Morality is trying to figure out what to do. The agent must translate knowledge about good- and right-making features into action. If an agent can see that justice and kindness are at stake, and that they conflict, she must take the next step, which is to make the choice between them and act appropriately. There are both hard comparisons and hard choices. Even agents who meet the threshold for being in our moral community will sometimes be stumped.[25]

This draws attention to another aspect of moral knowledge. For an agent to be in our moral community, it is not enough that she under-stands the substance of Morality, she must also understand that Moral standards apply to her. This is related to the debate in meta-ethics between motivational internalism and motivational externalism. Motiv-ational internalists claim that to sincerely make a particular moral judgment necessarily involves being motivated by it. I reject motivational internalism for reasons that I will not go into here.[26] But it is certainly the case that to understand Morality is to understand *that* it is reason giving. That doesn't necessarily entail that the agent is actually motivated.

---

[25] See Ruth Chang's recent work on hard choices, e.g. Chang (2012), for an account of the complexities involved in making comparisons between options. I think this bears on the debate about whether testimony can provide moral knowledge (see e.g. Hills, 2009; McGrath, 2009). Without a fair bit of a moral understanding, that is, understanding of the general good and right making features, and how they contribute to a final verdict, an agent will rarely be able to move to action, and on my view would not count as having a grasp of Morality.

[26] See Mason (2008). I come back to this in Chapter 7.

It is important to leave room for the possibility that someone understands the standards, but defies them, and is blameworthy. I shall return to this question in Chapter 7, where I contrast agents outside of Morality with Morality defiers.

Given that being in the realm of subjective obligation requires only that the agent meet a threshold, it is possible that an agent could be non-culpably ignorant of some moral fact, without being outside our moral community. How likely this is depends on how coherent Morality is. If Morality is a set of independent principles, it would be very easy to non-culpably miss some. If it is a set of closely related directives, supported by an underlying rationale, then it is much less likely that an agent could non-culpably miss some moral fact. The more coherent Morality is, the less likely it is that an agent could meet the threshold and yet be non-culpably ignorant of some important part of it.

For now, I conclude these remarks on moral knowledge without a firm or final account. My view is that threshold knowledge of Morality—a good grasp of Morality as a set of requirements—is needed for being in the realm of subjective obligation, and, I shall argue, for ordinary praiseworthiness and blameworthiness. I agree that it is not completely clear what counts as moral knowledge and I do not attempt to resolve all of the complexities here. The important point, which I will argue for in Chapter 4, is that, if we meet the threshold for moral knowledge, then even when we act without awareness of the badness of our act, there is a sense in which we *should have known* that our act was problematic.

Subjective obligation is indexed to M, the umbrella value system. This means that the agents to whom subjective obligation applies, the ones who accept M, are ordinary agents. The agents who are outside of our moral community, the ones who do not grasp M, are few and far between. Moral monsters, psychopaths, the historically distant and utterly different, plausibly do not grasp Morality, and therefore are outside the realm of subjective rightness.

I have argued that we should think of subjective obligation as relative to a particular value system, but, if we want it to be a useful notion, we should think of it as relative to a very broad and ordinary value system, not an abstruse theoretical one. This leaves room for non-radical normative uncertainty: sometimes agents must act on their best assessment of the moral situation in the same way that they must act on their best assessment of the non-moral situation.

6. Formulating Subjective Obligation: Beliefs

One might now think that an agent's subjective obligation is to do what she *believes* is most morally suitable, where we are assuming that she has a good grasp of Morality. However, the belief formulation is unsatisfactory. The first worry about a belief formulation of subjective rightness is that it will not meet the accessibility requirement. Clearly, I sometimes have beliefs that are not accessible to me. I may have beliefs about it that I do not know, or may think I have beliefs that I do not really have. What if the beliefs that would be relevant to what is best are not accessible?[27]

We need to know what we mean by accessibility. Many of our beliefs are tacit, in that we have never consciously formulated them, but would assent to them if asked. As Dennett pointed out, it comes as no surprise to us that zebras do not wear overcoats in the wild (1978, 104). Implicit beliefs are not inaccessible in the relevant sense. There are also beliefs that are not occurrent (not 'before the mind') but that we have stored somewhere in our mind. Again, such beliefs are not usually inaccessible in the relevant sense, though we may on occasion have trouble recalling them ('what is this person's name?').

Rather, the worry is presumably about beliefs that we have *unconsciously*, that we do not have any voluntary access to. Our implicit biases might be thought of as unconscious beliefs, though this is controversial (biases seem to involve both cognitive and affective elements, for one thing). I come back to the issue of responsibility for biases in the final chapter. Here, I am just using it as an example of a case where our beliefs may not be accessible to us. Another sort of example involves motivated burying of our beliefs: we sometimes engage in self-deception and motivated ignorance. And perhaps there are cases where for no particular reason a belief gets buried: we simply forget, or rather, almost forget, so that the belief is still there enough to count as one of our beliefs, but we can no longer access it.

It is notoriously difficult to tidy up the various ideas in play here. What is it to have a disposition to assent to a proposition? And how do we distinguish between cases where the belief is newly formed and cases

---

[27] Harry Gensler discusses problems for a belief based account of subjective obligation in Gensler (1987). Holly Smith raises some of these problems in her account of subjective obligation (2010).

where it was already there? I do not attempt to resolve these issues here, not least because I am rejecting a belief formulation of subjective obligation. But some of the same issues arise for my own proposal. There doesn't seem to be *any* element of our psychology that is always accessible to us. I do not always know what I believe, what I want, how I feel, what I am motivated to do, what I am doing. Any account of subjective obligation will face a version of this problem: there doesn't seem to be any type of mental state that is always accessible.

Given that any account of subjective obligation is going to face a version of the problem, how serious it is for beliefs depends on what proportion of our beliefs is inaccessible. If it is a very small proportion, the belief theorist can argue that in those rare cases, the agent has no subjective obligation, her subjective obligation rests only on the beliefs that are accessible to her.[28] We can safely ignore the inaccessible beliefs, precisely because the accessibility requirement is what is crucial in determining subjective obligation.

This solution might work, but there is a closely related, and more serious, problem here. The fact that our beliefs are sometimes buried to varying degrees means that we should sometimes check ourselves: 'is there a buried belief here?', 'Do I know more than I think I do?' A belief formulation of subjective obligation has to find a way to make sense of *that* duty. It is not obvious how to justify that duty in terms of beliefs. First, we do not necessarily start with a belief that we have a buried belief. Second, even if we have a belief that we may have a relevant buried belief, it is not clear how the instruction, 'do what you believe is morally most suitable' deals with conflicts and complexities. Imagine an agent has a fairly firm and conscious belief that P but suspects that she may have a buried belief that not-P. The instruction to do what she believes is P doesn't seem to give a clear direction for what she should do.

This is a version of a more general problem, that there may always be room for improvement in our beliefs. Frank Jackson mentions this issue briefly in his discussion of prospectivism. Jackson argues that culpable ignorance can be handled in terms of actual beliefs (1991, 464). Jackson argues that one of the options is always to get more

---

[28] This is Holly Smith's conclusion in her 2010 (see footnote 55, p. 95).

information, and that getting more information has an expected utility just as any other option does. So, if the agent forms a belief without getting the relevant information, in a case where the expected utility of getting more information is high enough to outweigh the costs, then she has acted wrongly.

Jackson's conclusion about something being amiss with the agent's conduct is intuitively correct, but his reasoning illustrates an important point that Jackson does not acknowledge. The aim that guides whether or not you should seek more information is not itself an internal epistemic aim. In thinking about whether or not I should seek more information I must think about my *practical* aim. Imagine that I must decide on where to invest my money. If I am only concerned to make as much money as possible, the only thing I need to know about is likely returns. If, on the other hand, I am concerned to be moral, I should find out more about the investment strategies of the various companies. But these are practical reasons, pointing in different directions according to the practical aim. There can be no purely epistemic reason to seek more information. Richard Feldman makes this point when he argues that epistemic justification concerns only the relationship between actual possessed evidence and belief (2004). As Feldman says, there may be further reasons to look for more evidence, but they are not epistemic reasons.[29] Thus formulating subjective obligation in terms of beliefs does not capture the requirement to seek more information.[30] It is essential that we are able to point out that an agent's beliefs should be improved *in the light of the Moral aim.*

Jackson's approach works fine for prospective rightness. We can base prospective rightness on what a reasonable agent would believe at a particular moment because we are talking about an idealized agent. So we can assume (stipulate) that the agent has found out all that she should

---

[29] Holly Smith expresses the point rather differently, but the underlying thought is the same, in her discussion of a duty to inform oneself before acting (2014). Smith rejects the view that there is a freestanding duty to seek information—such a duty would not necessarily help the agent fulfil later duties. Rather, she argues, the duty to seek information is derivative, it is a duty that applies conditional on information seeking being conducive to later doing well by Morality ('producing maximal deontic value', as Smith puts it).

[30] Prichard (1932) recognizes this issue and discusses it on pp. 90–1. Prichard's account of the issue is not completely clear. Julia Driver criticizes Jackson on the same point (2012, 115–16).

find out in the light of her aim. That's part of what it is to be a reasonable agent in this sense. We can assume that she has weighed the costs and benefits of seeking more evidence, and that she has weighed them correctly, and so that her beliefs are the most appropriate beliefs she could have.

However, this is not the case with subjective rightness. If we take a snapshot of an actual agent's beliefs we may be including lazy, hasty, poorly motivated, or self-deceptive beliefs. And clearly, what an agent subjectively ought to do should not be determined by beliefs that she could improve right now if she bothered. On the other hand, an account of subjective obligation is not subjective if it idealizes away from past mistakes, and bases rightness on beliefs that an agent *would* have had, but does not in fact have. If an agent does not know which drug will kill and which will cure her patient, and cannot now find out, then she has to deal with that ignorance, even if the ignorance was culpably acquired. My point is that at any particular moment an agent should be thinking about how good her beliefs are. She should not take her beliefs as fixed points. She should be prepared to examine them in the light of her moral aim, and see if they need to be improved.

It might be objected that either she has a belief (perhaps a suspicion) that her other beliefs are flawed, or she does not. In the former case, she has all it takes to know that she should find out more, and so her subjective obligation is to find out more. If the latter, if she has no suspicion that her beliefs are flawed, then how could it be the case that she subjectively ought to seek more evidence? Subjective obligation is supposed to be accessible. But if she has no suspicion that her beliefs are flawed, then she has no subjective reason to seek more evidence.

But this misses something out. What we ought to be doing is much more general and stretches over time. We ought to have a general *attitude* of alertness, a readiness to examine our beliefs, a disposition to double check our evidence in the light of our aim. This cannot be expressed in terms of beliefs, which are just one sort of mental state, and at any one moment a belief set may lack a relevant belief about possible flaws in the current belief set. So, formulating subjective obligation in terms of beliefs is too narrow. We need something that captures our ongoing duty to weigh the costs and benefits of seeking more evidence, and to be generally alert and sensitive to moral features of our environment.

7. Formulating Subjective Obligation: Trying to Do Well by Morality

I propose that we can capture the essential requirements by formulating the subjective 'ought' in terms of trying.[31] I am using the concept of 'trying' in a broad sense, so that it applies to doings as well as 'setting oneself'. When one tries to do something one takes steps that one believes will result in one's goal being achieved. I'll say more about the concept of trying in the next chapter, and I will come back to the relationship between trying and praiseworthiness and blameworthiness in Chapter 4.

Before I go any further I must address an inextricably related question, the question of what it is that the agent should be trying to do. Should she be trying to do what is right? Either that would be circular (it would be subjectively right to try to do what is subjectively right), or it must refer to one of the other sort of rightness. But subjective rightness is not parasitic on prospective or hyper-objectivist rightness. Trying to do what is hyper-objectivist right might be obviously foolish. This is what the choice situations described by Frank Jackson and others show. If I have a choice between three drugs, where A will certainly ameliorate the condition, and one of B and C will kill the patient and one will cure her, the best possible act is to prescribe the drug that would cure the patient. But given that I do not know which drug that is, I should prescribe drug A, a drug I know for sure is not the best drug to prescribe (Jackson, 1991, 462–3; see also Regan, 1980, 264–5).

Similarly, trying to do what is prospectively right might be foolish. Often, of course, what is prospectively right and what is subjectively right coincide, but this is not necessarily so. Sometimes we do not know which action is prospectively right. As Holly Smith (2011a) shows, the Jackson style counterexample to objective rightness can also be applied to prospective rightness: we might be in a situation parallel to the situation where aiming for the prospectively right action is risky. Trying to do the action that is prospectively right fetishizes the prospectively right action

---

[31] I argue for formulating subjective obligation in terms of 'trying' in my 2003. Andrew Sepielli (2012) also formulates subjective ought in terms of trying, and though his approach to the question is rather different to mine I think we end up in the same place for more or less complementary reasons.

in cases like this. Indeed, any account of what we should be trying to do that picks out a particular set of acts and says, 'aim for them', will be guilty of fetishization, and vulnerable to a version of the Regan/Jackson example.

So, if subjective rightness is not based on hyper-objectivist or prospective rightness, what is it based on? How do we characterize the thing that the agent should be trying to do? To see the answer we need to think again about what prospectivism is. The prospectively right action is a fixed point, and it is fixed by being the best balance of risk to benefit: the balance that a reasonable agent would choose. A real life agent may well be able to identify the action that is the best balance of risk and benefit. But she may not—what should she do then? She should try to balance the various moral considerations against the risks as well as she can. That is not the same as trying to do the action that best balances risks and benefits.

An analogy may help here. If I have lost my cake recipe, but need to make a cake, I am aiming for the best balance of ingredients. Too little baking soda and it will not rise, too much and it will taste horrible. Rather than aiming to do what the recipe says, I am aiming directly for a good balance of ingredients. Aiming to exactly replicate the recipe is a pointless fetishization of the recipe. My primary aim is to do well by the general standards of cake making, not to follow a particular recipe.

The subjective 'ought' tells the agent to try to do well by the right- and good- making features that are in the world. I propose that we should summarize an agent's subjective obligation as follows:

Subjective obligation (corresponding to the subjective 'ought' and subjective rightness): An agent should try to do well by Morality.

This formulation is neutral between deontological features and consequentialist features of the shape of Morality. Sometimes doing well by Morality may look more consequentialist, and would involve balancing risk and value, and in that case, that is what the agent should be aiming for. Sometimes, compromises may not be possible, and doing well by Morality requires doing only the very best acts. In that case that is what she should be aiming for.

Clearly, the notion of trying encompasses the injunction to seek out more information when appropriate. If I am trying to do well at something, I have a practical aim that gives me the resources to make expected utility calculations about whether it is worth seeking out more information. Sometimes I may not be sure of which moral features in a situation are relevant, and which are weightiest. Trying to do well by Morality involves thinking about those questions too. If I have a good grasp of Morality in general, I have a framework for resolving uncertainties within Morality.

Trying to do well by Morality captures the ongoing nature of the project. If an agent makes a mistake, she has to go from there, and what she should do next is carry on trying to do well by Morality. Part of that will be figuring out whether to go back and rectify the mistake, or whether and how to move forward. She should seek immediately helpful advice: she should ask her friends and family, ask morally wise people, read some books and articles, and so on. Seeking immediately helpful advice is part of trying to do well by Morality.[32]

8. Conclusion

The responsibility constraint tells us that there is some connection between deontic concepts and what an agent could be responsible for. But it is vague, and does not itself help us to choose between different concepts of rightness. I have argued that we should see weaker and stronger versions of the responsibility constraint as corresponding to more and less objective accounts of rightness. The most objective account of rightness, hyper-objectivism, says that the right action is the best available one. This only meets a very weak version of the responsibility constraint: an agent *could* be responsible for doing that action, but very often will not be. Excuses will abound: what is actually best is very often not accessible to an agent. Prospectivism is also an objective account of rightness, in that rightness is anchored in what a reasonable agent would take the appropriate action to be. Prospectivism meets a stronger version of the responsibility constraint—an agent will often be

---

[32] There may be some grammatical awkwardness here—new obligations come into existence only after the agent has the relevant information. If another agent tells her that she should Φ, it is not strictly true that she ought to Φ until she herself has the evidence that Φing is the best course of action. But this problem need not detain us here. We have more ideas than terminology, unfortunately, and there is bound to be grammatical awkwardness at points. See Peter Graham (2010) and Kolodny and MacFarlane (2010) for discussions of 'the problem of advice'.

praiseworthy when she does what is prospectively right, and will often be blameworthy when she does what is prospectively wrong, because prospective rightness and wrongness will often be accessible to her. But prospectivism does not guarantee accessibility, and is not necessarily correlated with praise- and blameworthiness. It may be that an agent cannot or does not know what is prospectively best, and is blameless for that ignorance.

There is another sense of rightness, subjective rightness, that has not been thoroughly explored, though we have a general sense that subjective rightness is accessible to the agent, and more closely connected to praise- and blameworthiness, and to action guidance, than the more objective senses. I argue that what we primarily want from this sense of rightness is that it should correlate closely with one sense of praise- and blameworthiness. This is not the way that subjective obligation is usually understood, and so subjective obligation may not be quite how we imagined it. First, it is not going to be action guiding in the sense of giving immediately helpful instructions to the agent. However, subjective obligation is action guiding in an important sense, the sense that links up with praise- and blameworthiness. The subjective 'ought' is a genuine imperative: it tells the agent what to do, rather than what it would be ideal, or good to do.

Second, subjective obligation is relative to a value system, and applies to agents who accept that value system. I argued that we should opt for a broad value system, Morality, as I call it. The realm of subjective obligation is restricted to those agents who have a good grasp of Morality. A 'good grasp' does not mean having perfect knowledge, it means being in the ballpark. Thus this account leaves room for the agent to act subjectively rightly even given some normative uncertainty.

Finally, subjective obligation is not based on beliefs. Rather, an agent's subjective obligation is to try to do well by Morality. This makes sense of her continuing obligation to seek information and be alert to the possibility that her beliefs are flawed. In the next chapter I shall say more about the concept of 'trying' as I am using it here, and flesh out the notion of trying to do well by Morality.

3

Trying to Do Well by Morality

In the previous chapter I argued for an account of subjective obligation that is tied to our broad system of morality ('Morality', as I call it), and for the sake of argument I assume that we have Morality roughly correct. That does not imply that we always know what to do, sometimes we need to work hard to decide what Morality requires. Our subjective obligation is to try to do well by Morality.

The notion of 'trying' is crucial here. The basic argument was that we cannot base subjective rightness (and hence praise- and blameworthiness) on belief, because that does not capture the ongoing duty to improve beliefs, and to be alert to the relevant features of the environment. Belief is static, whereas trying is dynamic, continuous. Our common sense pre-theoretical notion of trying makes good sense of the conceptual requirements of an account of subjective obligation. In this chapter I say more about what is involved in trying to do well by Morality. I do not pretend to be providing a full account of the concept of trying. I don't think we need one. The word 'trying' is used for many different purposes, and I am just delineating, and neatening up some aspects of the concept that I am particularly interested in.

I argue that on the best understanding, trying involves knowledge of the aim, that is, knowledge of what one is trying to do. In order to count as trying to do X the agent must know that X is her aim, and must understand, at least roughly, what X entails. Trying is thus the perfect candidate for the activity that captures subjective rightness. As I argued in Chapter 2, subjective rightness involves having the aim of acting rightly (the agent must be acting rightly by their own lights), and furthermore, the agent must have a good grasp of Morality, so that her idea of acting rightly is aligned with Morality's account of acting rightly.[1]

In this chapter I take it for granted that the agent grasps the details of what is involved in her aim sufficiently well, and I focus on arguing that trying to achieve an aim requires accepting the aim as an aim. I argue that what I call a 'reflexivity requirement' applies here: roughly, the agent must know what she is doing to count as doing it. I argue that the knowledge of the aim that is necessary for a course of action to count as trying need not be full conscious knowledge in the moment. It can be in the background, tacit, or implicit at the time of action. The idea is that the agent, if asked, would agree that it is one of her aims. This allows us to make sense of 'indirect strategies': sometimes one can try to do X by consciously trying to do Y.

I go on to argue that we should understand trying in a strong sense, such that trying is not 'merely' trying. Rather, 'trying' means taking steps that the agent believes most likely to achieve her goal. However, goals can be complex, they can include more than one sub-goal. In trying to achieve our overall goal, we need to achieve a good balance of the various values at stake. I illustrate these points with an analogy: trying to do well by Morality is a bit like trying to be a good parent. It involves many complex steps, lots of uncertainty, some moments of full blast effort, and sometimes merely being alert to red flags.

Lastly, I give an account of failing to try as opposed to merely not trying. Most importantly, failing to try, like trying, involves a conscious, though not necessarily conscious in the moment, grasp of the relevant aim as a required aim. Thus only those who have a grasp of Morality as an aim they ought to have count as failing to try to do well by Morality.

---

[1] To put this in *de dicto/de re* terminology, the agent must have the aim of doing well by Morality *de dicto*, i.e. she wants to do whatever would actually count as doing well by Morality, but she must also have a good enough grasp of what Morality involves that her *de dicto* pursuit coincides closely with what is actually required by Morality. I think all cases of trying have the same structure. I count as trying to go to Brazil if I both aim to go to Brazil in the *de dicto* sense: I want to go there, wherever it is, but I also must have a good enough grasp of where Brazil is. If I book a ticket to Basildon under the false impression that Basildon is the capital of Brazil, I do not count as trying to go to Brazil.

1. Trying Over Time

One traditional question about trying is whether it precedes action, or can also be an action.[2] We might think trying should be conceptualized as the thing that you do before an action: a mental effort, a 'setting oneself', as Prichard puts it (1932). Alternatively, we might think that trying can itself be a doing: taking the steps that are involved in pursuing a larger aim. I take a broad view of trying. Sometimes trying is a setting oneself, but trying is also doing. Sometimes trying to do well by Morality *just is* figuring out what would happen, seeking more information, prescribing a drug, and so on. Usually, in trying, an agent does more than set themselves. The rest of the sequence continues, they actually take some steps towards their goal. So, in judging whether someone tried to achieve a certain goal, we look at what they did.

Long-term goals, such as doing well by Morality, being a good parent, or having a fulfilling career obviously involve both a general attitude of alertness, a general orientation towards the goal, which directs the agent's attitudes and responses to relevant cues, and taking concrete steps. When we judge whether someone was trying, there are different perspectives we may take. If we look at a narrow snapshot of someone's behaviour, it may not seem that they are trying to achieve a given goal. Imagine an athlete, trying to reach the Olympics. Is she trying when she eats her breakfast? Not in that moment, but that is not the right way to assess her trying with respect to that goal. Rather, the question should be,

---

[2] Another question that has been discussed in philosophy of action is whether every action involves trying. Jennifer Hornsby (1981) and Brian O'Shaughnessy (1980) both argue that we try to do everything we intentionally do. The fact that we only talk of trying when there is failure is irrelevant: an onlooker may know that an agent has an incentive to perform action A, but the onlooker also knows that the agent will fail. The agent does not know this. So the onlooker says, correctly, 'the agent will try'. But if the onlooker is wrong about the failure, what has changed? Nothing has changed for the agent. However, as Anscombe points out (1957, 25–6), not all intentional actions have an aim, and thus not all intentional actions were things I 'tried' to do. I might idly peel the label off a beer bottle. I am not *trying* to do this, though I am certainly doing it intentionally. So it seems that not all our actions are preceded by tryings. I can remain neutral on this issue, because I am interested in the notion of trying rather than the notion of action. It is worth noting that the term 'volitionism' is used differently in the philosophy of action literature and in the moral responsibility literature. In the moral responsibility literature, the terms 'volitionalism' and 'volitionism' are used to refer to the view that some sort of voluntary control is necessary for responsibility. In the context of philosophy of action, volitionism refers to the view that all actions are preceded by volitions/tryings.

when we look at her choice pattern overall, can we see the individual bits of her behaviour as part of, or consistent with, a serious effort to reach the Olympics? Sometimes we may assess a particular step she takes: is moving to a high altitude part of making a serious effort to reach the Olympics? Is taking weekends off training consistent with trying to reach the Olympics? Our judgments about particular acts should be judgments about those acts in the relevant context.[3]

In most contexts, the trying that is most salient, because it is the trying that we can easily observe in others, is trying-as-taking-concrete-steps. However, we can infer something about an agent's general attitude— whether she has set herself to do well or not—by looking at the things she does. So when we think about whether an agent is trying or not, we think both about whether what she did on this occasion counts as trying, and about whether she is overall trying. We might say about an athlete that she should not have taken the weekend off training, that that was not part of the best strategy and she should have known that. So, on Friday, she was failing to try. However, we might concede that overall she is seriously trying.

In sum, trying to achieve long-term goals is something that takes place over time, and we should judge whether someone is trying or not in the larger context. We can make judgments about particular acts, but we should be aware of how those acts fit into the agent's overall strategy. We can also make judgments about an agent's general outlook, whether they have set themselves to try, and that judgment is somewhat independent of our judgment about individual acts: an agent may be trying overall without managing to try on every occasion.

2. Trying and the Accessibility Requirement

It seems central to the idea of subjective obligation that our subjective obligations are accessible, that is their raison d'être. But, as I pointed out in the last chapter, it may be that there is no type of mental item that is always accessible through introspection. It is obvious that we don't always know our own goals and motivations. What we are *really*

---

[3] This is a familiar lesson from discussions of the apparent inconsistency of act and motive utilitarianism. We should recognize that any act is part of a larger pattern of acts and should be judged in that context. See Adams (1976), and Fred Feldman's discussion (1993).

motivated by may not be what we think we are motivated by. Similarly, although we usually know what we are trying to do, it does not seem like a conceptual confusion to say, 'I think he was trying to hurt you, even though he was not aware of that'.

The worry about trying being inaccessible is that we may think we are trying to do one thing, and we are in fact trying to do a different, possibly incompatible thing, and not in fact trying to do the first thing at all. I may think that I am trying to help you do a better job of dealing with your students, but in fact I am trying to take you down a peg or two, get you to see that I am a better teacher than you are. Or, I may think that I am trying to be a better teacher, but actually I am trying to appear to be trying to be a better teacher, or trying to get people to stop nagging me. And it is a commonplace that 'attempted suicide' is sometimes not an attempt at suicide at all: the aim is an attempt, not a success.

In a moral context, there are cases where it is fairly obvious that an agent is trying to appear to be trying to doing well by Morality rather than actually trying to do well by Morality. The business person who gives a small amount of money to charity with a great fanfare, or the department chair who makes a big song and dance about having women on the shortlist but never actually hires any women, are good examples. But there are also more subtle cases, where the agent's mistake and motivations are less clear. The expression, 'moralizing' captures a version of this phenomenon. We might say that someone is moralizing when they are presenting an objection to someone's behaviour as if the objection is on moral grounds, and there plausibly are such grounds, but there is something inauthentic about the moral claims made, the real impetus is something else: prejudice, dislike, fear, or some such. In such cases, the moralizer may take herself to be trying to do well by Morality, but actually she is trying to dominate or insult her interlocutor, or make herself feel better.

In such cases, clearly, an agent is not trying to do well by Morality (although she thinks she is). Intuitively then, she does not count as acting subjectively rightly. The problem is that from her own point of view she *is* trying to do well by morality, and given the accessibility requirement, it seems that we have to use the agent's own assessment of whether she is trying rather than an objective one. It is tempting to say that, for subjective obligation, the agent's point of view reigns supreme. But this seems to give us the wrong answer in moralizing cases and the like.

The alternative is to go the objective route, and say that when an agent is not (in fact) trying to do well by Morality, she is not acting subjectively rightly, even if she thinks she is. This invites the objection that the view is no longer subjective: an agent's point of view is no longer central, rather, what is central is whether an agent is, as a matter of objective fact, actually trying. I will defend the objective route here, and I admit that in the end subjective obligation depends on something that is not necessarily accessible to the agent. An agent is acting subjectively rightly when she is, as a matter of fact, trying to do well by Morality.

The justification for this is that no sensible view could be based only on what is accessible to the agent. As I suggested in the previous chapter, there is no mental state that is fully accessible. The problem here is that we are slightly mysterious to ourselves, and so we don't always have a grip on what we are up to. As a result, we cannot always tell whether we are acting subjectively rightly. In other words, the accessibility requirement has a limit, a limit that comes from the nature of our psychologies. So sometimes we may think we are acting subjectively well, but in fact we are not.

It may be surprising that an account of subjective obligation delivers the result that we cannot always know that we are acting subjectively rightly. After all, the point of the subjective view seemed to be that it is distinct from, and serves a different purpose to, objective accounts of rightness, accounts which anchor rightness in an idealized agent. But notice that the reason we cannot tell whether we are acting rightly is importantly different to the reasons the hyper-objective or prospective senses of rightness are inaccessible to us. I do not know whether I am acting hyper-objectively rightly because I do not know various facts about the external world. I do not know whether I am acting prospectively rightly because I do not know how to weigh utilities and probabilities as rationally as an idealized 'reasonable person'. These gaps in knowledge (or understanding) do not seem morally important.

By contrast, the reason that I may be mistaken about whether I am acting subjectively rightly or wrongly (on the rare occasions when that is the case), is that I do not always know what my own moral motivations are. We are all capable of degrees of self-deception. And it is not an unfamiliar experience to find that our motives are (or were) less noble than we had imagined at the time. The moralizer may look back at her own moralizing, and realize later that she was not really trying to do well by Morality at all. When we think we are trying to do well by Morality but are in fact not, it makes sense that we should lose credit, that we should miss out on praiseworthiness. To put it another way, praiseworthiness cannot be bootstrapped—an agent is not praiseworthy just because she thinks she is.[4]

So it makes sense that an agent can fail to be acting subjectively rightly even though she thinks she is. But perhaps the more worrying issue is the other side of this coin: can an agent be acting subjectively rightly without realizing that she is doing so? This seems absurd. Acting subjectively rightly does not seem like something we should be able to do by accident. Yet it is possible to be trying to do P without being aware that you are trying to do P. If you are acting subjectively rightly when you are trying to do P, it seems that you are acting subjectively rightly when you are trying to do P even when you are not aware that that is what you are trying to do. In the next section I shall show that my account can deal with this worry.

3. Awareness of the Aim

I shall argue that trying requires awareness of the aim *as an aim*. This means that the class of cases where agents are trying to do well by Morality without realizing that they are is fairly restricted. It is true that we have many aims that we are not aware of having, in the sense that we may be motivated towards a certain end without acknowledging that end as something we value. We might say that an agent is 'trying' to hurt another agent, in a situation where, if asked, she would sincerely deny that that was one her aims. But commonsensically, it stretches the idea of 'trying' if we talk of trying to do things that the agent is not even aware of having as an aim, and I will argue that that is not the best way to use the concept.

---

[4] One might worry that the inaccessibility of subjective obligation means that a Jackson style counterexample could now be applied, of the form, 'one of these options is what it would be subjectively right to do, but this other option is clearly the one you should choose'. But that will not happen: as soon as there is another option in view which is better by your lights, that is the subjectively right option. The relevant uncertainty here is uncertainty about what your motives are. If you don't know your own motives, you can unknowingly be incorrect, or retrospectively be unsure, about whether you were acting subjectively rightly, but as soon as we think about a present choice (which Jackson style counterexamples must be about), whatever seems sensible in the light of whatever uncertainty there is, is what you should choose (see Chapter 2 for my discussion of Jackson style counterexamples).

Imagine a politician who thinks he is trying to govern in a fair and just way, but who is actually ruthlessly pursuing his own political ambitions. Of course, there may be overlap between these aims, but they often come apart, and the politician's behaviour when they come apart reveals that his real priority is his own career. Such a person, call him Boris, is sometimes confused about what he is trying to do, but he knows what his aims are. He knows that he has ambitions. In some cases he has clear plans aimed at (for example) 'becoming prime minister', and is open to himself and his friends about that being what he is trying to do. At other times, he makes a plan of action, and he himself is not honest with himself or anyone else about which of his goals he is really aiming for with these plans. He may think that in championing a certain cause he is trying to lead his country into a brighter future. In fact, his real aim is to further his own career, and the cause he champions means very little to him. In such a case it seems fair to say that Boris is really trying to further his own career, even though he himself is not aware of that.

Intuitively, part of what makes it the case that Boris is trying to further his own career, is that furthering his career, under that description, is one of his conscious goals. He need not be conscious of it all the time, but he knows that it is his goal. Contrast a case where someone's behaviour is causally influenced by some end, but not an end the agent consciously holds as a goal. Imagine that a shopper is unconsciously influenced by the smell of the baked goods, and, without realizing it, is heading towards the bakery end of the grocery store. Would it be fair to say that she is trying to get to the doughnuts? We might *say* it, of course, just as we might say that a flower is trying to get more sun by turning towards the light, or a spider is trying to catch a fly by building a web. But we can see a clear difference between these cases and the case of Boris. That the *behaviour* has an aim is not enough to say that the agent has an aim, and so, I suggest, not enough to say that the agent is trying to achieve that aim.

We can put this in terms of a 'reflexivity requirement'. Some of the things that we attribute to agents require that the agent herself be aware, in some way, that the attribution applies. There are many things to which the reflexivity requirement does not apply: an agent could be sad or angry, or unkind, or acting objectively wrongly, without knowing that she is. But there are some things that require some self-knowledge, the agent must (in some sense) know that she is acting that way in order to count as acting that way. Here, I am arguing that trying is subject to a reflexivity requirement. However, this is not a requirement that the agent know exactly what she is doing in the moment. The reflexivity requirement for trying (and, I shall argue, for subjective obligation) requires only that the agent have the aim as a conscious aim, conscious in the sense that she would assent to having that aim, but not in the sense that it must be occurrent, before her mind at the moment of action. In other words, the reflexivity requirement is weaker than the accessibility requirement.

Our pre-theoretical notion of trying allows that trying itself can be unconscious, but in cases where the aim is also completely unconscious—an aim the agent doesn't know she has—we are much less likely to think of the behaviour as trying. Of course, we are not strictly bound by the ordinary concept. But, the ordinary concept, delineated in the way I have suggested, is in fact the one that works for my purposes. On my account, an agent is doing what she subjectively ought when she is trying to do well by Morality, and she is trying to do well by Morality only when she knows that doing well by Morality is one of her goals.

To see that the most useful account of trying entails that the goal must be consciously held, consider the case of Huckleberry Finn. Huck's best judgment about his situation is that he ought not to help Jim, a slave, to escape. Yet Huck does help Jim, acting *akratically* (against his own best judgment about what to do). Philosophical commentators, and I think Twain himself, see moral virtue in Huck's *akrasia*. In Chapter 4 I will come back to the question of whether and how Huck is morally praiseworthy in doing this. The point here is that although we might judge that Huck is acting well in some sense, it would be absurd to say that he is acting *subjectively* rightly. The whole point of the example is that Huck does not know that his act is morally right. From his own point of view he is acting wrongly.

But of course, Huck is not someone who takes Morality as his aim, and plausibly, Huck does not have a good grasp of Morality. Contrast a case where the agent does have a grasp of Morality, and the background aim of doing well by Morality. Imagine an ordinary agent, Dolores, who is feeling depressed. She has a good grasp on Morality, and takes it seriously as an aim. However, her depression has been going on for a while, and she is exhausted and demotivated. She does not feel like doing what she usually does on Saturday mornings, which is to help out at a homeless shelter. She decides to do something utterly selfish instead, so she cancels at the last minute, much to the inconvenience and disappointment of various people, and buys an expensive train ticket to the seaside.

Later, she might realize that what she was doing was trying to shake herself out of her depression, and as such, she was taking steps to get back on track as a normally functioning moral agent. She sees that she would not have done well at the homeless shelter that day. At the time it seemed to her like weakness of will when she cancelled, but, although she didn't realize it, she was engaging in some much needed self-care. Ensuring that one is a normally functioning moral agent is part of what is involved in trying to do well by Morality. So Dolores was trying to do well by Morality after all.

The question is, how counterintuitive is it to say that in this situation she was acting subjectively rightly? It is obviously at least slightly counterintuitive, because she was not aware that she was acting well; she thought she was acting badly. But remember that the ignorance is quite local: she has a good grasp on Morality, and she is conscious of this, she is not like Huck Finn whose grasp on Morality is deeply unconscious if it exists at all. Dolores has a general aim of doing well by Morality. She is generally oriented towards trying to do well. On this occasion, her deeper motivations were in line with her background commitment to trying to do well by Morality, and that is not a coincidence.

We might think of her psychology as being a bit like that of a habitually safe driver, who reaches her destination without any consciousness of how she did it. She may find it disturbing that she has no memory of how she drove the vehicle and avoided crashing, but in fact she does not need to worry. Her instincts and reactions are so well trained that she can set herself to auto-pilot and allow her conscious mind to wander. Of course, Dolores did not deliberately let her auto-pilot take over, and did not see that she could trust her auto-pilot. But this lack of accessibility does not seem fatal to the claim that she was, nonetheless, acting subjectively rightly.

Huck is not at all like a habitual safe driver. Huck is like someone who has never learnt how to drive, and in fact believes that cars are magical beasts, controlled by the mind. Such a person may have a very instinctive grasp of car mechanics. And so when she jumps in the car and tries to control it with her mind, she feels her hands and feet doing strange things, things that in fact get the car moving in the right direction. But it all seems much too precarious to say that she is *trying* to drive the correct way. If we focus on her instinctive grasp of car mechanics, we may think her a prodigious talent in that department. We may be in awe of the way that her instinct took over, despite her firm belief that the mind alone would control the car. But we certainly wouldn't say anything straight-forward, like, 'She is a good driver'. Our response must be nuanced. And so with Huck and Morality.

This, of course, gets us into the debate about Huck's case in the context of praiseworthiness. Nomy Arpaly and Timothy Schroeder (1999) argue that Huck is praiseworthy despite his false beliefs about Morality. According to them, Huck is praiseworthy because his deep motivations are oriented the right way. I come back to this in the next chapter, where I will argue that although Huck is praiseworthy in one sense, he is not praiseworthy in the ordinary way. This is the first step in that argument: on my view, acting subjectively rightly and being praiseworthy in the ordinary way go hand in hand. Here, I am arguing that although there is something good about Huck's behaviour, we should not say that he is acting subjectively rightly. He is not trying to do well by Morality, because he does not have a good grasp of Morality. To allow that we can be trying to achieve goals we do not hold as goals, is to collapse useful distinctions.

I started with the accessibility requirement: the idea that subjective obligation should be accessible to the agent. Trying is *mostly* accessible to us, we mostly know when we are trying, but we do not always. It is possible that an agent takes herself to be trying to do well by Morality when she is not. She may be in the grip of motivations other than the ones she ascribes to herself. Thus it is possible for an agent to think that she is acting subjectively rightly but be mistaken about that.

The converse situation, where an agent is acting subjectively rightly without realizing that she is, is more complex. This is because trying is subject to a reflexivity requirement. What that requires is that the agent have the aim in question as an aim, she would assent to it if asked. It does not require that she be aware of her aim at every moment. Hence, while it is conceivable that an agent is trying to do well by Morality without realizing that she is doing so at that moment, it is essential that the agent has doing well by Morality as a conscious aim. My example of Dolores illustrates this possibility: Dolores may not realize that she is trying to do well at a particular moment, but we can see that her behaviour is part of a general pattern of aiming for doing well by Morality, and Dolores herself would agree that doing well by Morality is one of her aims.

There may be cases like that of Huck Finn, or my doughnut seeker, where an agent is guided by an aim that they themselves do not understand or see as an aim. In such cases I think it makes best sense to say that the agent is neither trying to achieve that aim, nor acting subjectively rightly. There may be other reasons to be interested in their motivations, but we should distinguish acting subjectively rightly—being guided by a conscious aim of Morality—from other ways of being well motivated.

4. Trying and Indirect Strategies

The above discussion leads us to another issue about how we understand trying. One might worry that my account ignores the lessons we have learnt from discussions of indirect theories. Directly trying to achieve one's aims can be self-defeating. We would sometimes do better to forget about our aim and go along on instinct, or something like that. Yet my view is that a conscious aim is necessary.

However, there are two ways to understand 'conscious aim', and I need to disambiguate them. My account of subjective obligation says that the agent only counts as trying to do well by Morality if she has 'doing well by Morality' as a conscious aim. But as I say, that is not the same as having it before her mind all the time. Someone who decided to focus on playing a game instead of winning still counts as trying to win so long as they adopt the indirect strategy *in order to win*. In most cases, an agent who has adopted an indirect strategy would readily assent to the proposition that they are trying to achieve their aim. Furthermore, there is no problem for praiseworthiness here. Strategic burying of your rationale does not undermine praiseworthiness.

In some cases we adopt an indirect strategy quite consciously, because we know that it will work better. It sounds slightly odd, but it seems psychologically possible to do that. In other cases we may not be pursuing our goal quite so consciously and, as I argue above, we may not even take ourselves to be pursuing the goal, but we may nonetheless count as doing so. My example of Dolores is obviously not an example of someone adopting an indirect strategy in order to do well by Morality. Dolores is hindered by depression, she does not consciously adopt a strategy at all. However, Dolores has an overall conscious aim of trying to do well by Morality. It guides her, in much the way that some consequentialists have imagined the consequentialist aim guiding the ideal consequentialist agent. As Peter Railton (1984) puts it, there might be a counterfactual condition on Dolores's behaviour: if it were to become the case that her actions no longer conformed to her aim, there would be some sort of mental red flag that stopped her, and made her consciously reconsider. But sometimes, Dolores should sacrifice short-term benefits for long-term ones. In order to stay sane, she has to take a break sometimes. The break is justified, it is not in conflict with her goal. Hence, trying to do well by Morality does not entail consciously aiming to do well by Morality at every moment.

5. Strong and Weak Senses of Trying

It is important to emphasize that trying to do well by Morality in my sense is not necessarily always making an effort at full blast. There are two points to be distinguished here. One is about trying itself, whether we are using a strong or a weak sense, and the other is about the nature of the thing the agent is trying to do, and what sort of effort that requires.

Take first the strong and weak sense of trying. In the strong sense of trying, it seems that if an agent is sincerely trying, she thinks she is doing the best that she can to succeed.[5] Success may be very unlikely, we can try to do things that are very, very difficult, or depend on luck to a large degree, in which we are unlikely to succeed. But sincerely trying seems to involve taking the steps, and exerting as much effort as the agent thinks is most likely to succeed. If I half-heartedly run for a bus, barely breaking out of a walk, and slowing down as soon as the bus doors start to close, I am not really trying. We do sometimes use the weak sense of trying, such that one can try to some degree, but not hard enough to succeed.

---

[5] Defining trying in such a way that an agent only counts as trying when she does what she believes will *actually* result in success is obviously too strong. We can try to do things we think unlikely to succeed. As I said, whether or not we should try depends on the costs of trying balanced against the value and likelihood of success. Terrance McConnell (1989) makes the point (which he attributes to Tom Hill) that we should sometimes try to do something we take to be impossible. I agree that there might appear to be such cases, but I would understand them as cases where what you are really trying to do is not what you are ostensibly trying to do—you are really trying to show others that you can't succeed.

One may take some steps along the road to completing the act, but for some reason, not take all the steps. The weak sense of trying is the sense in which one might say that someone *merely* tried, where trying is not closely connected to doing. This is the point of Yoda's oft-quoted line, "No! Try not! Do, or do not. There is not try."[6] In other words, we shouldn't try *instead of* succeeding. So why talk about trying at all? Why not just say that we should succeed? Yoda would argue that that we should not try to do well by Morality, rather, we should just do well by Morality.

This is related to a worry that William Frankena (1950) has about Prichard's view that obligations are obligations to try:

> But surely I have no obligation to try if I have no obligation to do. Trying is always trying to do; and, if I have an obligation to try, this is because I first have an obligation to do or think I have . . . This is shown by the fact that if I know I cannot do, I have no obligation to try in any sense . . .   (1950, 173).[7]

Roy Sorenson (1995, 257–61) illustrates the problem by referring to Kavka's toxin puzzle. In the toxin puzzle, an agent is offered a prize for forming an intention to drink a toxin, and although she has to sincerely form the intention to get the prize, she doesn't actually have to drink the toxin. The puzzle arises because it seems that the victim of the toxin puzzle cannot form an intention to drink poison. She has a reason to form the intention, but she has no reason to drink the poison. Sorensen thinks that an analogous problem arises if obligations are seen as tryings: this would put one "in the peculiar situation of aiming at a deed that is not itself morally meritorious" (1995, 258).

So we might appear to be in the grip of a dilemma. Either trying should be seen as independent of doing, in which case the obligation to try seems to be pointless: why should we care about trying? Alternatively, trying is essentially trying to do, and trying gets its value from the thing achieved, in which case, surely doing is the thing that matters, and then why talk about trying at all?

The answer to this puzzle is that of course trying is always trying to do. Trying is not an alternative to doing. In general, trying and doing

---

[6] The quote is from *Star Wars*: Episode V: *The Empire Strikes Back*.
[7] I have omitted references to Frankena's taxonomy of 'ought'. I discuss this debate in more detail in my 2003.

are crucially connected: whether you should try to do something depends on what would happen if you succeeded as well as on the costs of trying. There can be strange cases, like the toxin puzzle, where one would have a reason to try but no reason to do. But reasons do not respect anything like a responsibility constraint. One could have a reason to draw a square circle. When one has an *obligation* to try, it is not because one has an obligation to do, it is because doing would be good, and the costs of trying balanced against the chances of success make it worth trying.

That does not imply that we might as well omit the reference to trying, and say that we have an obligation to do well by Morality. We are looking for an account of subjective obligation here, an instruction to an agent. 'Do well by Morality' is ambiguous. It is fine if it means, 'do what you can', which of course means, 'try to do well by Morality'. However, it is tempting to understand 'do well by Morality' as picking out a particular set of acts, a set defined by how well they abide by the rules of Morality. As I argued in the previous chapter, subjective obligation cannot be an obligation to attempt to do some set of acts that are independently defined as right. Either that would be circular (if one's subjective obligation is to try to do what is subjectively right) or, if we said that one's subjective obligation could be defined in terms of some other sort of rightness, it would land us back in the fetishization problem (that is the point of the Jackson style counterexample I discussed in the previous chapter). There is always a possibility that aiming for the hyper-objectively or prospectively right act is a risky course of action, that compromise would be better. We should think of the aim of subjective obligation as being a good balance of the various good and right-making features in a situation, given any relevant uncertainty. Trying to do well by Morality is trying to balance complex considerations. It is not aiming for a particular predefined balance.

Let's return to the strong and weak sense of trying. The sense in which we should try to do well by Morality is obviously not the weak sense, which would allow that one could try in an entirely half-hearted way. We need something stronger. Trying to φ involves doing more than making some small effort. It involves something more decisive, something like, 'taking steps that the agent believes are most likely to achieve φ'.

It might be objected that this is too strong. Surely sometimes we can try to do something by doing what is second most likely, or even third most likely to achieve the aim. Imagine that an agent is permissibly trying to do various things at once, and if she does what is *most* likely to achieve φ she will have to give up on some other aim. But imagine that there is another route to achieving φ which she believes only slightly less likely to succeed, and also allows her to pursue her other aim. If she takes the second route, we would still want to say that she is trying to achieve φ, in concert with her other aims. For example, imagine that Bhavi is trying to finish her PhD as soon as possible, but she is also trying to earn enough money to survive the summer without going into debt. She thus takes on an extra teaching assignment, which slows her PhD down a little, but earns her enough money for the summer. Bhavi's overall goal here—doing what makes sense, prudentially—involves balancing her sub-goals.

Bhavi's situation illustrates that we should pay attention to the nature of the goal. It is not that Bhavi has stopped trying to achieve her original goal, it is rather that her goal is complex: she wants to finish her PhD soon, but she also wants to avoid going into debt. Her goal involves both of these things in the right balance, and *that* is what she is trying to achieve. In fact, she *is* doing what she believes most likely to achieve her goal, when we see her sub-goal in the proper context, where it must be balanced against other goals. Thus Bhavi is trying in the strong sense: she is doing what she thinks will result in success.

Let's refine the strong sense of trying to take the complexity of goals into account:

> **Strong Sense of Trying:**   An agent is trying to achieve her overall goal if she does what she takes to be most likely to achieve her goal to a sufficient degree. She is trying to achieve a sub-goal if she does what she takes to be appropriate to achieve her sub-goal, given the other sub-goals that fall under her overall goal.

There are a couple of clarifications to make here. First, it is worth stressing that trying hard is not a matter of putting in effort in a moment. One may be trying hard to get somewhere on time in the sense that one is running as fast as one can, arms pumping, heart pounding. However, trying is diachronic and multifaceted, it is not just effort in a moment. If you have to run because you didn't bother planning your day properly, or checking the time, or making childcare arrangements, then you didn't really try to get to your appointment on time. Trying involves a general setting oneself, as well as planning, taking concrete steps, alertness to relevant changes in the environment, and an active seeking of evidence. Trying *hard* is doing all of those things to a large degree.

Second, because my interest is in trying to do well by Morality, I am talking only about cases where there is an overall goal. Things may be more complicated than that in real life, and it may be that we face conflicting goals. This relates to the question of whether Morality is the sort of aim that permissibly can be overridden by other aims. One might think that sometimes, self-interested reasons are so strong that they override moral reasons. Or, one might think that moral reasons always override self-interested reasons. Neither view is attractive. But they can be reconciled. The clearest way to put this is in terms of 'moral rationalism' (Portmore, 2011, 28). The idea is that when there are very strong non-moral reasons, so strong that it would be irrational not to act according to those reasons, acting according to those reasons must be morally permitted. That does not mean that morality always overrides all other aims. It just means that if another aim is the one we should rationally pursue, morality must permit that. If morality does not permit it, it cannot be rational to pursue it. The point is most easily made with an example: if friendship is so important that I should pursue my friendship rather than do something that would help a stranger, then it must be the case that pursuing my friendship is morally permissible. I will assume, for the sake of simplicity, that something like moral rationalism is true.

It is also worth clarifying that not all goals are such that trying to achieve them is very demanding. Sometimes our goals are 'limiting goals'—they are limiting conditions on what we do, that do not require anything more than avoiding certain actions. I do not want to step in a puddle. It doesn't take much to avoid stepping in a puddle, and most of the time I am trying to achieve that goal without very much effort at all. Morality may be like that sometimes (though this is a matter of substantive dispute in normative ethics), in which case, trying to do well by Morality may be very undemanding.

Next, trying to achieve an overall goal involves balancing the sub-goals, and this must involve a judgment of importance. The importance of any particular sub-goal is relevant both to how sub-goals interact with each other, and how they interact with other considerations, and these are relevant to how much effort we should put into each sub-goal to count as genuinely trying.

Imagine that Bhavi has a deadline for handing her grades in. Imagine then, that there is some sort of computer glitch at the university that prevents her from grading for a couple of days in the period right before the deadline and now, in order to get her grades in on time, she would have to miss a night's sleep. Given the simplifying assumption that that the delay is not her fault, Bhavi should accept that the grades are going to be a day or two late. It is plausible that she still counts as having tried *hard enough* to get the grades in on time. You may object that she should have left more contingency time. But that raises the question, how much contingency time is it reasonable to leave? And that, like the question of how much sacrifice we should be prepared to make, depends on the importance of the goal. The more important the goal, the more precautions we should take, the more contingency we should build in. If Bhavi were a surgeon, scheduled to perform a life-saving operation at a critical time slot, she should make sure that she would be there no matter what. However, if she is a PhD student grading undergraduate papers on Descartes, the standard for making sure she succeeds in doing things on time is much lower.

These are normative claims, of course. My point is that they are built-in to our everyday notion of trying. What counts as trying to do something depends on the relative importance of that sub-goal in the bigger picture. If an agent is late for a lunch date because of a relatively unusual traffic jam, it is fair for her to say, 'I'm sorry, I tried to get here on time'. However, if she is a surgeon, late for a time-sensitive operation that only she can perform because of the same traffic jam, we are less likely to accept her claim that she tried. The surgeon should have built in more contingency time—the traffic jam is only relatively unusual. Of course, there are reasonable limits to what the surgeon needs to have done: she does not need to make sure to the point beyond which *nothing* could prevent her arriving on time. What counts as reasonable here depends on the balance of the various relevant considerations.

So agents can count as trying even if they are not doing all that they can to ensure success for a particular sub-goal. This is because sub-goals must be balanced against each other. The agent is trying in the strong sense because she is trying to do what she thinks most likely to achieve her overall aim, the aim of doing well by her overall goal. But she may be trying only as hard as she deems appropriate to achieve a sub-goal, and still count as trying, and be praiseworthy.

Another complication in understanding the notion of trying is that some of our goals involve scalar values. This is why my formulation above says that an agent counts as trying if she does what she thinks most likely to achieve her goal *to a sufficient degree*. In trying to tidy my child's room, there are different levels of tidiness I might achieve. We have to think of there being a threshold here: the room is tidy enough at a certain point, and that is the minimum I should aim for. Doing enough to reach the threshold will count as properly trying. And again, what determines where the threshold is, is the relationship of that particular sub-goal to other sub-goals and other values. What counts as tidy enough depends on what else is going on, how much time I have, what my preferences are, and so on. However, in this case, I could try harder (make more effort and take more of the relevant steps), and make it tidier. Trying harder would not be wasted energy, as I would create more of the value that I am aiming for, namely tidiness.[8]

The scalarity issue is important to praise- and blameworthiness, because the overall goal, doing well by Morality, is scalar. Imagine an agent, Amin, who is thinking about his obligations to those less well off than himself. Amin counts as acting subjectively rightly when he tries as hard as he thinks is required. He does not put in as much time as he could—he is a busy teacher—and he does not think he should spend a great deal of time researching the efficiency of different charities, or spending hours thinking about what percentage of his income he should give. So it is plausible by his own lights that he is doing well enough when he narrows it down to a few reasonable options and distributes 10 per cent of his income between them. That counts as

---

[8] There are two ways to think about this. First, we could think in terms of different goals: I might have the goal of achieving tidiness level 1 and try very hard to meet that goal, or the goal of achieving level 2, and try very hard to reach that goal. Or, we might think that there are degrees of trying, such that a reasonable level of trying to tidy will achieve tidiness level 1 and trying to tidy harder will achieve level 2. I am thinking in the latter terms because it makes better sense of the relationship between trying and praiseworthiness when values are scalar. Consider Amin, he might be trying hard, very hard, and in his mind he has a sense of the minimum required by Morality. If he overshoots because he deliberately erred on the side of doing extra well, he seems praiseworthy. He did not fail to meet his goal (doing the minimum).

trying as hard as the goal requires, and so counts as fulfilling his subjective obligation.

Of course, Amin could try harder, and trying harder would be morally better. We might put that in terms of supererogation—he is doing more than is required. Or we might say that rightness is scalar—Amin is acting rightly but he could act in a way that is even more right.[9] However we characterize the deontic notions here, we can say that Amin is trying hard enough to count as trying in the strong sense when he tries hard enough (by his own assessment) to meet the minimum level of achievement. He can try even harder, and be more praiseworthy. I come back to this in the following chapter, where I talk more about praise- and blameworthiness.

We can contrast cases where there is no scalarity, where overshooting the target is not better than simply meeting the target. Take the surgeon who is trying to arrive at the operation on time. She must try hard enough to arrive on time. Let's assume that her sincere assessment of what is required is that she should think about the worst regular journey time, and then add some extra time on top of that. To simplify things, we can assume that that is objectively reasonable too.[10] She could spend the previous night at the hospital, but that would be doing more than is required. She needs to be there in time for the operation. Being there earlier does not get her extra credit. Trying beyond the minimum requirement does not always contribute more value, and is not always more praiseworthy.

I have argued that we should think of trying in the strong sense, where an agent counts as trying when she does what is most likely to achieve her goal. However, when we are considering whether an agent is trying to achieve sub-goals or not, we have to take into account how those sub-goals interact with each other and with other considerations. Agents may be trying as hard as is appropriate even though they do not take themselves to be doing all that they could to ensure success.

---

[9] See Norcross (2006 and forthcoming) for more on the idea of scalar rightness. I come back to this in the next chapter.

[10] The agent counts as trying when she does what is appropriate by her own assessment, and of course her own assessment could be flawed, in which case we have a situation where she is praiseworthy despite having acted objectively wrongly. I focus on the simpler sort of case here.

6. Trying to Do Well by Morality: An Analogy

The view I am defending is that our subjective obligation is to try to do well by Morality. In this chapter I have clarified various aspects of the concept of trying that I am using here. An analogy may be helpful to draw these points together. Think about another, narrower thing that some agents ought to try to do: be a good parent.

First, we can think of our appraisal of people's parenting as being like our moral appraisal. It is indexed to a broad value system. There is a certain substance to being a good parent, and this is more or less objective and agreed on. Good parenting, other things being equal, results in morally good, happy, secure children who develop into morally good, happy, secure adults. When we talk about someone who is trying to be a good parent we take for granted that we share the same overall view of what being a good parent consists in. People who take themselves to be trying to be good parents but who have a wildly different view of things from ours, are outside the realm of ordinary assessment here. They are in a different category. There would be something misleading about saying of someone who gives their children to a devil worshipping cult that 'they are trying to be a good parents, it's just that they have rather different ideas to us'. Of course we could say that, but it would be more useful to point out that their conception of parenting is wildly off the mark. The way in which the devil worshippers are ignorant of what good parenting involves goes much deeper than the ignorance the rest of us contend with.

The rest of us, those who share a broad conception of what it is to be a good parent, may lack bits and pieces of knowledge and know-how. When we try to be good parents we are trying to figure out what to do as well as how do it. Some actions may be risky, very harsh discipline for example. It might be a great thing, but it might be a terrible thing. As with moral value, the values involved in being a good parent often involve risks, when faced with uncertainty we are pushed towards compromise. And we do not know what the best balance is. Is the pay-off of harsh discipline, or of controlled crying worth the risks? Hard to say. We do our best.

When our goal is being a good parent, we have to be flexible, thoughtful, responsive. We don't identify a set of acts in advance and aim for them. If we turn down a blind alley we need to decide where to go next, how to adjust our goals, and of course, when to give up. If we make mistakes we have to adjust our plans. We have to be alert to situations where the best thing to do is to gather more information, including about the nature of being a good parent.

As parents, we sometimes ought to be focusing fully on parenting. Sometimes only the best will do. But sometimes trying to be a good parent is just a 'limiting goal'. There are things I must not do, but beyond that I have freedom to do what I want. (We may not be sure where these freedoms lie and what their limits are, and of course, part of being a good parent is thinking about those issues.) But it is at least very plausible that good parenting is compatible with a fulfilling career, and that it is permissible to balance our efforts so that even if we accept that nothing is permissible that is incompatible with being a good parent (which would be parallel to accepting that nothing is rationally permissible that is immoral), we are sometimes permitted to do things that have nothing to do with being a good parent in themselves.

Having said that, it is also true that we sometimes try to be good parents, and yet don't try quite hard enough. We are sometimes a little bit self-deceptive, or a little bit lazy or distracted. We don't pay quite enough attention, or listen carefully enough, and we miss places we should be more supportive. Sometimes, of course, this is unavoidable, and not subjectively wrong at all. However, sometimes we are trying, but not trying hard enough for our behaviour to meet our own standards; by our own lights we are not awful, but we could have tried a bit harder. In the next section I say more about failing to try.

7. Failing to Try

I need to give an account of what it is to fail to try, because that is what renders an agent blameworthy in the ordinary way. I will argue that only agents who have a good grasp of Morality can fail to try in the relevant sense. Other agents, agents who do not have a grasp of Morality may in fact *not* be trying to do well by Morality, but that doesn't render them blameworthy in the same way as someone who does grasp Morality and *fails* to try. The difference is like the difference between failing to send someone a birthday card when you knew it was their birthday, and not sending them a birthday card when you had no idea when their birthday was.

Just as trying requires that the agent have a conscious aim, failing to try involves some awareness of failure. The reflexivity requirement applies to failure to try as well as to trying. If it seems fair to say that Imani *failed* to send Fred a birthday card, we would normally think that Imani knows when Fred's birthday is, and furthermore that Imani accepts that she ought to send a card. To count as failing to try, Imani must understand the relevant standards, and accept that they apply to her.

I will say more about what it is to accept that standards apply to one in Chapter 7. For now I will just note that 'accepting that the standards apply' leaves room for someone who defies the standards. Imani may think, 'I know it is Fred's birthday, and I know I ought to send a card, but I don't care about that, I can't be bothered, I am not going to do it'. So long as she understands that she ought to send a card, her not doing so counts as failure in the relevant sense, and correspondingly, she can be blameworthy in the ordinary way. Contrast an agent who (non-culpably) thinks that younger people do not have to send birthday cards to older people, and so does not think she needs to send a card on this occasion. This agent is not failing to try, she is simply not trying.

Thus the agent needs to understand the standards and accept that they apply. But, again, awareness does not have to be fully conscious in the moment. It is not that Imani only counts as failing to try if she was fully aware of the upcoming birthday and didn't bother to put a card in the post. It is enough that she had the date in her diary. Or, for a more complex case, take Tony Blair's decisions in the run-up to the invasion of Iraq in 2003. We can assume that Blair was not fully conscious in the moment that there were no weapons of mass destruction in Iraq. One possible analysis of Blair's behaviour is that at some point he stopped trying to govern in a fair and democratic way. He was swayed by thoughts about his own legacy, or by the power and charisma of George Bush, or by rivalries and disagreements within his own party. He believed what he wanted to believe. He was deflected from his Moral goal, and so the answer to the question, 'did he do what he subjectively ought to have done?' is 'no', even though he may have told himself that he was acting rightly.

The way in which Blair acted wrongly is very ordinary and familiar. When we blame him, we do so with that in mind. We expect him to be able to acknowledge (even if he never in fact does) that he did wrong. By contrast, agents outside of our moral community are acting wrongly in a very different way to agents who grasp Morality. We do *not* think that they have acted subjectively wrongly, in that we do not think that they are aware of what they have done. That seems like a very important difference. They have acted wrongly, but without self-awareness, and not through temporary self-deception, but through deep ignorance. It seems appropriate that we should say something different about a moral monster from what we should say about Tony Blair.

So, an agent counts as failing to try to do A only if she has a background knowledge of what A involves and accepts that A ought to be her aim. If she lacks that background knowledge, there may be other things to say about her, but she is not failing to try. In the next chapter I will argue that blameworthiness correlates with failure to try. Blameworthiness and failure to try both require reflexivity: we need something that the agent herself has a grip on in order to get blameworthiness.

In the moral case, failure to try hard enough is probably more common than complete failure to try. Consider again, Amin. As I imagine him, he is trying fairly seriously, and he is trying hard enough to meet the threshold for trying in the strong sense. However, the reality is probably that most of us suspect that we are not doing quite enough by the standards of Morality. We suspect that we should be spending more time thinking about the situation of the very poor, giving more money, making more sacrifices. We know we could try harder, and we think trying harder is very likely morally required. We try to do well in the weak sense: we take some steps towards the goal, but we are not trying in the strong sense: we are not doing what we think most likely to constitute doing well by Morality. This is the way most of us end up being blameworthy. Of course, there is a hard question in normative ethics here about how much is required. Perhaps our duties to those less well off than ourselves are not as stringent as I am assuming. Part of what we need to do, in trying to do well by Morality, is to think carefully about those hard questions.

8. Conclusion

I have given an account of 'trying' as I am using the idea in subjective obligation. An agent is trying to do well by Morality when she sets herself to do well by Morality, where that includes her general outlook and attitudes as well as taking the steps she thinks most likely to result in doing well by Morality. Trying involves background knowledge of the thing the agent is trying to do, and accepting the goal as a goal. However, it is possible that we don't always have full introspective knowledge of when we are trying to do something. I argued that so long as the agent accepts the aim as an aim, it can be plausible to say that she is trying even when she is not aware of doing so. The reflexivity requirement does not demand full knowledge in the moment, it requires only that the agent have the general background knowledge that that is an aim that she has.

We should understand trying in a strong sense, so that trying to do X is taking the steps that the agent believes most likely to achieve X. However, much of our day-to-day activity involves trying to achieve sub-goals, and part of what we must do in trying to achieve our overall goals is to balance those sub-goals. We count as trying when we do what is appropriate to achieve a sub-goal, given how it weighs against other relevant considerations. We don't always need to be doing all that we can to ensure success. It is often the case that we must accept some level of risk of failure, in order to allow space for other more important sub-goals.

In the next chapter, I will link this account of trying with praise-worthiness. Trying to do well by Morality is praiseworthy. Not trying hard enough, or failing to try, is blameworthy. Crucial to my argument is the point that praiseworthiness and blameworthiness, like the notion of trying, require background knowledge. There is a reflexivity requirement.

4

Ordinary Praiseworthiness and Blameworthiness

In the previous two chapters I have developed an account of subjective obligation according to which the subjectively right thing for us to do is to try to do well by Morality. In this chapter I will defend my claim that subjective obligation correlates with ordinary praise- and blameworthiness.

There is a controversial feature of my understanding of subjective rightness. On my view, moral knowledge (a good, though not necessarily perfect, grasp of Morality) is necessary for acting subjectively rightly and hence for ordinary praiseworthiness. And so, an agent who does *not* have a grasp of Morality does not have any subjective obligations, and as a result is never praise- or blameworthy in the ordinary way.

There are various possible worries about this. First, it might be objected that this account of subjective obligation is not subjective enough: surely agents should be judged on what is accessible to them, not on something (knowledge of Morality) that is not necessarily under their control. However, the real issue is not that subjective obligation is inaccessible: it *is* accessible to all those who grasp Morality. The worry is rather that my account leaves a lot of people outside the realm of subjective obligation and hence ordinary praiseworthiness. In Chapters 5, 6, and 7 I return to the question of agents outside our moral community, and what we should say about the way in which they might be praise- or blameworthy.

In this chapter I defend the connection between subjective obligation and praise- and blameworthiness. I start with subjective rightness and ordinary praiseworthiness. I start by arguing that merely acting on conscience is not enough for praiseworthiness. On the other hand, merely being motivated towards what is actually good is not enough for praiseworthiness either. I argue that praiseworthiness is subject to a 'reflexivity requirement', it requires some recognition of the grounds for praiseworthiness. The agent must both act on conscience and have a good grasp of Morality.

I go on to compare different approaches to understanding praise- and blameworthiness. Nomy Arpaly uses the example of Huck Finn to argue that an agent can be praiseworthy without having a good grasp of morality, and without acting as they believe they ought. On a competing view, which I refer to using George Sher's term, the 'Searchlight View' (2009), full awareness of every relevant aspect of the act at the moment of action is necessary for praise- or blameworthiness. I argue that both of these views fail: Arpaly's view does not meet the reflexivity requirement, and the Searchlight View meets too strong a version. Some awareness, some background knowledge is required, but it need not be as bright as a searchlight.

In the final section I sketch some of the details of this account of ordinary blameworthiness. My account is primarily an account of the praise- or blameworthiness of an agent for her general approach to life, but we can extrapolate, in an approximate way, to blameworthiness, and degrees of blameworthiness, for particular acts.

1. Competing Accounts of Subjective Obligation

I have been giving an account of subjective obligation according to which subjective obligation requires a good grasp of Morality, the broadly correct value system. I need to show that subjective rightness in this sense, and praiseworthiness, go hand in hand. In order to do that, I will examine other possible accounts of subjective obligation, and argue that, although they are internally coherent, they do not make good sense of praiseworthiness, and thus are not the conception that is most useful to us.

There are two competing accounts of subjectivism, as I discussed in Chapter 2. First, is theory-relative subjectivism. Subjective obligation might be relative to more fine-grained moral theories, such as Utilitarianism, or Kantianism, so that a utilitarian acts U-subjectively rightly, and is U-praiseworthy when she does what she believes she ought to do by utilitarian standards. Second, is pure subjectivism. Prichard and Ross both argue that subjective rightness is fully subjective. An agent acts rightly when she does what, by her lights, is most morally suitable. Acting subjectively rightly is relativized to the values an agent happens to have, so that acting subjectively rightly is itself a morally neutral notion. I will argue that neither of these accounts correlates with praiseworthiness.

We can give theory-relative subjectivism fairly short shrift. It offers much too narrow an account of subjective obligation.[1] The sense of praiseworthiness that we are after is broader than the theory-relative sense. That is not to say that praiseworthiness floats free of value systems. In fact, I think that praiseworthiness, like rightness, must be relative to a value system, but that the relevant system is broader than academic theories. We can think of praiseworthiness in narrower and broader ways: agents can be U-praiseworthy or K-praiseworthy and so on, or we can use praiseworthiness more broadly. The narrow usage is clearly not very interesting. I will defend the broader usage in what follows. An agent is praiseworthy when she tries to do well by the lights of Morality, the broad moral system that we share.

The second alternative account is pure subjectivism, which implies that the agent is praiseworthy when she does what *she* takes to be morally appropriate. The whole point of subjective rightness, it might be thought, is to get away from the vagaries of actually getting the correct answer, and focus on the agent's *will*, and whether or not an agent has the correct value system is just a matter of luck, just like whether or not they have the right credences, or the right factual beliefs. It is not necessarily up to agents whether or not they have the correct moral views. So it is tempting to think that an agent is praiseworthy when she acts on her conscience, even when she has a false moral view.[2] In the next section I discuss the

---

[1] There is a further point here. It is not just that we have a concept of praiseworthiness that applies regardless of the academic theoretical stance (or lack thereof) of an agent. Academic theoretical stances are very difficult to have knowledge of in the right way to be praiseworthy. This is a problem that Arpaly and Schroeder run into, in their recent account of what it is to be motivated by good-making features. Arpaly and Schroeder claim that an agent has a good will if she can conceptualize the right-making features of her actions in the correct way. But if that requires us to grasp complex and arcane concepts like autonomy, almost no one would be praiseworthy. See Lord (2017) for a critique of Arpaly and Schroeder's view that develops that worry.

[2] In Chapter 2 I argued that there can be some reasonable uncertainty about the content of Morality at the margins, and lots of reasonable uncertainty about how to balance and interpret the different elements of Morality. Thus one can be in the ballpark, and acting subjectively rightly, even when one has made some moral mistakes. When I talk about someone who has an incorrect moral view in the discussion below, I am referring to deep moral ignorance.

sort of credit that accrues to someone for acting on conscience, and distinguish that from a richer notion of praiseworthiness.

2. Pure Subjectivism and Conscience Respectworthiness

As I said, it seems that the whole point of being interested in subjective obligation is to focus on how things seem from the agent's point of view, not how things actually are. In thinking about subjective obligation we are accepting that an agent may not be ideally rational or even reasonable, that she may have limited knowledge and also limited skills, for example, she may not be very good at interpreting evidence. Similarly, we are not focusing on how things turn out, rather, we are focusing on what an agent does, the efforts she makes, the core of her action that is (I use this phrase very loosely) 'up to her'.

It might appear, then, that we should also abstract away from mistakes that the agent has made about the nature of morality, and focus on whatever it is that is purely *her*, her 'good will'. But this is a misleading way to look at things. The moral quality of an agent's will cannot be so easily isolated from the accidents of the environment. The way that an agent thinks about morality may be explained by the evidence that was available to her, but it nonetheless makes a difference to what her will is *like*.[3] As a purely descriptive matter, an agent with a false view of morality has a different sort of will to one who grasps Morality.

Compare two art critics, one of whom tries very hard to point out beautiful art, and because she genuinely understands beauty, successfully picks out beautiful art. The other also tries very hard, but through no fault of her own she has a corrupt and degraded aesthetic, and so fails. In one sense it is just luck that the second one picks out the wrong stuff. But

---

[3] An agent may be culpably ignorant, in that she brought about her own moral ignorance. In that case, we can blame her for a prior 'benighting act', as Holly Smith terms it (1983). Michele Moody-Adams (1994) argues that we should think more clearly about the motivations for ignorance like that of the ancient slaveholders. Charles Mills (2007) argues that ignorance is often 'active', motivated by group interests, but also maintained by the structural forces of oppressive societies. In a recent paper, Elizabeth Anderson argues along similar lines (2016). It is worth pointing out (as William FitzPatrick emphasizes in his 2008) that there are not necessarily clear benighting acts, but a general bad attitude to the situation, and that is what causes the ignorance. I come back to culpable ignorance in Chapter 7.

it is relevant to how we assess her will in aesthetic terms: her will, though good in some sense, is aimed in the wrong direction aesthetically. Her aesthetic sense is flawed, and so she is not 'aesthetically praiseworthy', even though it is not her fault that she is not praiseworthy here. The crucial point is that substantive motivations are relevant when judging an agent's quality of will.

This line of thought is closely related to arguments that Nomy Arpaly and other so called 'attributionists'[4] about moral responsibility have put forward. On this view, praiseworthiness is correlated with moral concern. In an early version of the view, Arpaly says:

> deficiency in good will is insufficient responsiveness to moral reasons, obliviousness or indifference to morally relevant factors, and ill will is responsiveness to sinister reasons—reasons for which it is never moral to act, reasons that, in their essence, conflict with morality. In other words, the person who is deficient in good will acts without regard for the wrong-making features of his action, while the person who has ill will performs his action exactly because of its wrong-making features.   (2003, 79)[5]

Arpaly's terminology doesn't make it explicit, but in referring to 'morality' and 'wrong-making features', she is referring to the true value system, 'Morality' as I call it. Her point here is that the notion of ill will (bad will) just is the notion of a will that is directed away from the actual substance of Morality. On Arpaly's view, the substance of the agent's motivation either matches or departs from the substance of morality, and when it matches, the agent is praiseworthy, when it departs, the agent is blameworthy.[6]

I think that things are more complex than this, and I will come back to the various ways in which agents can have bad and good wills. The point

---

[4] See Watson (1996, reprinted in 2004), Arpaly and Schroeder (1999), Arpaly (2003 and elsewhere), Smith (2005 and elsewhere), Scanlon (1998 and elsewhere), Sher (2009 and elsewhere), Talbert (2008 and elsewhere).

[5] In recent work (2014), Arpaly and Schroeder explicitly defend the condition that the agent must conceptualize the reasons for which she acts correctly. This does not mean that the agent must understand that her act is right, or even morally good, rather, the agent must conceptualize the reasons for which she acts in terms of the right-making features (164). This brings the view closer to my view but Arpaly and Schroeder insist that awareness of the overall moral status of the act performed is not necessary for praise- or blameworthiness. There are problems with Arpaly and Schroeder's view, see Lord (2017) for a critique.

[6] See also Markovits (2010). Markovits puts the point in terms of 'the Coincident Reasons Thesis', arguing that the reasons that an action was performed and the reasons that make it right must be the same reason for an action to be praiseworthy.

I want to make here is that we have a good reason to keep two different concepts apart: on the one hand, a will that is 'morally good' in the sense of matching the substance of Morality and on the other, will that is 'morally good' in the sense of aiming to act as the agent thinks she morally ought. As these are different qualities of will, we should acknowledge that, and acknowledge that there may be correspondingly different notions of praiseworthiness.

It seems undeniable—platitudinous—that our ordinary sense of the word 'praiseworthiness' refers to the case where an agent is both acting on conscience and her will is directed towards the content of Morality. But the two aspects of an agent's will can come apart, as in the case of an agent who does what she thinks she ought but has a terrible morality, or the case where an agent acts against her best judgment about what she ought to do but is in fact motivated by the right concerns. Given that my aim here is to refine our concepts, to come up with the best account of them in the context of our needs, I will examine these two different sorts of case on the initial assumption that we might find it useful to make a distinction here. I will call the content matching sense of praiseworthiness, 'Moral motivation esteemworthiness', and the conscience following sense, 'conscience respectworthiness'. In the end I will argue that both an agent's moral motivations and her conscience must be good for her to be praiseworthy in the ordinary way. Here I focus on showing that conscience respectworthiness is not sufficient for praiseworthiness.

It is worth noting that conscience respectworthiness is more than mere practical rationality. Practical rationality, doing what one thinks one has, all things considered, overall reason to do, is obviously not morally praiseworthy for its own sake *at all*. But following one's conscience involves some moral content in the will. To put it in Kantian terms, it involves acceptance of a categorical 'ought' as well as the hypothetical 'oughts' that might end up contributing to an all things considered 'ought' of practical rationality. And this is why the question about whether or not it is praiseworthy arises: an agent who accepts and abides by categorical 'oughts' has something in common with other agents who accept categorical 'oughts'. There is surely something respectworthy in that.

We might put the point in terms of virtues. An agent who is conscience respectworthy has a trait that is usually a virtue, something like integrity, or constancy. But if it is not paired with the right aims, the right motives, it does not function as a virtue. Nonetheless, we can respect that trait in a limited way, we respect it in isolation from the motives with which it is actually paired.

We have two different appraisal concepts here, and in ordinary contexts they are sometimes conflated. In giving them different names, motivation esteemworthiness and conscience respectworthiness, I make sure to avoid accidental conflations. But of course, the real question is, is the difference between the concepts important? And if so, which is the one that we are interested in?

It is intuitively obvious that the difference is important. Take JoJo, the cruel and ruthless dictator who (we stipulate) is the way he is through deep enculturation (the example is Susan Wolf's, 1987). Imagine that JoJo realizes that his value system demands that he kill a friend. He takes seriously his duty to kill his friend, and resolves to do what he takes to be the right thing to do, despite the emotional cost, inconvenience, and expense. JoJo is trying to do well by his moral code. But it is a false morality and this is not merely incidental to our assessment of JoJo. His trying to do well does not seem fully *morally* praiseworthy. The sense in which it is a small positive strike in his favour is not that it is a small contribution to his praiseworthiness, that might be outweighed. Rather, this is a different sort of positive. Making a distinction between conscience respectworthiness and motivation esteemworthiness makes sense of our ambivalence about the case.

So, are we primarily interested in conscience respectworthiness or motivation esteemworthiness? It depends on the larger aim. I am giving an account of subjective obligation. Conscience respectworthiness might seem to be the notion I am after because it fits well with the subjective framework: it is easy to say that an agent is responsible for following her own conscience, because following her own conscience is up to the agent, it does not depend on environmental luck. An agent can try her best to do well, no matter what her values. Whereas, being motivated by the right things—the concerns that really do reflect moral value—does not seem to be up to the agent. An agent may have been raised in a terrible world, and so no matter how hard she tries to do well, she is limited by her ignorance of the true value system.[7]

---

[7] There are different reasons for which we might think that the substance of the motivations is not up to the agent. I am referring to the environmental case, where the

So we are right back at the beginning: trying to do well is up to the agent, whereas getting it right is not. But the situation here is not that we are looking for whatever is wholly up to the agent. Rather, we are engaged in a sort of reflective equilibrium. We want an account of subjective rightness that meets the strong responsibility constraint, where we understand that as having both an accessibility aspect (subjective rightness must be accessible to the agent) and a praise- and blameworthiness requirement (it should be automatic that an agent is praiseworthy when she acts subjectively rightly and blameworthy when she acts subjectively wrongly). We don't want to put all the weight on accessibility, and dilute the notion of praise- and blameworthiness so much that it is not weighing anything in the equation.

There is a richer notion of praiseworthiness than is covered by conscience respectworthiness, and this richer notion is useful to us. Saying that someone tries to do well is interesting, but what we really want to pick out is the people who tried to do well *by Morality*. These are the people we interact with, the people we learn from, the people we have personal relationships with. Our primary interest in praising and blaming is in praising and blaming those who start on the same page as us. Those outside our moral community are in a different category, we interact with them, if we do at all, in a very different way to how we interact with those in our moral community. It makes sense to restrict ordinary praise and blame to those who share our Morality, as I shall argue in more detail in the next chapter.

I have argued that acting on conscience is not sufficient for praiseworthiness. However, as I shall argue in the next section, I do think that acting on conscience in a sense (the sense required for acting subjectively rightly), is a necessary condition. I am thus in disagreement with those, like Nomy Arpaly, who argue that acting on or against one's conscience does not make a difference to praiseworthiness at all (2003 and elsewhere).

environment is misleading. So an agent can be 'trying her best' and yet not have the right value system through no fault of her own. It is also true that an agent's motivations are not up to her because we think her motivational make-up is not up to her, but it is equally true that her ability to act on conscience is not up to her. In that case we have taken too many steps back, and we are staring into the abyss of a determined world.

3. The Moral Concern View, the Searchlight View, and the Reflexivity Requirement

Nomy Arpaly and other attributionists argue that having moral concern, where that means being motivated towards the right things, is sufficient for praiseworthiness. In other words, they argue that praiseworthiness depends on motivation esteemworthiness, and there is no reflexivity requirement. The agent need not think of herself as acting well, she just needs to be well motivated in fact.

In the previous section, in defending my view that following one's conscience is not enough for moral praiseworthiness, I endorsed the thought that an agent's motivations must be oriented in the right way for her to be praiseworthy. But that is not to say that correct orientation is sufficient. This is where my account departs from moral concern views. On my view, an agent must be trying to do well by Morality, and trying, as I argued in Chapter 3, requires background knowledge of the aim: it involves acting on conscience. Correspondingly, failing to try, which entails moral knowledge, as opposed to simply being motivated towards the bad, is essential for ordinary blameworthiness. It is not enough to be oriented towards the bad, one must also know (at some level) that one's acts are morally wrong.

Arpaly presents Huck Finn as an example of someone who seems praiseworthy despite not having awareness of the true moral status of his acts. Huck believes that he is acting wrongly in helping Jim, a slave, to escape, and yet finds himself helping Jim anyway. Huck's deep motivations are good, he does not think in these terms, but he is moved to help someone who needs and deserves help. In my terms, Huck is motivation esteemworthy: his motivations are aimed at the right things, but he is not conscience respectworthy, in fact, he is acting against his conscience. Arpaly argues that Huck is praiseworthy. The challenge for my view is the suggestion that an agent can be praiseworthy without trying to do well by Morality—she is praiseworthy just because she has good motivations.

Proponents of the moral concern view also give examples of cases where an agent seems *blameworthy* for some act or omission, despite not knowing what she is doing. In Angela Smith's example (2005), the agent forgets her friend's birthday. She didn't forget deliberately, and there is (let's assume) nothing she deliberately did that caused her to forget, so blameworthiness cannot be traced back to a prior culpable action. Smith's point is that if her forgetting is caused by her flawed will, by the fact that she does not care enough about her friend, the agent can be blameworthy even though she didn't know what she was doing.[8]

Arpaly and Smith might be interpreted as arguing that there is no reflexivity requirement on praiseworthiness and blameworthiness: it doesn't matter how the agent assessed her own behaviour. We can contrast that view with a view like Michael Zimmerman's (1997; 2008, ch. 4) or Gideon Rosen's (2002; 2004), according to which an agent is only praise- or blameworthy if she made a conscious choice to act as she did. Zimmerman and Rosen both claim that if you don't know what you are doing, the act does not count as being under your control in the right way. The same point could be made in terms of simple excuses: if I don't know that the lever I pull is connected to a device for killing puppies, killing puppies is not under my control, so I have a simple excuse. The act of killing puppies is not really my act, and I am not blameworthy for it.[9] Similarly, they might say, if I forget a friend's birthday, and there was no point at which I knowingly acted wrongly in creating that state of ignorance, I cannot be blameworthy, I have an excuse.

Following George Sher (2009), I will call this view the Searchlight View.[10] On the Searchlight View, responsibility requires awareness. On attributionist views, such as Sher's and Angela Smith's, responsibility does not require awareness. As Smith points out (2005, 238), what is really at issue between the two camps is what is attributable to an agent. On the attributionist view, what is attributable to an agent is whatever of her motives count as really hers,[11] whereas on the Searchlight View,

---

[8] One might also understand the forgetting as entirely inadvertent, not caused by bad will at all. I come back to that possibility in Chapter 8.

[9] Zimmerman and Rosen both argue that there are more simple excuses than we might think, because when we act in ignorance we are off the hook unless we acquired the ignorance culpably, and acquiring the ignorance culpably would have to mean acquiring it with open eyed awareness of wrongdoing. This, they both stress, is rare. See also Neil Levy's work, particularly his 2013.

[10] As Sher characterizes it, "an agent's responsibility extends only as far as his awareness of what he is doing" (2009, 4). Searchlight views fall into the general category that Angela Smith labels 'volitionalist' views (2005), though that label is not completely illuminating. See McKenna (2008) for a critical discussion of the taxonomies.

[11] There has been a lot of discussion about what exactly is required for attributability. Shoemaker (2011) argues that attitudes can be attributable to an agent just because they are his, but more is required for answerability. Shoemaker thinks that an agent must also have

conscious choice is necessary for an action be properly the agent's. My concern here is not with basic responsibility, it is with praise- and blameworthiness, but we get the same division of views. Attributionists tend to a moral concern view, arguing that praiseworthiness depends on moral concern. By contrast, Searchlight theorists argue that praiseworthiness depends on what is consciously chosen.

Moral concern proponents try to convince us by giving us examples, such as Angela Smith's birthday forgetting example, where someone is not aware (or apparently in control) of what they are doing, and yet seems culpable. On the other hand, Searchlight advocates try to convince us by emphasizing that, when an agent acts without knowing what they are doing, and there is nothing that an agent knowingly did that led to their ignorance, it is hard to say what we are blaming them for, and so it seems inappropriate and harsh to blame them.

However, on careful reflection, it is clear that many of these examples are ambiguous. It is certainly the case that the agent who forgets a friend's birthday acts in ignorance *in the moment*. She lacks awareness of the relevant moral properties of her act as she acts. But it is not clear how deep her ignorance goes. And, I shall argue, we lose confidence in the blameworthiness (or praiseworthiness) of the agent when we imagine a situation in which her ignorance is deep moral ignorance. I shall argue that the dispute between the Searchlight View and the moral concern view is not really a dispute over *whether* awareness is required for blameworthiness, it is really a dispute over how much and what sort of awareness is required. At bottom, everyone agrees that there is a reflexivity requirement on praise- and blameworthiness. The disagreement is over exactly what the reflexivity requirement requires.

On a crude understanding, moral concern theorists think that no awareness is necessary for praise- or blameworthiness, but in fact, the terrain cannot clearly be divided into two, rather there is a continuum of levels of awareness that might be deemed necessary for blameworthiness. At one end of the continuum is the view that all that is necessary is that the agent's motivation matches the true moral content. We can imagine an agent who is drawn to the good like a moth to the flame, an agent with

access to the reasons for his attitudes in order to be answerable for them. Angela Smith (2012) responds that answerability is the only sort of responsibility, but points out that it is not easy to say what exactly it is for an attitude to be connected to reasons in the right way.

no conscious representation of the good as good at all. As even Arpaly and Schroeder admit (2014, ch. 7), this is not an attractive account of praise- and blameworthiness. An agent does not seem praiseworthy unless she is able to conceptualize the morally relevant features of her act correctly, for example, as 'kind', or 'persons respecting', or even, 'happiness maximizing'.

We can see Arpaly and Schroeder as being some steps along the continuum, they think that some awareness of the act's moral properties is necessary. But they deny that the agent needs to see her act as right or wrong. Searchlight advocates tend to cluster at the other end, in the most extreme case insisting that clear eyed akrasia—involving clear eyed knowledge of the wrongness of the act at the moment of action in the moment—is necessary for blameworthiness. But some Searchlight advocates, such as William FitzPatrick, allow that a slightly more bleary eyed akrasia establishes blameworthiness (2008). On FitzPatrick's view, as on Moody-Adams's (1994), many cases of moral ignorance are actually cases of affected ignorance, and the agent is aware at some level that their behaviour is problematic.[12]

The issue, as I say, is over *how much* subjective awareness is necessary for blameworthiness. Everyone agrees that some is. So how can we establish how much is? I will argue that what we need to meet the reflexivity requirement for praise- and blameworthiness is the same as what we need for the common sense account of trying and failing to try that I argued for the in the last chapter, namely, background knowledge of the aim. What we are aiming for is to make sense of the claim that the agent should have been motivated differently, or should have known, or should have acted differently. Merely failing to meet a standard is not blameworthy. We need to make sense of a subjective version of that claim, such that the agent has failed by their own lights.

---

[12] FitzPatrick goes on to argue that in cases where the ignorance genuinely goes all the way down, we might still be able to blame the agent on the grounds that they *should have known better*. As I argue later in this chapter, this is a puzzling notion. FitzPatrick cashes that out as follows: first, there are no relevant limitations on the agent's social context, second, the ignorance is the result of "the voluntary exercise of vices" such as overconfidence, incuriosity, and so on, and thus, third, the agent could reasonably have been expected to do better (2008, 605). The problem here is that it is not clear what we should think 'voluntary exercise of vice' involves—does it involve clear eyed exercise of vice?

In arguing for her earlier account of blameworthiness, Arpaly considers three versions of a hurtful remark (2003, 80). In the first one, the agent is from a different culture, and has no idea that her remark is hurtful, in which case, she has an excuse, and is not blameworthy. I have no disagreement with that, when the agent is non-culpably factually ignorant, we should all agree that she has a simple excuse for her behaviour. In Arpaly's second and third versions, the agent is badly motivated in the sense that her motivations depart from the substance of morality: she either has insufficient concern for the recipient of the remark, or direct motivation to hurt him. Thus according to Arpaly the agent is blameworthy in those cases.

In the second version of the hurtful remark, Arpaly imagines that the agent is motivated by insufficient concern for the moral reasons:

she acts the way she does because she desires to vent the tensions of a long day by saying exactly what comes to her mind, which happens to be offensive to Joseph in an obvious way. In this case, she is blameworthy, because her action indicates a failure to respond to morally relevant considerations; she should be motivated by the fact that Joseph is likely to be hurt by what she says, but she is unmoved by this and so acts in an inconsiderate manner. (2003, 80)

The crucial point here is Arpaly's claim that the agent *should* be motivated by the fact that Joseph is likely to be hurt. In what sense should she be motivated? To see that there is a problem here, let's return to the first version of the hurtful remark, where the agent does not know that the remark is hurtful, and thus has an excuse. Could we say in that case, 'the agent should not have made that remark'? Yes, we could. We would simply be saying that making the remark was in fact hurtful, and that it would be better if had not been made. But we would not be saying anything about whether the agent was blameworthy.

This point about how we use the 'should have' construction has a similar structure to the distinction between hyper-objective, prospective, and subjective accounts of rightness and the way in which they are action guiding. I argued that hyper-objective and prospective accounts of rightness are not truly action guiding, in that they do not actually purport to tell agents what to do. Rather, they point out what is actually good or rational, and that is independent of the agent and her point of view. And so, I argued, that is why blameworthiness does not attach to objective and prospective wrongdoing, it attaches only to the genuinely action guiding sense of rightness and wrongness, the sense in which they point to a genuine imperative, the sense in which they appeal to the agent's own point of view. When we say that an agent 'should have' acted differently, it is ambiguous between objective and subjective uses.

So, returning to Arpaly's second version of the example: she says that the agent should have been motivated differently. In the objective sense this is clearly true. The agent should have been motivated differently in the sense that it would have been better to be motivated differently. But why should we think that she 'should have been motivated differently' in a sense that renders her blameworthy? If she did not know what she was doing, there is nothing that makes it true that she should have done things differently in a *subjective* sense. There is no reference to the agent's own point of view.

This is not to deny that her motivations are morally bad. I agree with Arpaly that these motivations can be criticized from a moral point of view because of their substance. And that is the crucial difference between the first version of the insulting remark, in which the agent believes her remark to be acceptable, and the second and third version in which, I am assuming, the agent has no particular beliefs about the morality of her action but doesn't care whether or not it is insulting. In the first case, the agent's motivations cannot be faulted, and that is why it is uncontroversial that she is off the hook. By contrast, in the second and third versions the agent's motivations are morally deficient, and so she is not so clearly off the hook. But she is not clearly on it either. The worry is that we need a subjective sense for the claim that the agent should have been motivated differently.

Imagine that the agent in Arpaly's example makes the insulting remark, and we confront her: first we might ask, 'Did you know that that was going to hurt him?' If the agent looks aghast and says 'No! I had no idea! I just meant it in a jokey way!', and we have good reason to believe her, then we will, as Arpaly suggests, think that the agent has an excuse. But imagine the agent says grudgingly, 'well, I wasn't thinking about that at the time, but I suppose so.' Then we are likely to think the agent blameworthy. Even though she didn't have the knowledge that the remark would be hurtful before her mind, there is a fairly clear sense in which she *should have known* it would be hurtful. And in most everyday cases we take something like that for granted, that the agent could easily have accessed her background knowledge that the thing she did had the properties that made it morally problematic. If the agent didn't know *at any level* that the remark would be hurtful, then the case is like the first version of the example, she is off the hook.

Imagine a slightly different version of the case: when we ask the agent if she knew that her remark would be hurtful her response is, 'no, I didn't know, but I didn't care about that'. Then surely we have to ask another question. We have to ask, 'do you know that it is not OK to hurt people?' And if the agent replies sincerely that she doesn't know that hurting people is problematic, something dramatic changes in our view of her. We may be baffled by such an agent, and of course it seems so unlikely that an agent could have missed the fact that hurting people is morally problematic that we are likely to distrust her at first, to take her as confabulating. But assuming that we establish that she is sincere, that she does not know that hurting people is problematic, our reaction to her is likely to change. Most importantly, the fact that she didn't care that the act was hurtful seems much less significant. Not caring about something that you take to be morally irrelevant is very different to not caring about something that you take to be morally relevant.

Again, I should emphasize, it is not that the agent has *no* bad will in such a case. But the agent's will, in doing the hurtful act, is bad only insofar as she is atavistically an uncaring person, an insensitive person, who lacks a natural aversion to hurting people. I agree that the substance of her quality of will is morally criticizable. But this is not the same as being blameworthy in the ordinary sense.

The point of my imagined dialogues is to make clear that when we blame people we usually take for granted that they have background knowledge of Morality, that they know, at some level, that their behaviour is problematic. And the reason we take that for granted, I suggest, is that this background knowledge is what makes sense of the subjective version of the claim that they should have been motivated differently, or should have known, or should have acted differently. In saying that, we are not just saying that the agent acted badly. When we use the phrase 'should have' in the subjective sense, we are genuinely saying that she should have done things differently. She should have done things differently, because, by her own lights, she should have. So, crucially, in not doing things differently, she is blameworthy.

Notice that on my account of moral knowledge (see section 5 of chapter 2), it is possible that an agent could meet the threshold for moral knowledge and yet not know everything about Morality. So it is possible that an agent could be non-culpably ignorant of a moral fact. Perhaps the agent in Arpaly's case could plead that she didn't know that hurting people by making offensive remarks was wrong, that she thought that there was a blanket exception for hurt by offence. Given that, in general, Morality is fairly coherent, it would be surprising to come across someone who had missed an important part. However, assuming that it is possible, such an agent would have the simple excuse of ignorance, and would not be blameworthy.

The sort of case that I am imagining where there is a valid 'should have known' is not one where a simple excuse applies. Rather, I am imagining someone for whom it is true that if they had thought about it a little longer, if they had thought more about their dispositions and alertness to red flags, if they had tried harder, in other words, they would have seen that this was a problematic act. For most of us, when we act wrongly without full awareness, it is just that we didn't bother thinking: it would not take much at all for us to admit that the act was problematic. There may be cases where things are more complex, and there can be border-line cases, cases where we are not sure if there is a simple excuse of non-culpable ignorance, or subjective wrongdoing.[13]

An essential element here is that the agent does not just see that her act might be hurtful, or cruel, or not persons-respecting, but that she sees that it *ought not to be done*. Merely understanding, and avoiding or pursuing, the properties that as a matter of fact are the morally relevant properties doesn't get us to a praiseworthy quality of will. We need to be

---

[13] Elizabeth Harman (2011) suggests that an agent is blameworthy if she *could have* come to the true view. Harman's examples are all cases where we are likely to assume that an agent has the relevant background knowledge (a parent forgetting to collect their child, a doctor forgetting to check the patient's chart for allergies, and someone who lights a match even though they smell a gas leak). If these are cases where the agent has background knowledge and some bad will, then the agent is blameworthy—but not simply because she could have come to the truth, rather, because she was already in possession of the truth. It is possible that these cases fall into a different category, pure negligence, where there is no bad will—I come back to that issue in Chapter 8. See my 2015 for a critique of Harman. In a recent article (2017) Errol Lord argues that what is required for praise- and blameworthi-ness is a sort of 'know-how'. Lord's conclusions are similar to mine, though his route to them is a little different. Like me, Lord sees that it is important that the agent be able to access the moral reasons: "The reasons that one possesses are the reasons that are within one's ken. In order to be in one's ken, one has to have epistemic access to the fact that provides the reason" (2017, 459). Sandy Goldberg (2017) gives a different account of how we should understand the 'should have known' charge: on his view it reduces to a criticism of the system or structure, and is not truly a criticism of the individual.

able to distinguish a mere desire or aversion from a moral motivation. In other words, we need an element of motivation by duty for its own sake: we need some conscience respectworthiness as well as moral motivation esteemworthiness.

Kant famously makes this point in the *Groundwork* by giving us pairs of examples in which someone does the right thing out of a sense of duty or out of inclination. As numerous commentators have pointed out, we do not need to interpret Kant as saying that inclination *undermines* moral worth.[14] Rather the point is that acting on mere inclination is not praiseworthy. A sense of duty is necessary for praiseworthiness. And that is the thought that I am defending here. An agent must grasp not just that some acts are kind and some are cruel, but that we morally should do the kind ones and avoid the cruel ones, and if she does not grasp that, it is hard to see her behaviour as other than mere inclination.

In sum, all accounts of blameworthiness depend on some sort of knowledge or awareness to link the agent to the problematic aspect of her action in the necessary way. On the traditional ways of carving things up, my account of ordinary praise- and blameworthiness is neither a Searchlight View nor a moral concern view, and I have suggested that the distinction between Searchlight views and moral concern views is less solid than is generally thought.

Like the Searchlight advocate, I see knowledge of Morality as a necessary condition for being in the realm of ordinary praise- and blameworthiness. But, I have argued, the strong Searchlight account is implausible, an agent can be blameworthy without clear eyed akrasia. What we need is somewhat weaker. We do not need for the agent to have known that her act was wrong, we just need a sensible application of the idea that an agent *should have known better*. We get that by saying that the agent had background knowledge of Morality. She should have known better in the sense that she herself grasps that there are better and worse ways to do things, and she could have found a better way here. This allows us to say that an agent such as Angela Smith's birthday forgetter is blameworthy in the ordinary way: she has the background knowledge necessary to assess her own action as problematic, and she was not trying hard enough.

---

[14] See e.g. Herman (1981), Baron (1995).

My account is like a moral concern account in that I agree that insufficient moral concern is important. However, what renders an agent blameworthy is failing to try hard enough, and that requires that the agent have a background knowledge of Morality.[15] It is the background knowledge that makes sense of Arpaly's claims that the moral concern is *insufficient* (as opposed to merely low) and that the agent *should have been motivated differently* (as opposed to merely saying it would have been better if she had been motivated differently). The agent's quality of will only has what is needed for ordinary blameworthiness when it includes the subjective element, the conscious understanding of the act as bad.

Praiseworthiness behaves the same way. An agent is not fully praiseworthy just because she has good motives. She is praiseworthy when she is trying to do well by Morality, which requires a background knowledge of Morality. An agent who is drawn to the right sort of thing without having any knowledge of Morality may have what Aristotle calls 'natural virtue'.[16] But this does not seem enough for being praiseworthy in the ordinary way. When we praise agents in the ordinary way, we think of their action as reflecting on their conscience, not just their motivations.

I have argued that praise- and blameworthiness are subject to a reflexivity requirement. In order for an agent to be praiseworthy or blameworthy, she must know what she is doing in some sense, she must recognize the moral status of her action. I have argued that this need not be full conscious awareness in the moment, but is rather knowledge of Morality in the background.[17]

---

[15] Or, as I said earlier, when she is culpably ignorant.

[16] Though unlike Aristotle I am not committed to the claim that natural virtue is in place from the moment of birth (2000, book 6, 13, 1144b5–6).

[17] There are some parallels here with Bernard Williams's account of the relationship of blame to an agent's reasons. Williams argues that there are only 'internal' reasons, that is, reasons that appeal to something that the agent already has in her motivational set (1981). He argues that blaming someone is a matter of appealing to internal reasons, though often, ones that only indirectly relate to the blameworthy act. Williams imagines someone who was not motivated to do the thing they are being blamed for not doing, but they have an ethically loaded disposition to avoid the disapproval of other people. Williams says that "to blame someone in this way is to tell him he had a reason to act otherwise, and in a direct sense this may not have been true. Yet in a way it has now become true, in virtue of his having a disposition to do things that people he respects expect of him..." (1995, 42). Williams is interested in the agent's existing motivations, whereas I am interested in the agent's existing knowledge, but the structure of the argument is the same—the relevant

4. Ordinary Praise- and Blameworthiness

So far I have argued that my conception of ordinary praise- and blameworthiness as correlated with subjectively right and wrong action meets the reflexivity requirement in the right way. In this section I shall say more about ordinary praise- and blameworthiness. This is not a complete account, I aim only to describe some of the broad contours of the view.

In the previous chapter, I gave an account of trying, and I will show here that this everyday account of trying serves well as the activity for which we are blameworthy or praiseworthy. We are praiseworthy when we try to do well, and blameworthy when we fail to try. The notion of trying can be understood in a weak or strong sense. Roughly, in the weak sense, to try is merely to make some moves in the right sort of direction. This does not correlate with praiseworthiness. Rather, to be praiseworthy, one must try to do well by Morality in a much stronger sense. One must set oneself to do what one takes most likely to achieve the goal. Of course, most of the time, in thinking about whether someone is blameworthy or praiseworthy, we are not thinking about whether they have overall set themselves to do well by Morality. Rather, we are interested in praise- or blameworthiness for particular acts.

Blameworthiness for acts is not a very easy thing to measure on this sort of view. What we are ultimately blameworthy for is a much longer range thing: not trying hard enough (or failing to try completely) to do well by Morality. However, my account of trying makes room for trying to achieve sub-goals, and we can think of particular acts, or courses of action, as sub-goals. When we are trying to achieve a sub-goal, we must first think about how it fits into the overall goal, and how it must be balanced against other sub-goals. We only have limited time and resources. Any act must be judged in the context of the agent's overall strategy. In my account of trying I argued that the level of trying that is necessary to count as trying (and hence to be praiseworthy) to achieve a sub-goal is thus not necessarily the level that the agent thinks most likely to result in success on that sub-goal. Rather, it is the level that the agent deems appropriate, given the other relevant considerations. There are

requirement (in Williams's case the internal reasons requirement, in mine, the reflexivity requirement) can be met indirectly. Williams also stresses that there is vagueness at the boundaries, it is not always clear whether blame will be felicitous. I come back to Williams's account of blame in Chapter 5.

costs to trying, and those costs must be weighed against other values in play. We should put in only as much effort as appropriate. Doing that is part of trying in the strong sense, doing what seems most likely to achieve the overall goal.[18]

Let's return to my analogy of trying to be a good parent. My overall goal is to do well as a parent, and I am praiseworthy if I do what I think most likely to constitute good parenting. In my everyday life, however, I must think about particular actions and courses of action. There are two ways I must balance my sub-goals. First, I must think about what to aim for: I want to spend time with my children, but I know that I can't spend all my time with them, so I need to think about what constitutes a reasonable amount of time. Second, when I have a goal, such as regularly spending at least one weekend day with my children, I need to decide how hard to try and achieve that goal. Clearly there are situations where that goal would yield to other more urgent or important goals. So long as I am trying as hard as is appropriate, I am praiseworthy.

It is a commonplace that praiseworthiness and blameworthiness come in degrees. In general, agents are more praiseworthy the harder they try, and more blameworthy the more they fail to try. However, there are a couple of complexities here. First, some moral values admit of degrees and others don't. To put it another way, it seems that rightness is sometimes scalar.[19] In the previous chapter I used the example of an agent, Amin, who knows that he ought to be doing something to help those less fortunate than himself, and gives 10 per cent of his income to charity. Perhaps he could try harder, but that seems like enough to keep him on the right side of the boundary between blameworthiness and praiseworthiness. In other words, in giving 10 per cent of his income to charity, Amin is acting subjectively rightly, even though he knows he could do better. If he tried harder, perhaps in giving more, perhaps in thinking more carefully about where to donate his 10 per cent, Amin would be more praiseworthy. This is our common sense view, praiseworthiness comes in degrees. People who try very hard are

---

[18]   In what follows I sometimes drop the qualification 'seems *to the agent*' to keep the text uncluttered, but that is what I mean throughout. E.g. when I talk about the 'required level of trying', I mean the *subjectively* required level.

[19]   See Norcross (2006 and forthcoming) for more on the idea of scalar rightness. Note that my account leaves open the possibility of supererogation (acts that are good and/or praiseworthy but not required), but I do not address that here.

more praiseworthy than people who try just hard enough to count as seriously trying.[20]

However, rightness may not always be scalar. It may be that in some cases there are particular actions that are required, and there is no second best and no better action. This would be a feature of Morality—a deontological requirement to do a particular action. Take for example the requirement to pick one's children up from school on time. In order to count as acting subjectively rightly, an agent must try hard enough that she will succeed, barring highly unusual and unpredictable barriers. It is not enough to put in a level of effort such that, if there is no traffic at all, she will get there on time. Predictably, there will be traffic, and she will be ten minutes late. The agent must try hard enough that other things being equal, she will arrive on time. But she is not more praiseworthy for trying harder than that: her efforts beyond that are wasted; they do not realize more value or earn her more credit.[21]

Blameworthiness is not quite symmetrical. Praiseworthiness tops out when the agent tries hard enough (i.e. at the level that makes sense given the balancing of different values) to achieve a non-scalar value. Blameworthiness does not bottom out in the same way.[22] An agent who,

---

[20] Arpaly and Schroeder suggest that the term 'creditworthy' might be better than praiseworthy, because praiseworthiness suggests a level of good behaviour above merely doing what is required (2014: 161). I address that worry to some extent in the next chapter.

[21] The trying account thus avoids one problem of Arpaly and Schroeder's moral concern account, on which an agent with a lot of moral concern implausibly seems more praiseworthy for the same act then someone with less, but enough, moral concern doing the same act. Arpaly and Schroeder amend their account to say that praiseworthiness depends on how much moral concern an act 'manifests', which is not the same as how much moral concern the agent actually had (2014, 188). Because it focuses on trying, not on moral concern, my account gives us a clearly non-arbitrary way to explain why the moral saint is not more praiseworthy than anyone else for that particular act (in most cases), and also gives us a way to explain why she is more praiseworthy in general. Of course, the main advantage my account has over the moral concern account is that it meets the reflexivity requirement, as I argued above.

[22] Compare Björnsson's account (2017a and 2017b), according to which the degree of blame that is appropriate for an act A depends both on the degree of concern that can be required of the agent, and on what deviation in that concern was necessary to explain the gap between A and what should have been done (2017a, 151). Thus the badness of the act is part of what determines how blameworthy the agent is. The agent could in fact fall further short, but would not be more blameworthy on Björnsson's view. By contrast, my view is not concerned directly with the badness of what is done, but primarily with the state of the agent. As I suggest below, the badness of the thing done is relevant, but only because the agent herself should take that into account.

through poor planning, is ten minutes late to pick up her kids is a little bit blameworthy. An agent who thinks to herself, 'it doesn't matter, the school will call eventually', and settles down to watch another episode of a day-time soap opera is much more blameworthy for the same degree of lateness. Both agents have failed to the same degree of objective wrongness (being ten minutes late to collect their children), but their levels of subjective wrongness differ.

This raises the worry that blameworthiness does not connect with the objective wrongness of the thing done at all. However, on my account blameworthiness connects *indirectly* with the badness of the act. It is important to remember that trying to do well by Morality involves weighing the relative importance of different things. It might seem that an agent is more blameworthy for being late to a lecture she is giving than she is for being late to a lunch date, even though she failed in both cases through laziness. But it is not simply because being late for a lecture is worse than being late for lunch that the agent is more blameworthy. It is because the agent is falling short of the required level of trying by different degrees in these cases. Part of what we need to do is to think about how much we need to do to ensure we will not be late. For important things, more precautions are required, and so the first step is to make sure we are clear about what is important, and then we should take the relevant precautions.

Lectures are generally more important than lunch dates, and so the agent who is late for her lecture has usually fallen farther short of the appropriate effort levels than the agent who is late for lunch. Imagine, however, that the agent is late for lunch because she was lazy and didn't bother trying to get there on time, but the reason she was late for the lecture is that she stopped to move a stray trash can from the middle of the road, in order to minimize the risk of accident. Being late for the lecture is still worse, objectively, but nonetheless the agent is not as blameworthy as she is for being late for lunch. My account reflects our common sense view.

Ordinary praise- and blameworthiness can thus apply both to agents over the long term, and to acts they perform. An agent who sets herself to do well and tries very hard is a praiseworthy agent. She might sometimes slip up, and fail to try hard enough on particular occasions, and my account has the resources to say that she is not praiseworthy for those acts. The borderlines of what exactly she is blameworthy for may not be very precise, but that matches an imprecision in our everyday practices. Commonsensically, it is hard to isolate blameworthiness for a particular act: we need to know the context and the agent's general patterns of behaviour before we can make a good judgment of blameworthiness. My account gives us the resources to make complex judgments.

One more aspect of the subjective wrongness account of blameworthiness deserves a mention, and that is the possibility of an agent's being actively motivated by bad things. I have argued that the less an agent tries to do well by Morality, the more blameworthy she is. An agent who doesn't try at all is very blameworthy indeed. But some agents seem to have a bad will, to be motivated to do bad things for their own sake. What I have to say about that is somewhat complex, and I say more about various sorts of case in Chapters 6 and 7. To anticipate briefly: in general, it is not bad motives we are blameworthy for, but failing to resist them. However, there are people whose motivations to the bad are strong and consistent, and those motivations seem to reflect on the agent in an important way, even when she is trying hard to overcome them. In Chapter 6 I examine Gideon Rosen's case of Kleinbart, whose problematic motivations triumph, despite his trying to do well. In Chapter 7 I examine cases where agents really are motivated towards the bad *qua* bad, and make no effort at all to do well. I argue that if such people genuinely understand Morality, and see that it applies to them, they are blameworthy in the ordinary way for failing to try. However, both Kleinbart and the thoroughly bad-willed agent might be blameworthy for their bad motivations in a different way. I argue for the relevant type of blame and blameworthiness in the following chapter.

5. Conclusion

My account of ordinary praise- and blameworthiness is a quality of will account. It falls into the category of views according to which, to be praiseworthy is to act out of good will, and to be blameworthy is to act out of bad will. I have identified a very particular kind of quality of will that I think is involved in ordinary praise- and blameworthiness. It is a precondition for having this sort of quality of will that the agent is in our moral community, that she grasps Morality. Agents who are in our moral community can be assessed according to whether or not they try to do well by Morality. I have argued that we get the plausibility of blameworthiness from the reflexivity that is inherent in acting wrongly by one's own lights.

It is worth stressing again that my mention of desert here is very low key. My aim has been to identify the sort of wrongdoing that it makes sense to blame people for. When people act subjectively wrongly, they share our assessment of what is morally problematic about their act. Thus it makes sense to think them blameworthy: we have identified a relevant fault in the agent.

It also makes sense to blame them, as I shall argue in more detail in the next chapter. My accounts of blameworthiness and blame go hand in hand, as will become clear. I think that actually blaming—engaging in the activity—is usually optional, but that is not to say that blameworthiness can be defined entirely independently of the sort of blame that is applicable. The sort of blameworthiness that I have identified here is essentially dependent on shared moral understanding, the shared community, that makes blame possible. When we blame in the ordinary way, we are blaming someone who understands why we are blaming them.

We can now see how the various elements of my account of subjective obligation fit together. In Chapter 2 I argued that subjective obligation is an obligation to try to do well by Morality. There, I based my argument on the nature of subjective obligation as a deontic concept. We have various deontic concepts, and they range from being objective to being subjective. We can think in terms of a 'responsibility constraint': all deontic concepts meet at least a weak version of the responsibility constraint. That's what distinguishes them from merely evaluative concepts, like goodness, but there are various ways that we might understand the responsibility constraint. I argued in Chapter 2 that we should think of subjective obligation as meeting a strong version of the responsibility constraint. As I put it, there are two ways to understand the strong version of the responsibility constraint: we can understand it in terms of accessibility, and in terms of praise- and blameworthiness. My account of subjective obligation as trying to do well by Morality explains how subjective obligation is accessible. I argued that subjective obligation must make sense as a direct instruction to the agent. The instruction, 'try to do well by Morality' makes sense as a direct instruction to those who have a grasp of Morality.

In this chapter I have argued that my account of subjective obligation, grounded in Morality, correlates with one important sense—the ordinary sense—of praise- and blameworthiness. An agent who acts subjectively rightly is praiseworthy: she may not act objectively rightly but, because she is trying to do well by her own lights, and her own lights are beamed in the right direction, she deserves praise. I do not mean to invoke anything new in talking of desert here. Rather, the point is that my talk of subjective obligation does the work of explaining what we might mean by desert in this context. I have defended that idea by demonstrating the importance of background knowledge in both subjective obligation and praise- and blameworthiness.

Being motivated to the right things without any conscious grasp of the values involved is not sufficient for praiseworthiness. As almost everyone admits, an agent is not praiseworthy for a 'moth to the flame' style motivation to the good, she must understand her own actions as morally required, she must meet a reflexivity requirement. This does not mean that she must be fully aware of what she is doing at the moment of action. Both trying, and ordinary praiseworthiness, require that the agent have a broad background knowledge of her aim as an aim.

Ordinary praiseworthiness is correlated with acting subjectively rightly, which is a matter of trying hard enough. Rightness, and hence praise-worthiness, are sometimes scalar, and sometimes not. Blameworthiness is always scalar, even when wrongness is not. I have talked about ordinary praise- and blameworthiness, but I have not talked much about ordinary praise and blame. In the next chapter I sketch an account of ordinary praise and blame according to which they are communications, and I show how that fits with my account of ordinary praise- and blameworthiness. My point is to have identified one central and important sort of blame-worthiness, to which a corresponding sort of blame applies. But I think that we respond to wrongdoing in many different ways, and that we are not always responding to quality of will, far less the particular quality of will that I have identified here. In the following chapter I say more about other blame responses.

5

Praise and Blame

In the previous chapter I argued that that it is essential to ordinary praise- and blameworthiness that the agent have a grasp of Morality. I argued that this is how we can make sense of the crucial idea that the agent should have done better. I now want to link these conclusions to an argument about the nature of blame: that ordinary blame is communicative.

It is worth setting out a threefold distinction that appears in our concepts as they currently stand, which is intuitively attractive enough to be worth taking seriously as a starting point in the project of conceptual engineering. The distinction is between judging blameworthy, blaming, and punishing. It might turn out that judging blameworthy and blaming are extensionally equivalent, that is to say, that they amount to the same thing, but we should be aware that that would need an argument. Judging blameworthy and blaming are conceptually distinct. Likewise, there is a distinction between blaming and punishing. Again, it might be that we cannot make sense of blaming other than as punishing. But that is not necessarily the case: blaming may be distinct from punishing. Blame is the least well understood idea out of these three, and has been neglected as a topic in its own right until relatively recently,[1] so it is not surprising that it often gets collapsed onto one of the other two things, judging blameworthy or punishing.

J. J. C. Smart (1961) is an example of someone who thinks that we must collapse the distinction between blaming and punishing. He argues that blame is only interesting when conceived of as an action, and that it is justified by its consequences. Smart was motivated chiefly by worries about the meta-level question, whether we have free will or not. He argues that because we don't have free will, it is not justifiable to blame

---

[1] For an overview of accounts of blame see Coates and Tognazzini's *Stanford Encyclopedia* article (2014), and also Coates and Tognazzini's edited collection (2013).

people in any way other than a forward looking way. But as I have said, I am leaving that sort of worry aside here, and focusing on what we can make of our normative responsibility concepts. Blame in the traditional backward looking sense, blame that identifies a fault in the agent and responds to it, is an important part of our interactions with each other. It is worth trying to make sense of it.

An alternative to conflating blaming and punishing is to collapse the distinction between blaming and judging blameworthy, as Michael Zimmerman (1988) does. He argues that to blame someone is just to judge that they are blameworthy. Anything further, Zimmerman thinks, is a different act, a punishment, that is in need of its own justification.[2] But it is a central tenet of our intuitive concepts, our pre-engineered ideas, that we can judge that someone is blameworthy without actually blaming them.[3] Blaming seems to be something over and above judging blameworthy. The challenge is to find a place for blame as a part of our responsibility practices, where it goes beyond a mere judgment, but does not go as far as punishment.

The parameters for an account of blame can be roughly sketched. Clearly someone who is entirely unmoved by a judgment of blame-worthiness is not actually blaming. And clearly, blame must come from within the relevant value perspective, we are not blaming if we take delight in someone's wrongdoing, or if we disapprove but for perverse reasons. We can say that blame is a response to wrongdoing that goes beyond a mere judgment, and is intimately related to the blamer's acceptance of the value system from which she blames. But blame, unlike punishment, does not necessarily aim at the blamee's suffering, though it may. This is not intended as an account of the necessary and sufficient conditions, rather it is intended to provide a rough template, such that if something fits this description, it is plausible as an account of blame.[4]

---

[2] See also Haji (1998) and Oshana (1997).

[3] I do not address sceptical positions, such as Pereboom's (2001) that argue that we could and should eliminate blame from our practices. See Shabo (2012) for a response to Pereboom that emphasizes the role of interpersonal relationships in our responsibility practices.

[4] Some philosophers have argued that an emotional reaction is essential—see Bell (2013a), Bennett (1980), Fischer and Ravizza (1998), Owens (2012), Strawson (1962), Wallace (1994; 2011), Watson (1996), Wolf (2011). George Sher argues that emotion is not essential, but some sort of conative reaction is. Sher argues that a certain desire–belief pair is what is essential to blame (2006). Another view is that blame can be a judgment alone, but it is a special sort of judgment. Pamela Hieronymi (2004) and Thomas Scanlon

In this chapter I argue that there are different sorts of blame, that correspond to different sorts of wrongdoing. I start with ordinary blame, which I claim is communicative, and applies to agents who have acted subjectively wrongly. I argue that ordinary praise is, likewise, communicative, and also depends on the agent knowing what she is doing. I contrast these with detached praise and blame, which apply to agents outside our moral community. Detached blame is a mixed bag, but I give a general account of how such blame reactions work. They are not communicative, rather they function from a distance. That does not entail that they are mere appraisals: they are genuinely a species of blame, in that they are a response to wrongdoing that goes beyond a mere judgment.

1. Ordinary Blame

On the communicative view of blame, blame is a way of interacting. There are various different, often overlapping stories in the literature about what the blamer is saying, and to whom.[5] My own view is that there are several things that the blamer could be saying, and that the context determines what it is appropriate to say. It is useful to put this in Michael McKenna's terms (2012). McKenna thinks of responsibility itself as a conversation, where the opening move is some sort of expression of quality of will, and blame is the rejoinder. I do not want to argue

(2008) both defend a view according to which the judgment of blameworthiness has force because it modifies the relationship between the blamer and the blamee. Many philosophers have argued that blame is essentially *communicative*: the blamer is saying something— Christopher Bennett (2002, 2008), Darwall (2006), Duff (2001), Fricker (2016a), McKenna (2012), Macnamara (2015a), Angela Smith (2013), Talbert (2012a), Watson (1987). Blame communicates something important to the blamee and/or to the rest of society.

[5] Chris Bennett (2002) argues that blame expresses moral condemnation, and aims to bring about guilt and repentance; Stephen Darwall (2006) argues that we are giving the blamee a second person reason to change her behaviour; Gary Watson (2011) argues that the blamee is being asked for a justification of some sort; Matthew Talbert (2012) and Angela Smith (2013) both argue that blame is a form of protest; Michael McKenna (2012) argues that blame is a communication of disapproval. David Shoemaker (2015, 107) argues that the aim of communicative blame, which is understood in non-cognitive terms on Shoemaker's view, is not to sanction, but to "make the slighter aware of what he has done". Miranda Fricker (2016a) argues that the aim of blame is to inspire remorse in the wrongdoer, increase alignment of moral understanding, and change the wrongdoer's behaviour for the better. See Macnamara (2015a) for an account of how exactly blame could be communicative.

that we can think of the whole responsibility system as a conversation, but I think it is very useful to think of ordinary blame on the model of a conversation. As Chris Bennett (2002) puts it, blame has a 'call and response' structure. Like a linguistic conversation, it has rules and conventions, and the relationship between the parties makes a difference to what those rules and conventions are. The victim has a different relationship to the wrongdoer from that of the bystander, and the blame conversation that is appropriate is different. What all ordinary blame conversations have in common though, is that they aim to achieve recognition in the blamee.

On my account of subjective obligation, when we judge that someone has acted subjectively wrongly, we judge that she has failed by her own lights. Recall that to act subjectively wrongly is to act with the background knowledge that one's act is morally problematic, even if that knowledge was not at the forefront of the mind at that moment. This is essential to my account of ordinary blame. Because we think that the blamee has failed by her own lights, we are entitled to expect that she will come to recognize the problem with her behaviour. This is why subjective wrongdoing merits communicative blame. We can engage with the wrongdoer, and we can expect a response.

To make this point more vivid, think about an ordinary case. Imagine that a friend lets us down in some way: forgets to turn up for a meeting, or fails to stand up for us in an important context. She forgot, or failed, because she wasn't trying very hard. When we blame her, we are doing various things. First, we are making a judgment about her blameworthiness: that she really did act subjectively wrongly. But our blaming her is not just a judgment about her subjectively wrong action, it is also a communication of our expectation that she will recognize her fault, feel remorse, apologize, and, if appropriate, make amends.

Of course, blame can legitimately come from various quarters, not just the victim, and it is only usually the victim who has the right to demand an apology, or to offer forgiveness.[6] In cases where the victim blames the wrongdoer, as in the case where someone is let down by their friend,

---

[6] Darwall gives an account of blame in very much these terms (2006, 65–78), though his bigger picture is different to mine, as he thinks that all moral reasons and thus all legitimate blaming boils down to the second personal demands—the demands that we have authority to make of one another.

blame contains a sequence of demands and assurances: the exact sequence may vary according to the complexities of the case, but a victim's ordinary blame often features, first the communication of disapproval, and then further, a demand that the blame is accepted, which is to say that the wrongdoer recognizes their wrongdoing; a demand that the wrongdoer feels remorse, which indicates that the wrongdoer cares about what she has done;[7] an expectation of apology; an assurance that after an apology we can move towards forgiveness; and an expression of a further expectation that forgiveness will be met with gratitude and relief.

The length of the blame conversation varies with context. Forgiveness is not always part of the process. Some slights may not be the right sort, or may not be grave enough to require forgiveness. Not all blame conversations require the whole sequence. In a case where the blamer is not the victim, the sequence may be even shorter. The blamer calls the wrongdoer's attention to her own commitment to acting differently. The only demands and expectations might be a demand for acceptance of the blame and the expectation of remorse, which need not necessarily be expressed in an apology.[8]

Crucial here is the claim that we are entitled to expect that an agent who fails in her subjective obligation will come to recognize her own fault. She may not come to that immediately: it may take some convincing her, or even educating her. To understand Morality is not to have every detail correct. There are both innocent mistakes and motivated mistakes. If the mistake is innocent then, usually, the agent has a simple excuse. Rather than blame her, we should try to educate her. However, many of our mistakes, both moral and non-moral, are *motivated* mistakes. We turn away from hard questions and undesirable answers. In such cases, we can be brought around to seeing that we have been acting wrongly by our own lights, but it may take some patience.

To reiterate: the communication that I think is essential to ordinary blame is not simply a communication that the blamee has done wrong, but that she has done wrong by her own lights. Thus the blamer is entitled to expect acceptance of blame, and remorse, and entitled to

---

[7] I come back to the demand for remorse in Chapter 8.

[8] See Bennett (2002) for an interesting account of the way that the sequence of blame and appropriate responses might work. Unlike Bennett, I do not take a retributivist line, but I agree with his basic 'call and response' picture.

expect (if applicable), an apology. When I say 'entitled to expect', I mean it in both a predictive sense and a normative sense. It is reasonable to expect that the wrongdoer will recognize the problem because it is a problem by her own lights. In blaming her, I am acting as a proxy for her own conscience: I am simply reminding her of what she already knows to be the case, and making vivid that she has failed. There is thus nothing mysterious about my expectations here, they make sense in the context of a shared moral community. Through the full blame sequence the blamer and the blamee mutually affirm their commitment to trying to do well by Morality, and if it goes well, reconcile with each other.[9]

We are entitled to expect the blamee to engage with our communicative blame in a normative sense because that is part of what being part of the moral community involves. It is important to recognize that the normative sense here is not a first order moral norm. Of course, there may be first order norms related to making amends that apply here. If someone steals my yoghurt from the communal fridge they ought to buy me a new one. That is a first order moral duty of reparation. However, I do not think that the yoghurt thief has a first order moral duty to accept my blame. Rather, if they want to carry on in good standing in the moral community, they ought to accept my blame. This is a broader hypothetical requirement—accepting blame, and engaging in blame exchanges is what we have to do if we want to be fully engaged in our moral community. I come back to this in Chapter 8 when I discuss taking responsibility. Taking responsibility, accepting the blame of others, and moving through the blame conversation, are important elements of our responsibility practices.

Of course, it is possible that the blamee will not engage in the blame conversation right now. Perhaps she is too angry, too ashamed,

---

[9] It is worth briefly contrasting this with George Sher's account (2006, ch. 7). He argues that being committed to morality entails being committed to blame. His thought is that it is a conceptual truth that if we are committed to morality, we must desire that others act in accordance with it. That desire is the essential conative component in blame. My argument here is different, I am arguing that blame reminds people of their commitment to morality, and relies on their commitment in expecting that there will be a response. James Lenman emphasizes the importance of shared moral understanding in his contractualist account of responsibility (2006). His main concern is to defend a sort of compatibilism given worries about free will, but many of the details of his account are congruent with mine.

or too shy.[10] But if I know that deep down she accepts that a response is called for, my blame is not being thrown into the void. It is being directed towards a receptive agent. It is also possible that an agent refuses to engage in the blame conversation out of defiance but, again, if the agent can understand what she is being blamed for, communicative blame is not missing its mark. I come back to this issue in Chapter 7, where I say more about the distinction between agents who understand Morality but defy it, and those who do not understand it.

My focus here is on the communication itself, the idea that we are appealing to the agent's own sense of having acted wrongly. My argument is closely related to the point I argued for in Chapter 4, that merely failing to meet a standard is not sufficient for ordinary blameworthiness. If the agent does not understand her own wrongdoing as wrongdoing, the reflexivity requirement is not met. Ordinary blame is a response to subjective wrongdoing that goes beyond a mere judgment of blameworthiness, in that it is a communicative act, an attempt to activate a sequence of moves. It may be angry or sad, but it need not be—what makes it blame on my view is that it is communicative. What makes it felicitous as a communication is that it reminds the agent of something that she already knows.

There is a parallel here with Bernard Williams's account of blame. Williams is concerned with the agent's existing motivations, not with the agent's grasp of Morality, but his basic thought is similar to mine, that blame appeals to something internal. It is not merely a registering of disapproval, a statement that *the blamer* accepts reasons that render the action condemnable. As Williams puts his criticism of the 'external' account (on which the blamer is appealing to reasons that the blamee does not recognize), "the image of blame that can be derived from its account of reasons, in failing to provide any way to engage with the agent's actual motivations, leaves us also without ethical resources. It gives us no way of understanding the difference between a blame that might hope to achieve recognition, and the blame that hopes by mere

---

[10] I will not say much about cases where the agent cannot respond because she is dead or distant. I think these cases can be dealt with fairly easily by saying that we simply judge them blameworthy—we judge that if we were in a position to blame them, we would. Alternatively, we might say that we blame such people in a way that is parasitic on ordinary blame—there is an 'as if' element.

force to focus on the agent's reasons a judgment that represents in fact only a rejection (perhaps an entirely justified rejection) of what he has done" (1995, 44).

In other words, if we think of blame as something that merely registers disapproval, and does not reach out to meet something in the blamee, we have missed something important. The interesting sense of blame understands blame as communicative. It is worth noting that Williams does not think that all blame is communicative. He hints here that there is another kind of blame, a blame that does not attempt to reach the blamed agent, but merely expresses the blamer's own reasons. I return to that idea, the sort of blame that I call 'detached blame', in section 3, but first I will briefly compare ordinary blame to ordinary praise.

2. Ordinary Praise

In this section I will say a little about praise, and how it relates to blame, and along the way I will diagnose some of the reasons why we are generally less concerned with praise than with blame. I will argue that ordinary praise and blame, like ordinary praiseworthiness and ordinary blameworthiness, work in pretty much the same way. However, there are some complexities, and some small differences between praise and blame. We are much more ready to engage in blame than praise. Praise is a delicate business, and our praise conversations are often muted to the point of imperceptibility. I explain this tendency by pointing out various features of the praise conversation. One major explanatory point here is that our praise habits are based on non-moral praise, and some features of non-moral praise seep over into our habits regarding moral praise.

Both praise and blame involve communication: in blaming someone, we are communicating to them that we disapprove of their efforts, and in praising someone we are communicating to them that we approve of their efforts, that we see that they have tried hard. In that sense praise and blame are symmetrical. But whereas blame, particularly in the case where the blamer is the victim, can activate a sequence of further moves, praise lacks the extras that come with being in a particular standing to the subject of the praise. When I praise someone, I ask that she accept my praise but I do not ask for more than that.

It might be simplest to start with a case of non-moral praise, so let's imagine that we are beginners at a ceilidh dance. It is hard work, and we keep stumbling and bumping into each other. After an hour or so we are doing better, and my partner pulls off the do-si-do with accuracy and panache, and I praise him: 'well done, that was brilliant!' I want him to understand that I see that he tried hard, and that he did well by his own lights, and I want him to recognize that I recognize that. What is communicated has this circular structure: the praiser wants the praisee to recognize the recognition of his efforts. More than that, the praiser wants the praisee to take some pleasure in the praise. Thus the implicit request for acceptance of praise is non-trivial. It involves an emotional imposition.

In moral praise, we have the same structure. Imagine that my friend decides to donate 10 per cent of her income to charity. I admire this, and I also want to praise my friend, which is a further thing. When I praise her, I am entering into a communication: I am telling her that I recognize the moral value of her act, and the effort she has put into it. I want her to accept my praise. Verbally she may brush it off, but that is compatible with her accepting it. We tend to say things like, 'oh, you know, it's not much'. But that can be a way of accepting praise. In accepting my praise, my friend does her part of the praise conversation, accepts my assessment, quietly takes pleasure in it, and we jointly affirm our shared values.

We can contrast a case where we admire but do not expect our admiration to be recognized. Praise does not work as praise when it is directed to someone in a context where there is not a relevant shared value system. Imagine I encounter an alien being, who, to me, appears to be performing incredible acrobatics. Given that I have no idea what is actually going on (perhaps this is a signal of distress, or a fit of some sort), I have no business praising the alien, though I may of course admire what seems to me to be aesthetic value. But I can praise those in my moral (or academic) community, because I know what they are up to, and see it in the same terms that they do. This is exactly the same for praise as it is for blame.

This picture makes sense of a common way in which praise misfires. Praise is often directed at accidental features of an agent, such as looks. The discomfort we feel about such praise is apt. Praise is not simply admiration, it implicitly demands acceptance, and acceptance requires that the praisee be able to take pride in the thing praised, to take credit for it. For many things, aspects of our appearance being the most salient here, we cannot take credit. So although a compliment or admiration may be acceptable, we feel uncomfortable being praised for such things.

This picture also makes sense of various ways in which praise is delicate, and easily blunders into something inappropriate. Praise does make a demand, and does insert the praiser into the picture in a way that may be unwelcome. The praiser is asking for something: she is asking for her approval to be recognized, she is asking for the praisee to respond with pleasure, even if only very faint. For that not to be presumptuous or patronizing, it requires a certain sort of equality. The equality point is important, and we need to make a distinction between two kinds of praise. The sort of praise I have been focussing on is 'peer-praise', such as when I praise my friend for giving 10 per cent of her income to charity. But there is also 'teacher-praise', which does not require equality. One reason that we are cautious with praise is that we don't want to seem to be bestowing teacher-praise when we in fact intend peer-praise.

Teacher-praise is like peer-praise in requiring shared standards. When I praise my student, I am referring to our shared values and expressing my happiness that my student tried hard and did well by those standards. Teacher-praise is relatively simple: I am very likely to praise my student openly, to say, 'you did so well, and I am really happy'. I may also express pride, though expressions of pride are complex, and it is crucial not to appear to be taking some of the credit. But teacher-praise does not rule out pride.

Peer-praise is harder to get right. It is crucial to avoid the appearance of teacher-praise, which would be patronizing when the praiser is not in fact in a teacher role. Go back to the ceilidh dance, and imagine that I have been criticizing my partner and correcting his moves throughout the event. If in fact my own dancing is no better than his, teacher-praise is not appropriate, but of course anything I say will be read as an attempt at teacher-praise. I might be self-aware enough to see that, and decide, wisely, to refrain from expressing my praise, or to express it only very obscurely. In the moral case, we are rightly anxious to avoid seeming as though we take ourselves to be moral teachers, and so we may avoid peer praise in order to minimize the risk.

Praise is particularly risky when the praiser is in some sort of superior position to the praisee, but is not in a teacher role. Imagine a senior academic who hears a junior colleague he has not met before give a talk. He can say, 'great talk!' But he should probably stop there, because there is a danger that if he goes on, and explains what he likes about the talk, he will be illegitimately assuming a teacher role, and that is patronizing.

Whereas someone at the same professional level is much less likely to fall into being patronizing if she carries on enthusiastically, 'great talk, I really liked your argument against Thomson, and the way you weave the various themes together is fantastic!'. There is a more general point here: when the praiser has much more social power than the praisee, praising appropriately is delicate. That's a familiar phenomenon.

Equally, peer-praise is difficult when someone is in an inferior position. Peer praise requires not being presumptuous about equality with respect to the relevant standards. When my undergraduate student says to me, 'I see that you know a lot of about philosophy, it is very impressive!', my reaction, is, 'who are you to praise me for that?' In order to avoid being presumptuous, the praiser must at least be on a roughly equal standing with the praisee with respect to the shared standards. I cannot praise my pilates teacher for her perfect plank, I can only admire her. Peer-praise requires a certain amount of equality with respect to the shared standards being invoked. The same applies to blame. When fans blame David Beckham for missing the vital penalty kick, they are acting as if they are on a par with Beckham with respect to that sort of thing, that they see where he went wrong and where he should have done better. But the reality is usually that their own football skills are massively inferior.

The explanation for why rough equality is a necessary condition for appropriate peer-praise is intimately connected with what ordinary praiseworthiness is. I have argued that ordinary praiseworthiness is correlated with subjective obligation, so an agent is praiseworthy when she has tried to do well by Morality. Praise expresses recognition of that. Thus peer-praise implicitly involves an imaginative identification with the amount of effort the agent had to put in to achieve what she did. Without rough equality such imaginative identification seems strained. When I admire my pilates teacher, I am inwardly saying, 'wow, that's great, I have no idea how you do that'. When I praise a peer, I am saying, 'I see what you had to do, and how hard you tried, and I am impressed'. We might put this in terms of the agent's standing to praise or blame—an agent who is seriously inferior or superior to the other, risks being presumptuous or patronizing.[11]

---

[11] My point is that in order to effectively peer-praise we must understand the sort of effort that was required to perform as the agent performed. This is an epistemic issue at heart: without rough equality we do not know what the other person's efforts were. So just

In the moral case, rough equality is more likely than it is in areas where particular skills are arduously acquired. I can morally praise and blame David Beckham for his conduct in his personal life, or over his tax affairs. I have no reason to think that he is morally superior or inferior to me. But the delicacy of distinguishing between peer-praise and teacher-praise means that we are often more cautious of moral praise than we need to be.

We can now see one reason that we often leave the praise conversation unspoken. We are cautious, perhaps too cautious about praising. We think that someone is praiseworthy, but we do not actually praise them. We want to avoid presumptuous or patronizing praise, and so it seems better to avoid praise altogether. After all, in praising, we are taking a situation where things are already good and trying to make it better. The risks of patronizing or presumptuous praise are not worth taking. By contrast, if blame is a possibility, things are already bad, and so the consequences of getting blame a bit wrong are less likely to be damaging.

Another reason we are reluctant to praise is that in praising we are imposing ourselves on the praisee in a certain way. We are making a demand, and we have to be sure that the demand is welcome. The praisee, unlike the blamee, is not in deficit, she does not owe us anything, and so if in doubt about whether praise would be welcome, we are rightly cautious. However, there may also be some bad reasons operating here. We may simply be shy, reluctant to say nice things, overly anxious about who our equals are, or about being intrusive. In the case of moral praise and blame, we do not usually need to worry too much about equality, but perhaps our wariness of non-moral praise bleeds into our tendencies regarding moral praise.

In sum, then, I suggest that praising and blaming are communications. Praising and blaming both appeal to shared values. Hence the felicity condition for both praise and blame is a shared value system. Essential to both is an expectation that the blamee or praisee will recognize and accept the blame or praise, and a hope that they will have the appropriate emotional reaction, remorse, or pleasure. Blame and praise come with an

as we should avoid praising or blaming, we should avoid judging praise- or blameworthy. Hence we might want to say that this is not really an issue about *standing* to praise or blame: usually, if you lack the standing to blame you can nonetheless judge blameworthy. But inequality disrupts both praising and judging praiseworthy (or blaming and judging blameworthy)—the two do not come apart. See Bell (2013b) for a critique of the idea of standing to blame, and in particular the hypocrisy condition.

RSVP, as Stephen Darwall puts it (2006, 40). The demand may be rejected for various reasons, and a rejection of the demand does not necessarily mean that the blame or praise was infelicitous.[12] The point is that in both praise and blame, something is being requested, an attempt is being made to start a sequence of exchanges. The exact details of the sequence vary according to context, but may involve the following steps: acceptance of blame (or praise), remorse or guilt (or pleasure), apology (or thanks), reparations, forgiveness, acceptance of forgiveness. The sequence is an essential part of our complex web of morality and responsibility practices, and has the function of regulating and rationalizing our social relationships, of affirming our commitment to trying to do well by Morality.

3. Detached Blame (and Blameworthiness)

I now turn to agents who do not have a grasp of Morality. Such agents are not praise- or blameworthy in the ordinary way. They do not take themselves to be trying (or failing to try) to do well by Morality, because they do not grasp Morality. Perhaps they have some other morality, perhaps they have none. Either way, our communicative blame will not make sense to them. However, there is a different way to blame them.[13] In this section

---

[12] Blame can be refused because the blamee is unrepentant, as Coleen Macnamara (2015b) points out. I come back to her discussion in Chapter 7.

[13] Pluralism about blameworthiness and blame has been gaining traction lately. Watson (1996) makes a distinction between 'two faces of responsibility', attributability and accountability, where attributability is the 'aretaic' face of responsibility, and accountability the face that attracts communicative blame. John Martin Fischer and Neal Tognazzini (2011) argue that if we zoom in there are even more faces. Their claim that there are two steps in the attributability category of responsibility has something in common with my suggestion that we can distinguish between detached blame and the truly objective stance. David Shoemaker (2015) has developed a tripartite account of blameworthiness, in which he distinguishes between attributability, which is a matter of the motives being truly the agent's, 'answerability', which requires that the agent grasp the reasons for her action, and accountability. Neither answerability nor attributability attracts a communicative sort of blame, according to Shoemaker. Shoemaker agrees with Watson that accountability is what merits communicative blame, and on Shoemaker's view, one is accountable when one has slighted someone by failing to take their normative perspective to bear on deliberative reasons (2015, 104–6). Some writers insist that we do not need to be pluralist: Angela Smith (2008) argues that we do not need accountability blame at all, attributability can do all the work. Neil Levy (2005) argues on the other side that we do not need attributability blame at all, we can just use the notion of a bad person. Miranda Fricker stresses that our blame practices are diverse (2016a, 166–7) though she goes on to argue that we should see communicative blame as the paradigm.

I defend an account of 'detached blame'.[14] Detached blame is similar to ordinary blame in some ways, but it is not communicative, and can be applied to agents from whom there is no prospect of a response.

The agents we are talking about here are agents who act objectively wrongly, but not subjectively wrongly. The relevant acts qualify as wrong, rather than just bad, because they meet a weak version of the responsibility constraint. To recap my account of objectively wrong action from Chapter 2: objectively wrong action is defined in terms of what a somewhat idealized agent would do in the circumstances. According to prospectivism, which I take to be the most sensible account of objective obligation, wrong actions are described in terms of what a reasonable agent with a grasp of Morality would do in particular circumstances. So we can say that agents who do not in fact have a grasp of Morality act objectively wrongly, and it doesn't matter that that point of view is not accessible to them. We can apply the objective standard even to those who do not understand how to meet it.

That should be distinguished from the point that any agent could act in ignorance, or lack of control. The sort of objective wrongdoing that is relevant here is not accidental wrongdoing, it is objectively wrong action that the agent would not disown as her action. It might be helpful to give an example. Imagine an agent, Hal, who does not grasp Morality. Hal routinely litters: he throws his rubbish out of the car window, out of boats, and onto the street as he is walking along. Hal doesn't know this is wrong. He doesn't pay much attention to what other people think, and Hal is a big scary looking guy, so people tend not to challenge him. His acts are objectively wrong: they meet a weak version of the Responsibility constraint, in that they are the sort of thing that people could be responsible for. Further, Hal *is* responsible for them, he does not have simple excuse. If challenged, he would not say, 'oh sorry, I thought that was a rubbish bin'. He would say, 'yes, I threw my rubbish onto the street'. So he would not disown his action.[15]

---

[14] In my 2015 I referred to this as 'objective blame'. I have refined my view in various ways since then, including changing the terminology.

[15] Of course there are possible descriptions under which he would disown it, and I am relying here on an intuitive level of description, such that it is fair to say that the action as described is objectively wrong, and that the agent would accept that action as theirs under that description.

Unexcused objective wrongdoing by someone who does not have a grasp of Morality is not in the realm of subjective obligation. It is not the case that the agent is acting subjectively wrongly. The agent does not have access to the right sort of moral understanding to see that her act is morally problematic. So her activity here, the thing that she does, does not make her blameworthy in the ordinary way. She is not knowingly failing to try to do well by Morality. And because she is not acting badly by her own lights, an attempt at communicative blame would be pointless—we would not be latching onto any receptors or recognition in her.

However, as members of the community that does grasp Morality, we cannot be indifferent to unexcused objective wrongdoing. We cannot blame in the ordinary communicative way, but we are bound to have some sort of reaction. I think the simplest story here is that we react with a different sort of blame. It is like ordinary blame in that it is not just a judgment of wrongdoing, it follows a judgment of wrongdoing, and goes beyond it, but it differs from ordinary blame in that it is not communicative, it is detached from the blamee.

Detached blame has something in common with Strawson's 'objective attitude'. Of course, Strawson contrasts the interpersonal reactive attitudes, which constitute praise and blame, with the objective attitude, but I will argue that the objective attitude can be a form of blame. Strawson himself readily accepts that the situation is complex, admitting that he is dealing in crude dichotomies and ignoring "the ever-interesting and ever-illuminating varieties of case" (1962 reprinted in Watson, 2003, 79). I agree with Strawson that the situation is complex. My aim here is to do some work in expanding our understanding of the objective attitude.

I will begin by highlighting the difference between ordinary communicative blame and detached blame. Strawson, in his discussion of exemptions says:

But suppose we see the agent in a different light: as one whose picture of the world is an insane delusion; or as one whose behaviour, or a part of whose behaviour, is unintelligible to us, perhaps even to him, in terms of conscious purposes, and intelligible only in terms of unconscious purposes; or even, perhaps, as one wholly impervious to the self-reactive attitudes I spoke of, wholly lacking, as we say, in moral sense.... We may say: to the extent to which the agent is seen in this light, he is not seen as one on whom demands and expectations lie in that particular way in which we think of them as lying when we speak of moral obligation; he is not, to that extent, seen as a morally responsible agent, as a term of moral relationships, as a member of the moral community.   (1962, reprinted in Watson, 2003, 85)

In this passage, Strawson sketches a version of the view that blame is essentially a sort of communication with those in our moral community, and contrasts those whom we can blame in the ordinary communicative way with those who are outside the moral community, to whom we must take a different attitude.[16] Strawson is not just pointing out that blame does not apply to those outside our moral community. He also says that *obligation* does not apply here. So it seems that Strawson is thinking along the lines of the sort of view that I have been defending. On my view, in order for the concept of subjective wrongness to apply, the agent must grasp Morality. An agent in our moral community, one who shares our morality, is one that we can make demands of, communicate with, and so, one that we can blame in the ordinary way. Agents who do not grasp Morality are not in the realm of subjective obligation, and so we cannot expect them to see that they have acted wrongly by their own lights. To them, we must take something like the objective attitude. But what exactly is the objective attitude?

Strawson suggests, at the end of the quoted passage, that taking the objective stance involves seeing the agent as 'not responsible to that extent' where 'that extent' refers back to the claim that we cannot think of demands and expectations as being appropriate for that agent. This does not imply that the agent cannot be seen as responsible at all. We need not think of the objective attitude as granting a full exemption. Strawson himself allows that the objective attitude can be emotionally toned (Strawson, 1962 reprinted in Watson, 2003, 79).

Strawson would probably be reluctant to characterize the objective attitude as a form of blame but, I will argue, it can be blame. Our normal reactions to ill-willed agents outside our moral community include elements that we usually think of as distinguishing blaming from merely judging blameworthy. Our reaction is not just a cognitive judgment about the agent's behaviour. Nor is it just an emotional reaction that we might have to bad things happening. Detached blame involves a reaction to the agent *qua agent*. However, I will argue that we should include a diverse mix of reactions under the umbrella of detached blame. More work might be done here, but I will rest content with exploring

---

[16] My account here owes a lot to Watson's account in 'Responsibility and the Limits of Evil'. Watson points out that the reactive attitudes are a form of moral address, and that there are limits to the applicability of moral address (1987/2004, 223–33).

some of the major detached blame reactions, and showing that it is very plausible to see them as blame.

First, when we react to something bad done by an agent, we usually react with emotion. The emotional tone that Strawson speaks of is a reaction to the fault identified and though, as Strawson says, it is not resentment, it can be a different sort of reaction that constitutes a different sort of blame. When we hear about the despotic dictators I mentioned earlier, we feel repugnance, anger, disdain, and so on. These are reactive attitudes, and they are not lessened when we reflect on the deep moral ignorance of such people. In fact, I think that our reactions to people who are deeply morally ignorant are not reactions to quality of will in a strict sense. They are, rather, reactions to agents who act wrongly; but beyond the judgment that the perpetrator is an agent, and their act is objectively wrong, I do not think we feel the need to delve further into what the perpetrator's exact quality of will is. In that sense, detached blame is in the same family as the objective attitude. It is more about the blamer than the blamee—the blamer's need to let off steam, to signal disapproval to her peers, to manage and manoeuvre around the offending agent.

Consider the reaction we might have to someone who behaves in a sexist way, but who has never been given any reason not to be sexist. Imagine that this person, Bill, has been raised in an entirely sexist environment, which of course has shaped the evidence that is available to him.[17] We can imagine that it is possible that he is entirely good willed, that his mistakes are purely due to bad evidence. He sincerely believes that women are too silly to be allowed any power or responsibility, and the kindest thing is to keep them safe at home, relegated to the simple domestic tasks to which they are suited. However, Bill has no hostility to women, he sees them as most of us see dogs. Dogs are wonderful, great companions, not to be mistreated, but certainly not our equals. Bill is not doing anything wrong by his own lights: he is not acting subjectively wrongly. However, he is acting objectively wrongly. We are bound to react to that, and to blame him in a sense. He is an agent, and his sexist behaviour is not accidental. He would not respond,

---

[17] Arpaly has an example with the same form (2003, 104). According to Arpaly, the agent is not blameworthy, because he has no bad will. We might dispute the premiss, and argue that moral mistakes always involve bad will—see Harman (2011).

'oh, I didn't realize that my wife wanted to get an education'. Rather, he will accept his acts as his own (though not as wrong): he will say, without embarrassment, 'yes, I did forbid my wife to read that book'.

Once we are sure that Bill is sincerely and thoroughly in the grip of his false moral view, it is clear that there is no point in blaming him in the ordinary way. It will not make sense to him, and he will not respond. At that point, we are faced with an agent whom we cannot reach, but who has acted seriously wrongly. I think that is all we need to know to have a blame reaction. We might be interested in Bill's motivations in a psychological or anthropological way, but we do not need to know exactly what his quality of will was in order to blame him. Bill is someone who stands outside our moral community, we are not going to engage with him on the topic, so it doesn't really matter what his exact motivations are. He forbade his wife to read a book! His having no bad will doesn't change the basis of our reaction, which is to the bad thing that he has done. So long as it was not an accident, a misunderstanding, he is not excused. He is outside of the realm of ordinary blame, but that is not a way of being off the hook.

What might someone who wants to convince us that we should not blame Bill at all argue? They might say, 'but he really thinks it is necessary to forbid his wife to read the book, he thinks he is doing the right thing!' But that shows that he is conscience respectworthy at best. Being conscience respectworthy is not the same as being praiseworthy, and is compatible with being blameworthy. My imaginary opponent might try arguing that Bill has no unjust, unkind, or cruel motivations. To which I reply that it doesn't matter. What he is doing is nonetheless unjust, unkind, and cruel. I am not interrogating his motives, I am thinking of his wife, and of the other women in his life over whom he has control, and I am reacting to the wrong done to them. My opponent might then respond that there is no difference between my reaction to Bill, and my reaction to a non-agent, a hurricane, or a fire. To this my response is that reactions to agents are different to reactions to non-agents.

Take first our emotions. Our emotional reactions to 'bad things happening' are very different when there is another agent involved. We react to objects, animals that are not agents, and forces of nature with emotions like sadness and disappointment. If it is foggy on a day I had hoped to climb a mountain for a beautiful view, I feel disappointment. There is nothing like blame in my reaction. There is simply no one *to* blame. If a raccoon steals my picnic, or the wind blows it away (assuming I have no reason to blame myself, which of course I might) I cannot blame anyone. My reactions are not about other agents, they are just about me, my own loss.

Emotional reactions are very different when accompanied by the judgment that the cause of the bad thing happening is an agent. Perhaps some emotions are such that they can only be directed at agents. Consider disdain. Plausibly, disdain only makes sense if directed at agents. Knowing that an agent, rather than an object (or an animal or a force of nature) behaved in a certain way makes an important difference to the reaction we tend towards. We cannot disdain a raccoon, or a car. But we can disdain agents, even ones who cannot respond appropriately. Another example is contempt. As Michelle Mason argues, we can take contempt to be a reactive attitude, a ranking of the other person on moral grounds (2003, 240–1).

Note that neither disdain (as Darwall points out, 2006 40) nor contempt requires a response. In fact, they don't make room for a response. Disdain and contempt then, are plausible candidates for reactive emotions that are particular to detached blame. Contempt and disdain are what is left when ordinary blame is not applicable, when we see that the transgressor is an agent, but not the sort who will walk through the ordinary blame conversation with us.[18] Contempt and disdain seem incompatible with ordinary blame, because they seem to shut off the possibility of a conversation. If I am contemptuous of you, it does not seem that I am asking you to accept that you have acted wrongly by your own lights and to move towards making amends. Rather, I have given up on you as an interlocutor.

[18] Michelle Mason sees contempt as in the same category as resentment, and in defending that view she must try to answer the powerful seeming objection that contempt is not a genuine reactive attitude because it is incompatible with forgiveness (2003, 255). We might understand that worry as being the worry that contempt is not compatible with communicative blame. On the view that I am defending, this worry does not arise: forgiveness is not applicable in the realm of detached blame. Macalaster Bell argues that contempt (unlike disgust) does demand a response (2013a), and so concludes that, whereas contempt is a reactive attitude, disgust is not. I disagree, I don't think either contempt or disgust demands a response. Contempt is always directed at agents, and so is a reactive attitude that qualifies as detached blame. Disgust can be directed at agents, but there are various complexities in disgust that I do not go into here. See Robert Wallace's discussion in 'Responsibility and the Limits of Good and Evil' (manuscript), for an interesting account of how disgust plays a role as a reactive attitude in cases of extreme evil.

There are other emotions that can accompany either ordinary blame or detached blame. Hurt and offence, for example, are complex. Clearly, they are reactions to agents: one can be hurt or offended by agential action, in a way that one cannot be hurt or offended by non-agents. But it is plausible that neither hurt nor offence demands a response. They can be entirely private emotions, and make sense even when there is no possibility that the target will understand or accept the reaction. I might feel hurt that I was not thanked in your award acceptance speech, even though I know that you do not value my contributions and will not see that I should have been thanked. I might feel offended by a racist joke, even though I know that you can't see the problem. However, these emotions can also coexist with communicative blame. I can feel hurt by you, and still move forward with a blame conversation. Other emotions are even broader, and can accompany both blaming and non-blaming responses. We can feel anger, annoyance, and irritation at all sorts of things, though, arguably, the way in which one is angry with a non-agent is different to the way in which one is angry with an agent.[19]

The point is that agents are an important category, even when they do not possess all the features that make ordinary blame felicitous. We respond to agential wrongdoing with a range of reactions. Our emotional reaction to wrongdoing by agents is plausibly a form of blame. The emotional reaction is a response to wrongdoing that goes beyond a mere judgment of wrongdoing, so on my rough template for blame, is at least a contender.

It might be objected that that there is not a clear judgment of *blameworthiness* here. When I distinguished blame from punishing and judging blameworthy above, I said that to blame is to go beyond a judgment of wrongdoing. In the case of ordinary blame, a judgment of wrongdoing is a judgment of subjective wrongdoing, and so *just is* a judgment of blameworthiness, as I argued in Chapter 4. In the realm of subjective obligation, our judgment of blameworthiness is prior to blame: it is because we are identifying something in the agent's quality of will—her acting subjectively wrongly—that we move on to actual blame.

[19] See David Shoemaker's account of the reactive emotions for a detailed analysis of the different reactive emotions (2015). My account is not sentimentalist, I do not think emotion is essential to ordinary blame. I do think emotion is usually present when blaming, and I am arguing here that detached blame is often constituted by emotion.

In the case of detached blame, the judgment of blameworthiness is a very different sort of thing. There is a judgment of wrongdoing, and a judgment that the perpetrator really is an agent, not an object. But, beyond that, we are not making a judgment about what the agent deserves or merits in virtue of a fine-tuned judgment about the agent's quality of will. A judgment of objective wrongdoing is not a judgment about blameworthiness in that sense. When we have a case of unexcused objective wrongdoing by an agent, a certain sort of response is fitting, it makes sense for us to react with a species of blame, but this is not something we could express well in desert terms. The wrongdoer is worthy of blame insofar as detached blame makes sense, but that is not the way that the term 'blameworthy' is usually used.[20] I am using it in a weaker, but nonetheless appropriate and useful sense.

I have argued that reactive emotion in response to an agent's wrong-doing is one sort of detached blame. In that sort of detached blame, the emotion constitutes the blame. But it is not the only sort of detached blame, there are other ways to react that go beyond the judgment of wrongdoing. This brings us to Scanlon's account (1998; 2008). He argues that blaming someone is taking them to have attitudes that are incompatible with a particular sort of relationship that should have obtained, and so modifying or withdrawing from that relationship in response. He emphasizes the importance of recognizing that an agent has the basic capacities of agency. According to Scanlon's account, we can blame anyone, so long as they have attitudes. We do not need them to be able to respond, or understand the blame. Critics have worried that this does not capture all that we mean by blame, and I agree: this does not capture

---

[20] This brings out the difference between my pluralism and Gary Watson's distinction between attributability and accountability (2004, 260–88). On Watson's view, attributability, or self-disclosure, is the fundamental form of responsibility, and is to do with the agent's quality of will. My account of detached blameworthiness here is not equivalent to attributability, it is not the fundamental kind of responsibility, and it is not dependent on quality of will beyond the basic capacities of agency. Watson, and also Scanlon (1998), think that we first identify the agent's quality of will, and then move on to a social practice of holding responsible, which depends on concerns like fairness—whether it is fair to hold people responsible when they have had poor formative circumstances, for example. As Watson puts it at one point, "accountability blame is a response to the faults identified in aretaic blame" (2004, 278). My account of ordinary blameworthiness is not equivalent to accountability in this sense: ordinary blameworthiness is not defined by whether punishment might be appropriate or fair. Rather, ordinary blameworthiness is defined in terms of a certain sort of quality of will, a quality of will that contains self-awareness of wrongdoing.

the communicative element that is essential in ordinary blame. However, it does capture what is often going on in cases where we blame those who do not have a grasp of Morality.

One might worry that the modifying of a relationship is not blame, but rather a form of Strawson's objective attitude, in that we are simply avoiding the object of our disapproval, and not treating them as a person at all. This is what happens in the most extreme case: when we take the truly objective stance, we are merely managing the person, taking measures to reduce their bad effects on us and others. However, in detached blame, our avoidance is also *intrinsically* motivated, motivated by our sense of the agent as an agent. When an agent acts badly, and communicative blame is not fitting, we avoid that agent not just in order to minimize contact, but on principle. We shun them.

Imagine that the university you work for has taken an endowment from an evil dictator, and the dictator's son, JoJo is enrolled in courses. Of course we give JoJo the benefit of the doubt, and we may work on bringing him around to our way of seeing things. This is often successful: we are usually optimistic about the prospects for transformation in such cases, as we should be. Imagine, however, that we hear that while enrolled in courses, JoJo is also working for his father, and is involved in espionage, reporting on his fellow students in order to support terror campaigns at home. It seems that JoJo is outside our moral community after all, he doesn't get it, he has not been changed by his experiences.

Inevitably, in real life this sort of case is complicated by our uncertainty about whether someone really is beyond the pale. I think that we rightly give people the benefit of the doubt as long as we can. But let us stipulate here that JoJo is deep in the grip of a terrible value system, and our value system means nothing to him. In this case, we would not blame him in the communicative way: that would be pointless. But we would not treat him merely as an object either. We would blame him, but in a detached way. We would avoid him, but not just out of caution, we would avoid him simply for the sake of avoiding him. We do not want to symbolically condone his behaviour, even though the condoning would mean nothing to him and make no difference to anyone. We may feel it professionally incumbent on us to continue teaching him so long as our university requires us to do so, but we would certainly refuse to socialize with him or spend extra academic time with him—we would surely be reluctant to take on an independent study, for example.

Of course, not all of our detached blame can be understood on the Scanlonian model. Sometimes there is no relationship with an agent at all, as critics of Scanlon have pointed out. In those cases, detached blame may consist of emotional reactions. We can have emotional reactions to people with whom we do not have relationships, and to the dead as well as the living.[21] Detached blame may also take the form of a protest, as Matthew Talbert suggests (2012a). There are various reactions that can fairly be characterized as detached blame, what unifies them is just that they are blame type reactions (reactions to wrongdoing that go beyond a mere judgment of wrongdoing, and are not essentially an imposition of suffering) that are not communicative, and can thus be applied to agents outside our moral community.

Detached blame has a function, just as communicative blame does. Both detached blame and ordinary blame are social practices. Ordinary blame is a practice that makes sense in the context of a moral community, reminding each other of the values we share. But our moral community is not an entirely isolated community, it is not entirely homogeneous. Individuals sometimes slip through the cracks, and end up with no recognizable morality at all. There is no point in trying to communicate with such people, but we are bound to react to their trampling on the values we hold dear. When reacting to people outside our moral community, our reactions are more for the benefit of each other than for the benefit of the people blamed. We demonstrate to each other our commitment to our values, partly through contrasting our values with the bad values of outliers. Further, we can learn from the complexities of borderline cases, which helps us to reflect on our own values and moral disagreements.

It is worth contrasting my discussion of ordinary blame and blameworthiness with my discussion of detached blame and blameworthiness. In discussing ordinary blame, I started with ordinary blameworthiness: I started by describing what an agent *does* in order to be blameworthy (she violates her subjective obligation) and went on to argue that this meshes with understanding ordinary blame as communicative. I did not put my argument in terms of desert, but my aim was to do some of the

---

[21] By contrast ordinary blame, being communicative, depends on some sort of contact. In cases where there is no contact at all, there is a judgment of ordinary blameworthiness, but no blame. (Though we might be able to construct an account of ersatz ordinary blame that depends on an imaginary exchange with the person.)

work that talking of desert does: to make clear that ordinary blame is fitting when an agent has acted subjectively wrongly. In my discussion of detached blame and detached blameworthiness, the order is reversed. I discussed detached blame first, and that is because detached blame is the prior concept. Our reactive attitude is in the driving seat. This picture is thus more like the projectivist view that is sometimes attributed to Strawson: what makes detached blame make sense is primarily the values and attitudes of the blamer, rather than something in the blamee. Whereas in the case of ordinary blame I have done some work to explain and accommodate our everyday notion of desert, that is not a feasible aim for my notion of detached blame and blameworthiness. My account of detached blame is a species of objective stance but, as I have argued, an objective stance that we take to *agents*.

My account of detached blame is not a quality of will account, except in the very limited sense that the agent's act is not accidental. As I explained above, the sort of wrong action that attracts detached blame is objective wrongdoing by an agent outside our moral community. There is no requirement that the agent have a bad will, the only requirement is that the agent have acted objectively wrongly, and that she would not disown the act.

4. Detached Praise (and Praiseworthiness)

I have focused on detached blame, but I should say something briefly about detached praise and praiseworthiness. Reflecting on detached praiseworthiness lends support to my story about detached blameworthiness.

Ordinary praise, as I argued in section 2, makes a demand. It demands that the agent accept the praise. If someone acts well without understanding what they are doing, then clearly, they will not accept praise. Think of Huck Finn, who believes that he is acting badly in helping Jim to escape. He could not accept our praise in a straightforward way: he could not meet us in agreeing that he tried hard by the correct standards. Of course Huck is a child, and as with blame, praise to children is often proleptic, designed to bring them into our moral community.[22] But paradigmatic praise relies on a shared understanding of the moral situation.

---

[22] Bernard Williams (1995) argues blame can function as a proleptic mechanism, a sort of manipulation, in his 'Internal Reasons and the Obscurity of Blame' (though it is essential

Detached praise, like detached blame, can involve both emotional reactions and some sort of relationship modification. Detached praise is not communicative, does not involve a demand. We can feel admiration and approval, but we feel it in an alienated way, engaging with the agent about how we feel would not make much sense. We may also modify our relationship. On realizing that an agent does not actually understand that her acts are morally good, and is not actually trying to do well by Morality in doing them, we are likely to distance ourselves a bit, we take a step away from interpersonal engagement. We may approve of the agent, but there is still a sense in which we give up on them, when we see that the praise conversation will be infelicitous.

Of course, as in the Huck case, the temptation to praise proleptically is very vivid when an agent displays good motivations, and in that there is a slight asymmetry with blame, where we are more likely to move straight to detached blame. There are, I think, various reasons that proleptic praise is more tempting than proleptic blame. First, people who exhibit motivations to the good despite deep moral ignorance seem particularly susceptible to being brought into our moral community. Moral ignorance seems less stable when an agent acts well. Second, because appropriately offered praise is pleasant (usually both to bestow and to receive) it seems to be more likely to be effective in the proleptic mode. Finally, because it pleasant to bestow, it is less burdensome to engage in than proleptic blame.

Corresponding to detached praise is a sense of praiseworthiness, detached praiseworthiness. As with detached blameworthiness, it is not the paradigmatic sense of 'worthiness': it is not desert. Detached praise is fitting when an agent non-accidentally acts well. Detached praiseworthiness is more or less that quality that Aristotle calls 'natural virtue' (2000). It clearly invites a reactive attitude. It is a fine thing, and we enjoy it in others, but it is not full virtue or (as I would have it) ordinary praiseworthiness. Someone who is drawn to good things, that is to say, has a good will in the content matching sense, is certainly admirable. But natural virtue lacks the element of awareness that is necessary for ordinary praiseworthiness.

---

that the agent have some motivations that relate to the motivation the blamer is trying to induce). Miranda Fricker (2016a) points out that understanding the proleptic function of blame supports the view that blame is essentially communicative.

5. Conclusion

In this chapter I argued that we should think of ordinary praise and blame as communicative. I sketched a model, which I acknowledged is variable according to different circumstances and relationships, according to which blame is like a conversation: the blamer points out to the blamee that she acted wrongly by her own lights and, in blaming, the blamer is attempting to initiate a series of moves, which may involve acceptance of blame, feeling guilt or remorse, apology, acceptance of apology, forgiveness, acceptance of forgiveness. Praise involves a shorter sequence, the praiser communicates her approval to the praisee, she hopes for her praise to be accepted with pleasure, and that may be the end of the conversation.

Both ordinary praise and ordinary blame rely on shared moral community. Both make sense because it makes sense to expect a response from the recipient of the praise or blame. Thus ordinary praise is fitting when an agent acts subjectively rightly. Subjective rightness requires background knowledge of Morality. Likewise, ordinary blame, a communication, is fitting when an agent acts subjectively wrongly.

By contrast, when we blame those outside our moral community, those from whom it is not reasonable to expect a response or recognition, our blame is a different sort of thing. Detached blame is not communicative (though it may communicate something to other members of our moral community). I argued that there are various reactions we may have to objective wrongdoing that count as detached blame. What makes something plausible as a form of blame is just that it is a reaction that goes beyond a mere judgment of wrongdoing, and yet is not essentially a harm to the blamee. Both emotional reactions and relationship modifications fit the bill, and both are plausibly blame reactions to objective wrongdoers.

It is worth noting briefly a couple of small points that I have only hinted at in the arguments above. First, both ordinary blame and detached blame are optional: they are further steps beyond a judgment of wrongdoing, and even when they are fitting, whether or not we should engage in them depends on the details of the situation, on the inclinations of the blamer, or on what good will come of it. Of course, often we cannot help ourselves blaming (this applies to both modes), even when blame is futile, or counterproductive.

Second, ordinary blame is often emotional, but it needn't be, and when it is emotional, there are lots of different emotions that could be involved. Sometimes, when we blame those in our moral community, we do it with love and sympathy: we aim to blame our children in this gentle way, for example. Sometimes we are angry, our blame—the call and response—is accompanied by strong hostility, and we usually hope to rid ourselves of that by the end of the blame conversation. But we don't always succeed. There are other possible emotions too—sometimes blame is sad, or bitter, or tinged with schadenfreude. It seems possible to me that we could blame someone in the communicative way with no emotion at all. However, I think that we use emotional reactions as a measure of sincerity. Because emotions are the human condition, emotionless blame is suspect.

Blaming may not involve a particular emotion, but it does request an emotional reaction from the blamee. Genuinely accepting blame when one takes responsibility involves feeling remorse. Thus, as I shall argue in more detail in Chapter 8, taking responsibility can be a sort of emotional work. What we aim for, when we blame in the communicative way, is partly for the person to take the blame conversation seriously, to care, not just about what they have done, but that others are holding them to account. The same applies to praise: someone who accepts my praise but takes no pleasure in it has not really engaged in the praise conversation. They have missed something important.

In this chapter I have been focusing on cases where the agent's act is unambiguous: either subjectively wrong, or objectively wrong (and the agent does not disown her act). But of course in real life acts are often ambiguous, there often seem to be mitigating circumstances, or background considerations that are relevant to blameworthiness. In the next chapter I examine the ways in which excuses work for ordinary blameworthiness and for detached blameworthiness.

6

Excuses

In the previous chapters I developed an account of subjective obligation, and argued that subjective obligation and ordinary praise- and blame-worthiness do indeed align very closely. I argued that we should under-stand subjective obligation, and correspondingly, ordinary praise- and blameworthiness, as depending on trying (or failing to try) to do well by Morality, which in turn relies on the agent having moral knowledge. This leaves some people out of ordinary blame but, I argued, those who lack a grasp of Morality may be blameworthy in a different sense: we can blame them in the detached way. Ordinary blame and detached blame both apply to agential wrongdoing, but whereas ordinary blame applies to agents who act subjectively wrongly, detached blame is applicable when an agent acts objectively wrongly but is not in the realm of subjective obligation. In this chapter I look at the different sorts of excuses that apply to the different sorts of blameworthiness.

I start this chapter by examining in more detail the question that I discussed briefly in Chapter 2, about whether an ordinary agent might sometimes have an excuse *for acting subjectively wrongly*. An agent who acts subjectively wrongly could not have a simple excuse of ignorance or lack of control. However, it is conceivable that an agent could have something like an excuse, despite knowing what she is doing, and having some sort of control. If it is possible to have an excuse in such a case it is not a simple excuse. I shall argue that it is possible that there can be mitigating factors that apply to those who act subjectively wrongly. I argue that mitigating circumstances, like excuses, show that what is really going on is that the agent is not acting as badly as it looks as though she is.

I go on to examine cases of mixed motivations, where an agent is trying hard enough to be acting subjectively rightly, but something goes wrong with her act, not through external bad luck, but through the agent's own flawed motivations. In such cases I argue that the agent is praiseworthy in the ordinary way for trying, but that we are bound to react with a species of detached blame to her bad motives.

Finally, I consider the role that unfortunate formative circumstances play in blameworthiness. I argue that formative circumstances do not undermine ordinary blameworthiness. There may be some marginal cases, people who are not clearly in our moral community and not clearly out either, but I argue that for those who are clearly in our moral community, formative circumstances are not relevant. However, bad formative circumstances can be relevant to detached blameworthiness. We move to the truly objective stance, in which we cease to see the agent as an agent.

1. Mitigating Circumstances

In this section I examine the idea that there can be excuses for subjective wrongdoing. There are two kinds of simple excuse. Some simple excuses are excuses of ignorance: the agent who is asking for an excuse is saying, 'I did it, but I did not know that it would have that result, or I did not know that it was an act of that sort.' In this case, assuming the ignorance is non-culpable, and that the ignorance is not deep moral ignorance,[1] it was just bad luck that she was ignorant. The other sort of simple excuse involves blocked agential efficacy or, more straightforwardly put, lack of control. Here it is not so natural for the one making the excuse to say, 'I did it'. The plea is rather, 'I did it, in the sense that my body did it, but for some (temporary) reason my body was not under my control: I was pushed, or I tripped, or I was suddenly paralysed . . .'. Again, we must assume that the back-story is innocent, that it was not the agent's own fault that she tripped, or was pushed. But assuming that she is not to blame for the problem, we see this sort of thing as an excuse. In fact, in both cases the plea is that the agent didn't really do the thing it looked as though she did: she did not do it under the relevant description.[2]

---

[1] See Holly Smith (1983) on culpable ignorance. On deep moral ignorance, see the next chapter. Note that I am not depending on a distinction between moral and factual knowledge. On my view an agent could have a simple excuse for not knowing a moral fact, so long as she has enough of a grasp of Morality to count as being in our moral community.

[2] There is another sort of excuse, which denies responsibility more globally, by indicating that there is something internal to the agent that means that her agency cannot be judged the same way that we judge the exercise of agency in ordinary agents. This basic

Simple excuses are relevant because we cannot see into another agent's head, so before we blame her, we want to know what her account of the situation is. The implicit question is of the form, 'did you really do what it looked as though you did?', and in presenting a valid simple excuse, the agent is saying, 'no, it looked as though I hit her, but I thought she was a shop dummy, or I was pushed, or . . . '. She is not attempting to justify the act, she admits that what happened was bad, but she is saying that she didn't really do it. In making a simple excuse, the agent denies responsibility for a particular act, as a result of a particular blocking factor.

Simple excuses apply to *objective* wrongdoing, agents did not know what they were doing, or were not in control, and so their act was not subjectively wrong. An agent who knows what she is doing, and understands the wrongness of her act (at least at the background level, as I argued in Chapter 2) cannot plead that she did not know what she was doing. Nor can she have a simple excuse of lack of control. Imagine an agent is pushed or (non-culpably) trips, and so steps on someone else's toe. In that case we can imagine that the agent admits that her act is objectively wrong, and pleads the simple excuse that she was not in control at that point.[3] In saying that she was not in control, she is saying that her act was not one that she was trying to do, and not a case of failing to try, and so she is precisely denying that her act was subjectively wrong. Thus she is not asking to be excused *from subjective wrongdoing*. Simple excuses work by admitting objective wrongdoing while denying subjective wrongdoing.

If agents can have something like an excuse for subjective wrongdoing, it must be more complex. The idea would be that an agent did not try as hard as she should have, but there is something like a mitigating circumstance that relieves her of some blameworthiness. I will argue that there are complex excuses that we sometimes refer to as mitigating

distinction in types of excuse comes from Strawson (1962). It is worth noting briefly that Strawson includes coercion in his list of type 1 excuses. I discuss coercion in detail elsewhere (2012). Coercion is a more complex case than being ignorant or being pushed: the agent makes an open-eyed choice, but the choice circumstance is designed by another agent to push the agent in a particular direction insofar as she is reasonable.

[3] In fact it is hard to imagine that an actual agent would admit that her act is wrong in any sense, once she is focusing on its being out of her control. This is because she is now focusing on subjective wrongness, and in this context, subjective wrongness is clearly the relevant sense, because the issue under discussion is praise and blameworthiness. So, other senses of wrongness fade away and seem pointless.

circumstances but that, in the end, there is no local excuse for subjective wrongdoing. The only case in which an agent is excused from blameworthiness for subjective wrongdoing is the case where her agency is undermined entirely.

First, it is worth reiterating some points from previous chapters. To act subjectively rightly is to try to do well by Morality. Trying to do well by Morality need not be a matter of trying as hard you can at every moment. The effort that is required in order to count as trying to do well by Morality is just what is appropriate to the goal, and the goal may allow other goals some space. Sometimes, we need to take some time off, and that does not count as not trying to do well by Morality. We can think of Morality as, on occasion, functioning as a limiting goal, such that so long as we stay within the boundaries of what is morally permissible, it is fine to focus on other things.

But even with that in mind, there are cases when an agent will fail, and not all cases seem completely blameworthy. Someone might be under stress at work, and although her work is not in fact important or stressful enough to justify spending lots of money on shoes, or snapping at her children, she does. We don't think that her bad behaviour is justified, but we do think that it is understandable. But what does that mean? Is being understandable the same as being excused? What about mitigating circumstances? As Austin points out, there is a whole raft of possible terms here. As well as excuse and justification he lists 'extenuation', 'mitigation', and 'palliation', and we use them in unclear and overlapping ways (1956, 3). Perhaps some of these are *partial* excuses, where the agent cannot say she did not act as she appeared to act, but she can say, 'I did it, although perhaps when you hear the background facts, you will see that my behaviour was not as bad as it seems'. We need to know what the background facts are.

One relevant background fact is that the agent may be balancing more sub-goals than is immediately apparent. As I argued in Chapters 3 and 4, it is important to remember that although an agent should be trying hard enough that she is doing what she thinks is most likely to constitute doing well by Morality, when we judge her approach to sub-goals, particular actions and courses of action, we should remember that she has to balance various different sub-goals, and it is not always the case that she must put maximal effort into achieving a sub-goal. In the normal course of events, if I arrive ten minutes late to collect my kids, I am blameworthy. But if I explain that I am caring for a sick relative at the moment, that alters the appropriate balance of goals, and pushes the level of effort that it is reasonable to require for other things down. In fact, I am offering a justification of my action here, I am saying I did not act subjectively wrongly.

It is worth noting that whether the agent is presenting an excuse or a justification depends on whether she is talking in terms of subjective or objective wrongness. As I say, an excuse usually works by claiming that the agent is not acting subjectively wrongly, even though she is acting objectively wrongly. One sensible way we might make the distinction between excuse and justification is to say that a justification claims that there was no subjectively wrong act and no objectively wrong act either. In our actual conversations, we often elide these things out of politeness. As Marcia Baron (2007, 31) points out, our reasons for *mentioning* excusing or mitigating circumstances is often to reassure our friends and associates that what looks like bad will to them is not bad will at all. It seems rude to insist that one's hurtful act was justified, whereas presenting one's justification as if it were an excuse is seen as polite. If I say, 'I am so sorry I can't come to your talk, my child is ill', I am presenting a justification, even if I dress it up as an excuse. In many cases where we mention mitigating circumstances we are actually appealing to a justification, the act is not objectively wrong.

As I said, it may be that there are features of the situation that are not immediately obvious from the outside, that quite reasonably affect the agent's priorities. It is also important to remember, that in balancing goals, the agent is balancing risk. She should leave enough time to arrive at the school to collect her kids, given reasonable assumptions about what might go wrong. If she has nothing else on her plate, she should be more conservative, take a smaller risk, than if she has lots of other important things going on. Either way she might be unlucky—things might be unexpectedly worse than she counted on them being. Thus being late is not justified, but it is not subjectively wrong either. The agent has an excuse, which is that despite her having balanced the risks in a reasonable way, things turned out badly. When an agent is unlucky, she has an excuse in the usual sense, her act was objectively wrong but not subjectively wrong.

The balancing excuse can be full or partial. It is possible that once we see the complexities the agent is dealing with, we see that she was unlucky, but it is also possible that she didn't try as hard as she should. Perhaps she didn't fall as badly short as it appeared (that's what the excuse is, a plea that things are not as they appeared), but she nonetheless fell short. Perhaps her assessment of the timing was not as careful as it should have been. Perhaps she stopped to chat to the nurse in the care home when she should not have. In such cases we can think of her excuse as only a partial excuse: it does not fully explain her failing.

There is a distinct excuse-like plea that an agent might make in this sort of case. She might point out features of the situation that show that she was trying harder than it at first appeared. She snapped grumpily at her kids, which usually indicates 'not trying'. But given the background, the stress she is under with her sick relative, we see that she probably was trying pretty hard, and yet still failed. To put it another way, mitigating circumstances could be circumstances that make it hard to succeed, and so the agent needs to try even harder than usual. In this case, it can be helpful to be reminded of the difficulties the agent faced, and that is the role of the plea of mitigating circumstances. In some cases, mitigating circumstances could constitute a full excuse: it might be that the agent's circumstances were so bad that despite appearances to the contrary she really was trying as hard as she ought. Alternatively, it might be that the agent did fall short, but not as far short as a superficial examination of the situation would suggest.

A more complex and unusual case where we might think an agent who acts subjectively wrongly has an excuse involves 'rogue' impulses. Imagine an ordinary agent, with a good grasp of Morality, who suddenly finds herself with a rogue impulse to do something wicked, or just to ignore her everyday duties and commitments, blow everything off and go skiing. The difficulty here is in defining a 'rogue' impulse. We all have somewhat unwelcome impulses as part of our normal psychology, and part of trying to do well by Morality is dealing with these impulses. Sometimes, the right thing to do is give in to them. Sometimes we need a break, we need to recharge. Sometimes we should have strategies to resist them: if I know that I lose my temper easily, I need some techniques to avoid losing my temper. Part of trying to do well is expecting the unexpected: anticipating the normal run of obstacles. It is very plausible that most 'rogue impulses' fall into the category of the predictable unexpected.

If an agent's rogue impulse is to be such that it means she is not responsible, it must be very rogue indeed. One way that philosophers manufacture such examples, of course, is by imagining evil neuroscientists, able to manipulate the brain, and create desires and intentions in the hapless agent.[4] If an evil neuroscientist has managed to gain control of our brain, and implant desires or intentions, clearly those meet the standard for rogue enough. Outside of science fiction cases, it is hard to say what would count as rogue enough. I will leave aside that question here. I leave it open that there might be mental states rogue enough to relieve the agent of responsibility. In such a case it is not clear that we should say that she is acting subjectively wrongly because it is not clear that she has agency *at all* in that moment. However, it is possible that the best thing to say is that the agent is acting subjectively wrongly, in which case, this is the very unusual case where it is possible to have an excuse for subjective wrong-doing. Her agency is blocked, as it is in simpler cases, but she herself doesn't realize that and takes herself to be agentially involved. However, this is a very special sort of case. As I have suggested, my suspicion is that most of our rogue impulses are ones we are indirectly responsible for.

So far I have suggested various factors that may constitute justifica-tions, excuses, or partial excuses: cases where the pressures on the agent affect what ought to be done, or how hard the agent has to try, and so the agent can make a plea that her act was not quite how it seemed: that she was not acting subjectively wrongly at all, or not as badly subjectively wrongly as first appeared. But there is another, more tricky case. We might think that there are circumstances that make it hard for an agent to try in the first place, and in such cases it seems unfair to blame an agent for not trying.

This brings us back to the question of what trying is. On my very broad view of what counts as trying, I think that in this sort of case we

---

[4] Harry Frankfurt contrasts two cases: in both, the agent is about to make an important decision about who to vote for, and in both cases there is a powerful neuroscientist standing by, ready to intervene and make sure that the decision goes his preferred way. In one case the neuroscientist has to intervene, in the other he does not. Frankfurt's point is that although the agent has no genuine alternate possibilities in either case, he seems more responsible when there is no intervention. The overall point, I take it (this is not an uncontroversial interpret-ation), is that what we take to be important about persons and their psychology is what should guide whether or not we think they are responsible, not whether they are ultimately free. If determinism is true, we are not ultimately free, but we do sometimes make our own choices. The difficulty is in giving a principled account of exactly what sort of 'intervention' (agential or other) undermines responsibility. See Frankfurt (1969). The secondary literature is too enormous to list in any way that would do justice to it.

should deny the premiss. We should say that whatever an agent is doing towards her good ends—trying to try, if you like—counts as trying. Imagine an agent, Dolores, who is slightly depressed and finding it difficult to get motivated to go about her normal life. From the outside, it looks bad: she is lying in bed watching daytime television. From her own point of view, she occasionally thinks, 'I should get up '. She focusses as long as she can on the thought that she should get up, but she lets it go without acting on it. In that case, I think we should say that that thought counts as trying. She is setting herself. She may frame her failure to take it further as 'can't be bothered', but of course that is part of what is so debilitating about depression: it appears as agency when it is not. It is very hard for the agent to take steps beyond setting herself, but that does not mean she is not trying.[5]

Before I close this discussion of blameworthiness and excuses, it is worth making a distinction between excusing and understanding. We sometimes think of the circumstances around bad behaviour as being mitigating, when in fact all we mean is that we would have behaved like that too. But bad behaviour is not mysterious. We do it all the time. And so of course we understand it. If someone gives in to the temptation to insult someone, we can see that we might have done that too. What we are seeing is that we would behave badly, and be blameworthy too. This is true even when the circumstances are unfortunate. If we have taken into account all the pleas I mention above, and it is still the case that the agent did not try hard enough, she is a little bit blameworthy, even when we see that we too would have buckled under that pressure.

Let's consider praise and praiseworthiness briefly. Ordinary praiseworthiness, like ordinary blameworthiness, is undermined by simple excuses. If an agent did not know what she was doing, or was not in control she is not praiseworthy. And, as for subjective wrongdoing, there may be more complex considerations that undermine the praiseworthiness of subjective rightdoing. We do not usually dwell on the mitigating circumstances that undermine praise, but intuitively it seems that praise

[5] As Dana Nelkin points out in her discussion of difficulty and degrees of praise and blameworthiness (2016, 362), this sort of case is hard for a moral concern view to make sense of. One can do easy things with a lot of moral concern, and difficult things with a little moral concern. Trying, by contrast, is more directly related to difficulty. For another account of the role of difficulty see Faraci and Shoemaker (2014).

(and praiseworthiness) and blame (and blameworthiness) are symmetrical here. Imagine a case where someone acts well, but we learn that it was incredibly easy for them to do well. Perhaps they had an unusual degree of help and support; perhaps they got lucky, with the task itself turning out to be easier than usual, perhaps they are lucky in having slept extremely well for the last ten years. In that case we are still inclined to praise the agent who tries to do well and achieves a lot, but we do not ignore the fact that she has not had to try as hard as others. There are circumstances that mitigate her praiseworthiness.

To conclude this section, an agent cannot have a simple excuse for acting subjectively wrongly. Simple excuses are relevant only when we are talking about objective rightness and wrongness, where it makes sense that the action can be labelled right or wrong even though it was not under the agent's control or purview. But something with the general form of an excuse can be applied to some subjectively wrong actions. An excuse claims, 'the quality of will behind my action was not quite as it seemed'. In a simple excuse, the idea is that there is no quality of will at all: the agent simply didn't do that act. With mitigating circumstances the idea is that the agent did the act, and may have had bad will to some extent, but much less than at first appeared.

2. Mixed Motivations and Local Detached Blameworthiness

There is one sort of case that remains to be dealt with. What should we say about an agent who does what is subjectively right—she tries her hardest, and has a good grasp of Morality—but who nonetheless performs badly, not through poor non-moral skills, or external obstacles but through problematic motivations? For example, imagine an agent who sincerely tries hard, as hard as she can, to be kind, but is thwarted by her own bitterness and misanthropy.[6] My view implies that that such an agent is not blameworthy in the ordinary way. She has, after all, acted

---

[6] Nelkin discusses this sort of case (2016, 368) and suggests the view I defend, that there might be different dimensions of appraisal here. Ultimately Nelkin defends a different view, according to which difficulty is relevant insofar as it affects the quality of one's opportunity, which meshes with her rational abilities view (I discuss that view briefly in the next chapter).

subjectively rightly, she is trying to do well by Morality. This sort of case is a direct challenge to my view, because it seems that the agent is not praiseworthy despite acting subjectively rightly. Thus my close correlation between subjective rightness and praiseworthiness is threatened.

If an agent does not try very hard, she is usually blameworthy. There are lots of reasons that people may fail to try to do well, such as laziness, selfishness, not caring, and so on. In other words, an agent is prevented from trying, or from trying hard enough, by her own bad motivations. For example, an agent knows full well that she should recycle more and consume more carefully, but she is simply too lazy, and does not try. In that sort of case, her bad motivation is not an excuse and not a mitigating circumstance. As I have argued over the course of the last few chapters, failing to try is precisely what we blame people for. Ultimately, not trying is always caused by something, but failing to try is not the sort of thing that can be excused by the nature of the internal cause of the failure to try.

However, it might sometimes be the case that an agent *does* try, even tries as hard as she can, and rather than something in the external world, it is her own bad motivations that prevent her from doing well. Imagine an agent who sincerely tries to be kind, but if they are naturally extremely misanthropic, they may end up doing something that is not kind at all, or simply falling short. Yet, if they have genuinely tried, it seems that they are acting subjectively rightly. What should we say when an agent has acted subjectively rightly, but nonetheless displays bad will? My view comes apart from the moral concern view here. On the moral concern view, the agent is blameworthy because the quality of her moral concern is poor. Arpaly discusses a relevant case:

To be sure, there are many occasions on which we do hold people blameworthy for failing, as it were, to check their mental brakes . . . Perhaps the akratic adulterer should have refused that invitation for dinner while her husband was out of town, and perhaps the angry person, before his outburst of rage, should have taken a deep breath and counted to ten. But this is not all that we blame such agents for. After all, it is sometimes the case that no such "count to ten" measures were available to the agent. It is also sometimes the case that the agent could not be expected to know of such measures in time to use them (perhaps powerful aggressive urges have never appeared in you before, and when such an urge appears it takes you so much by surprise that you do not notice it until you have already done some damage). There are also many cases in which the agent has already taken such measures and in general tried as hard as she could not to follow her "outlaw" desires, but her attempts and measures fail. In many such cases, we still blame the unautonomous adulterer, procrastinator, or angry aggressor. (2003, 141)[7]

Here we have someone who has tried their hardest, but failed, and failed because of motivations that are flawed. In this sort of case, the subjective obligation account of blameworthiness has to say that the agent is not blameworthy, because she tried her hardest. Yet it seems to Arpaly, and I agree that it seems plausible, that such an agent *is* blameworthy. To Arpaly, the flawed motivations are more important than the fact of trying.

It is worth pointing out that when we think about real life cases we probably do think that most of the time the agent is not trying hard enough. Trying to do well involves a constant (possibly low-level) alertness to red flags, adopting general strategies to avoid trouble, and learning from our mistakes. As I said above, in relation to rogue impulses, our bad motivations do not usually come as a total surprise. Most of the time, we have had ample opportunity to learn from our own past mistakes. So it might be that the first couple of times we experience the problematic motivations we genuinely have no opportunity to take preventative measures. But that will not be the case for long. When we encounter someone who acts out of disturbing motivations without realizing that he is doing it, who rages at his colleagues, or sexually harasses his students, our first thought is usually something like, 'why does he think this is OK?' We do not tend to assume that this person must have been taken by surprise by their own behaviour. We think, rather, that the person must not really care that their behaviour is awful. In real life we do not often encounter people whose bad motives prevent them from doing minimally well when they are sincerely trying. So the force of Arpaly's objection is diluted at least.

However, there may well exist some such cases. I will examine one presented by Gideon Rosen, who is defending the Searchlight View, the view that if there is no clear eyed akrasia, there is no blameworthiness at all. Rosen thus takes the opposite position to Arpaly: for Arpaly, the fact of trying is not important given the bad motivation. For Rosen, the bad motivation is not important given the fact of trying.

---

[7] Arpaly does not officially characterize the view she is discussing as one that formulates subjective obligation in terms of trying, but it is interesting that that formulation comes very naturally here.

Rosen imagines a man called Kleinbart. Kleinbart is trying to tell a funny story at a dinner party but the story is too personal, too other-revealing, and upsets his wife. However, Kleinbart is not aware, as he is talking, that this is the effect he is having, and his ignorance is not traceable to culpable negligence.

the only reason Kleinbart fails to notice his wife's distress is that he simply does not care that much about her. He is dutiful enough. He would never knowingly offend her and he takes care not to do so inadvertently. We may even imagine that he overcompensates in this regard. Aware that indifference dulls the sympathetic faculties, he is somewhat more attentive to his wife than he would otherwise be. I want to stipulate that Kleinbart has compensated adequately in this regard. It was neither negligent nor reckless for him to launch into the story in the first place, and as the conversation unfolded he complied with the procedural requirements under which he labored. I want to stipulate, in other words, that his ignorance cannot be traced to prior negligence or recklessness of any sort.   (2008, 607)

As Rosen points out, Kleinbart does not care very much about his wife, so he has an objectionable quality of will. If objectionable quality of will in this sense is what makes agents blameworthy, Kleinbart should be blameworthy. Rosen wants to resist this conclusion, although he admits that he has no decisive arguments. His strategy is to paint the view in an unappealing light. Rosen keeps pointing our attention back to the fact that poor old Kleinbart has done nothing deliberately wrong. In fact, all his deliberate actions are good. Kleinbart has done nothing to bring about his lack of regard for his wife, and he tries hard to compensate for it. Rosen insists that to blame Kleinbart seems unfair.

Kleinbart is the sort of case we need to focus on because he is acting subjectively rightly. He has the relevant background knowledge of relationships, morality, and so on, and he is trying his best to do well by those values. In that sense, his quality of will is good. But he is failing to achieve his goal, and he is failing because of his problematic motives. He doesn't love his wife, but more than that, he seems like a self-centred and insensitive guy. His faults go beyond merely not loving his wife. Rosen insists that Kleinbart is not blameworthy—for Rosen, subjective rightness swamps the fact of bad motives. The basic issue here is a methodological one. We are only forced into one of the extreme positions taken by Arpaly on the one hand or Rosen on the other if we insist that there is only one sort of blameworthiness.

The story that I have been telling so far has presented agents as if they are in two categories: those who are in our moral community, and those who are not. I admitted, of course, that the boundaries may be vague but, nonetheless, the categories are crucial, marking an important difference between the class of those it makes sense to blame in the ordinary, communicative way, and those whom it only makes sense to blame in the detached, non-communicative way. But here we have a mixed case: the agent is in our moral community, and yet a seemingly relevant feature of his behaviour is independent of his trying to do well by Morality, it is just the way he is. I argued that for those who understand Morality, ordinary praise- and blameworthiness attaches to efforts, but that we can still blame those outside our moral community (those for whom trying to do well by Morality is not applicable) because of the way they are. This case puts pressure on that division. It brings us back to the attributionist view, that deep motivations are crucial for praise- and blameworthiness, even for those who have a good grasp of Morality.

First, I should stress that I agree with Rosen that Kleinbart is not blameworthy in the ordinary way. It is important that Kleinbart has a good grasp of Morality and has tried his best. In one very important sense, the ordinary moral sense, Kleinbart is not at fault. This is not a case where Kleinbart can examine his own conscience and see that by his own lights he has acted badly, on the contrary, he has acted well. Indeed, Kleinbart is praiseworthy, though as I shall argue, his praiseworthiness is tempered by his blameworthiness in another sense.

So what is the sense in which Kleinbart is blameworthy? There are, I will argue, two possible responses. First, the approach I will defend in this chapter, according to which Kleinbart is praiseworthy in the ordinary way, but he is detached blameworthy in a local way. Kleinbart is generally eligible for ordinary blame, he is someone that we can communicate with on the general topic of Morality (or relationships, if we want to stick to the more limited framework of the example). But he does not love his wife, and this is not an activity, not a trying or lack of trying. Rather, his lovelessness is best described as something that he *is*, not something that he *does*: he is unloving, despite the efforts he makes to be otherwise. If we blame him it should only be in the detached sense: detached blameworthiness applies in a limited, local way here. Second, I shall argue in Chapter 8 that Kleinbart can become blameworthy in something more like the ordinary way by taking responsibility.

In Chapter 5 I argued for two kinds of praise- and blameworthiness. I argued that ordinary praise- and blameworthiness are an assessment of the agent's quality of will, and that the relevant quality of will is trying or lack of trying. I will not rehearse the whole argument here, but a crucial point was that this account meets a reflexivity requirement. It makes sense to blame an agent who has failed to try to do well because they have done something wrong by their own lights; they can recognize and accept blame. There is another sort of blame, detached blame, which applies to agents who do not have a good enough grasp of Morality to understand that they are acting wrongly. I argued that this sort of blameworthiness does not depend on quality of will beyond applying to agents who have non-accidentally done the thing in question. The paradigm cases of detached blameworthiness are agents like JoJo, the dictator's son, or Bill the encultured sexist. These agents do not understand Morality, and would not accept that their acts are problematic, but they would own their acts. I argued that we do not need to know much about the quality of will in such cases to react to these agents with detached blame. It is possible that there are ways to construe their wills as morally unproblematic in some ways, but that is not important to detached blame. What is important is that detached blame is a reaction to wrongdoing, that is, wrongdoing in our Morality. With detached blame, it is the blame reaction that is prior to a judgment of blameworthiness. Detached blame is fundamentally about the blamer, not the blamee.

Clearly, the case of Kleinbart is not a paradigmatic case of detached blameworthiness. First, it is not quite the case that he is acting wrongly. Rather, he has a bad motivation. Second, what seems really problematic is precisely his quality of will, his lack of moral concern, and this is why the moral concern account of praise- and blameworthiness seems to have the upper hand in this case. I will argue that despite these wrinkles, the best way to make sense of Kleinbart's apparent blameworthiness is by appealing to detached blame and blameworthiness.

Let's take first the issue of whether a motivational state is in the right category to be a candidate for detached blame. Recall that at the beginning of Chapter 5 I offered a template for blame, where something is a good candidate for blame if it is a reaction to wrongdoing.[8] My account

---

[8] I said that blame is a response to wrongdoing that goes beyond a mere judgment, and is intimately related to the blamer's acceptance of the value system from which she blames.

of ordinary blame essentially focuses on activity, and obviously having a bad motivation is not an activity in that sense. However, my account of detached blame also focused on activity—objective wrongdoing. But that doesn't seem relevant in Kleinbart's case. Kleinbart's *action* is not the main problem. The clumsy story is bad, of course, but to his wife, we might think, the real problem is what it reveals about his state of mind.

I think the answer here is to extend the account of detached blame so as to be able to include reactions to problematic psychological states of agents as well as problematic actions of agents. This is not to concede that detached blame is based on quality of will. As I argued in the previous chapter, there are many cases where quality of will is not important. Rather, detached blame is a reaction to things, agential things, that we take to be problematic. Some kinds of motivation or state of mind might be among those things. We are reacting to something we take to be morally problematic, that is essentially agential. There is no particular reason to restrict detached blame to actions. The major point about detached blame is that we apply it without expecting a response. We do not think that the reflexivity requirement is met: in doing (or being) the thing we blame her for, the agent is not consciously doing something wrong by her own lights. Detached blame, unlike ordinary blame, is a 'blame first' (rather than a 'blameworthiness first') reaction.

Consider the situation from the point of view of Kleinbart's wife: she cannot blame him for something he has deliberately done. As Rosen says, he has done nothing deliberately bad, and so there is no point in raising that with him. Kleinbart's wife cannot say that Kleinbart should have tried harder. However, she is bound to have some sort of reactive attitude. She is bound to feel something like anger, disdain, or hurt, something in the family of detached blame. In Kleinbart's case, detached blame is not a general stance. Kleinbart is generally a suitable candidate for ordinary blame. But he is not a perfect agent, and his flawed motivations sometimes win out over his good intentions. For Kleinbart's wife, in particular, this is relevant. She is not assessing him just as a moral agent, but as her husband.

We can imagine Kleinbart saying to his wife after the party, 'I'm sorry about that, but you can't blame me, I tried my hardest!', and his wife responding, 'I don't blame you in the ordinary way, I know you are trying your best. But that's not the end of the story is it? You don't really love me, you are not tuned into me, my needs don't register very strongly on your radar. In the end, though you try to ameliorate it, you care more about social success than about my feelings. That's not the sort of thing that I can "blame" you for, that's just how you are. But I cannot help but respond to it: I feel angry and hurt, and I feel disdain and contempt for you.'

No demands are made of the blamee, but the blamer, in engaging in detached blame, may be implicitly making resolutions about her own future behaviour and attitudes. Detached blame can be fierce and active, it can be motivating, and can result in changed relationships. But not by way of communication. It works rather, by motivating the blamer to withdraw from or avoid what she cannot change. As I suggested in Chapter 5, detached blame often involves changing a relationship, and this is particularly relevant in this sort of case. Our relationship with Kleinbart needn't change if we are simply a fellow member of the moral community. Our role is to commend Kleinbart for his efforts on trying to do well by his wife. But his wife has a different relationship to Kleinbart, and her interest is not just in his efforts but in his deep motives. Her reaction to Kleinbart's unfortunate storytelling might involve a modification of their relationship, which can also be a sort of detached blame, as I argued in the previous chapter. Kleinbart is not displaying the attitudes necessary for a loving relationship, and so she marks that by withdrawing, not just to protect herself, but because that is what is fitting.

One can imagine a further chapter in the Kleinbart story. Imagine that his wife finds out that Kleinbart has been poisoned over a long period of time, and that somehow the poison caused the erosion of his love. On finding out about the poisoning, we would expect his wife's attitude to change. Even her detached blaming would now be undermined. Kleinbart seem less like an 'unloving husband', and indeed, less like an agent at all. His wife has already taken one step away from engagement with him when she realizes that he simply doesn't love her. Now she takes another: Kleinbart is damaged, and so her feelings might change from something in the region of contempt to something more in the region of pity. I come back to the ways that detached blame can be undermined in the next section.

A final remark about Kleinbart: we should consider what he should feel about himself. It would certainly be odd if Kleinbart felt pride and self-congratulation. He may have tried his best, but it didn't work out well, and not through external bad luck.[9] On the other hand, we might

---

[9] Even if things go badly through external bad luck, it would be odd to feel nothing but pride and self-congratulation. I come back to the issue of agent regret in Chapter 8.

think, it would be odd for him to feel guilt or remorse, given that, as the story is told, he really tried his hardest, did his best to do well. However, it is plausible that he should feel the first-person analogue of local detached blame, which is shame.[10] Shame is a feeling of disappointment in, or distaste with oneself, one's performance, or character, or even extrinsic features, like upbringing. Shame is usually distinguished from guilt by referring to the level of control: one can feel shame about what one is, even what is not under one's control. It certainly seems apt that Kleinbart should feel shame. That is compatible with his reminding himself that he tried his best.

This might all be clearer and simpler if we take a moral example. Imagine an agent who tries very hard to be fair and just but is, for whatever reason, driven by racist motives. Insofar as she can indirectly control her racism she does, but occasionally she is in a situation that she could not have predicted, and her racist motives issue in action. As I said when discussing Arpaly's examples above, we should remember that in real life the scope for trying is broad: we are usually aware after not too long that we have some problematic motives, and there are lots of things we can do to ensure that those motives do not get to be causally efficacious. However, let's grant that it can happen, an agent can be trying hard and yet be hijacked by her own bad motives. In such a case, we need to recognize complexity in her praise or blameworthiness. In the ordinary way, such an agent is praiseworthy, and it is important to acknowledge that. But it is also important to recognize that her deep motives are problematic.

Quite how we react to that might depend on our position, our relationship to the agent who is acting badly, and I will return to the difference relationships make in Chapter 8. For now I am just pointing out that it is natural for at least some people to react with non-communicative reactive attitudes: with detached blame. Agents who are directly affected by the bad attitude are, of course, more likely to focus on the detached blame. Others, those who are in a teaching role with regard to the problem, for example, can legitimately focus on the way in which the agent is ordinary praiseworthy. For the rest of us, our reactions are mixed. The agent herself should feel both pride

---

[10] Detached blame in general does not have a first person analogue, as it does not expect any response at all.

(because she tried) and shame (because her motives were flawed). Her shame should motivate her to try harder, to focus on indirect strategies for controlling her bad motives, and to make amends to those she has hurt.

I have argued that although we cannot blame Kleinbart in the ordinary way, we can blame him in a detached way. But there is another possibility here. Think again about Kleinbart. What might he say when his wife says to him, 'you don't love me, do you?' One thing he might say, and might be wise to say, is, 'you are right, I have tried, but I can't do it, let's call it quits before things get any worse'. But another thing he might say is 'I take full responsibility for that awful story at the party. I see now how stupid and insensitive it was. I want to do better. I feel utterly remorseful'. This would be Kleinbart *taking responsibility*. He might consciously decide to take ownership of his own inadvertent bad behaviour, rather than focus on how hard he tried to do well. In that case, arguably, the appropriate reaction for him to feel would be remorse, and he would be giving his wife licence to feel resentment, and ordinary blame, not just detached blame. He would be stepping back into the ring, declaring himself thoroughly fit for ordinary praise and blame.

In the context of Kleinbart's failure, which does not seem to be primarily a moral failure, we think he would be justified in giving up. But consider the more clearly moral case, the agent who tries not to be racist but whose racist motives sometimes get the better of her. Such an agent could stop at feeling shame, and resolving to investigate and commit to more and better indirect measures to control her racist motives. She could do more though: she could take responsibility. She could tell herself, and others, that her racist motives are really hers, and that she ought to feel remorse. She could accept ordinary blame, and move forward on the basis that, as an ordinary agent, she qualifies for ordinary blame, even in this case. Such an agent seems more admirable than the agent who is content to stop at shame. In Chapter 8 I shall argue that that is indeed the case, and that we should take responsibility in these and other cases.

I have argued that we should countenance a complexity in the pluralist story. An agent can be simultaneously praiseworthy in the ordinary sense, for trying her best, and locally blameworthy in the detached way. Another possibility is that even if she is not blameworthy in the ordinary way, she should nonetheless be willing to take on responsibility, to situate herself in the guilt category rather than the shame category.

I return to the conditions under which we might take responsibility in Chapter 8.

3. Excuses and Detached Blame: Formative Circumstances

In this section[11] I come back to the question of detached blame, and what sort of excusing condition might apply there. In his account of type 2 (non-simple) excuses, Strawson lists the various ways that someone might be "psychologically abnormal", such as being "warped, deranged neurotic", and then he adds, "or peculiarly unfortunate in his formative circumstances" (1962, reprinted in Watson, 2003, 79). As Gary Watson points out, being unfortunate in formative circumstances seems to be an *explanation* for being the other things, not another of the same sort on the list (1987, reprinted in Watson, 2004, 242–3).

Having unfortunate formative circumstances does not automatically render one exempt from blame. After all, lots of people have unfortunate upbringings and yet go on to lead normal lives. Yet, intuitively, having unfortunate formative circumstances undermines blame in some sense. I will argue that we should see unfortunate formative circumstances as the sort of excuse that applies to detached blame. It does not work quite the way that type 1 excuses work with regard to ordinary blameworthiness. Unfortunate formative circumstances, as Watson points out, appear to explain bad will rather than to explain it away.

Think about the case of Robert Harris, as discussed by Watson (1987). Harris killed two people in cold blood, and apparently showed no remorse. It is plausible that Harris did not fully grasp Morality, that there was some fatal flaw in some aspect of his understanding of Morality. If so, on my account, he is only eligible for detached blame. It seems that, no matter how he got like that, Robert Harris is evil. However, when we reflect on Harris's terrible upbringing, as Watson points out, we start to see Harris as a victim. And when we compare the bad apple version of Robert Harris, someone who has had a perfectly normal upbringing and yet behaves as Robert Harris behaved, we are

[11] This section draws on my 2015. The material is reprinted by permission from Springer Nature, *Philosophical Studies* 172 (11): 3037–57, 'Moral Ignorance and Blameworthiness', Mason E., Copyright © 2015.

even less inclined to think of the real Robert Harris as fully blameworthy. The bad apple Robert Harris seems *really* blameworthy. The actual Robert Harris seems like a product of his environment.[12] This is not because the two versions have different qualities of will, we can assume for the sake of argument they have the very same quality of will.[13] Nonetheless, the bad apple version of Robert Harris appears to be importantly different to the version who had a brutally horrible upbringing.

Evidently, moral concern theorists must dispute this. On the moral concern view, all that matters is what the quality of will is like and whether it is truly the agent's. Our attributability judgments should be stable in the face of considerations of history. But that doesn't seem to be the case. If attributability judgments were simply shallow appraisals, as their detractors sometimes say they are, then of course attributability judgments would be stable in this way. A rock is hard, no matter whether it came from a volcano or a seabed. But blaming is not just making a judgment of attributability. Blame, even detached blame, is essentially about *agents*.

What happens, when we learn about a horrible history, is that we lose confidence in the agential status of our agent. When we hold Robert Harris to be blameworthy in the detached way, we take it that he is the author of his own acts, he is a bad person. But when we think about his history, we see that he is more object than subject: he is acted upon more than he acts. When we consider the damage that has been done to him as a moral agent, we retreat even further, into a 'truly objective stance'. Thus the clemency that we are inclined to grant in the light of bad formative circumstances really amounts to a retreat from detached blame to the truly objective stance. It is not a way of letting agents 'off the hook' (it is not an excuse), rather, it is further disengagement.

---

[12] Note that, as Watson points out in his discussion of Harris (2004, 247) the difference between Robert Harris and the bad apple Robert Harris is not a difference in *capacity*. Watson thinks that lack of capacity undermines accountability, but not attributability. I come back to capacity in the next chapter.

[13] David Shoemaker points out that, in fact, the bad apple version of Harris and the actual Harris are very likely to have different qualities of will, and that seems right to me. Shoemaker imagines a structurally similar case where two people, Agnes and Anastasia, have identical bad wills but Anastasia has an unfortunate history whereas Agnes does not. Shoemaker stands by his pure quality of will view—in that case, he argues, the same response is fitting, notwithstanding the difference between the two histories. He suggests that there may be other reasons not to punish the one with a bad history as much, but they are extrinsic reasons, not reasons of fittingness (Shoemaker, 2015, 201). The advantage of my view is that we can make sense of the relevance of bad history in itself.

The truly objective stance is probably what Strawson intended to be talking about in contrasting the reactive attitudes with the objective stance. I am pointing out that there is something in between ordinary communicative blame and the truly objective stance. We react to other agents as agents, even when they are not in our moral community. It takes a lot for us to permanently give up on them as agents. And as Strawson says, what makes us give up is reflecting on the object-like nature of such beings. The way that they have been caused to become what they are draws us towards seeing them as objects.

The difference between the agent who is blameworthy in the ordinary way and the agent who is blameworthy only in the detached way can now be further explained. When we blame someone in the ordinary way, we are setting aside considerations about how a person came to be the person they are, and focusing on what that agent does. The fact that the agent has enough of a grasp of Morality to accurately assess the moral status of their own actions indicates that the agent has not been severely morally damaged. We see them as a competent moral agent. Of course, they are what they are because of a certain history, but only in the sense that we all are, and so we do not, and cannot, take that as being an excusing condition.[14]

Think about our judgments about someone like Tony Blair who (let's accept for the sake of the example) failed to try to do well by Morality. He had a good grasp of Morality but, as prime minister of Britain, he got deflected from the appropriate goals. We blame him in the ordinary way, he should have tried harder. If we were to find out that Blair had a miserable childhood, one that explained his weaknesses and his tendencies to grandiosity and deception, would we change our view about whether or not he was blameworthy? I think not. As we say about growing up, there comes a point when you have to stop blaming your parents for your faults. The same is true on a larger scale here: as adults, as fellow members of a moral community, we must take ourselves and each other to be responsible. The fact that there is an explanation for the

---

[14] In her discussion of JoJo (1987), Wolf says that JoJo is similar to us in being a product of his environment: he is unavoidably insane and we are unavoidably sane. My point here is similar, though not identical. I am saying that so long as someone has moral knowledge, they are in our moral community and subject to ordinary blame, their upbringing is not relevant. By contrast, for those who lack moral knowledge (who are 'insane' in Wolf's terminology), upbringing is relevant, and can undermine responsibility.

way that our characters have been formed doesn't matter. So long as we are sufficiently developed to grasp Morality (and do actually grasp Morality), we are in the realm of ordinary blameworthiness.

By contrast, someone who does not grasp Morality is not in that realm. Such a person may or may not have been morally damaged by their upbringing. Either way, they are not part of our moral community, in the sense that they do not share our values, and so we cannot judge them by how well they react to those values. We judge them in a more detached way, focusing instead on what they, and their attitudes, are like. However, we *blame* them only if we take them to be agents. When we focus on the causes of their behaviour, and see what made them the way they are, we are less inclined to blame and more inclined to the truly objective stance. We lose faith in the agency of the blamee, and so are inclined to withdraw reactive attitudes and retreat to the truly objective stance.

A bad history undermines our sense that the agent's practical identity is robustly hers, that her evaluative commitments can be taken seriously. Hence our ambivalence about someone like Robert Harris is explained in at least two ways. First, we may feel ambivalence because we are not certain whether Robert Harris and people like him do, deep down, have a grasp on Morality. So we are not certain whether they are acting subjectively wrongly. That is why we are so interested when such people claim that they do know right from wrong.[15] But I suspect that the main source of our ambivalence about such cases is that we are slipping between detached blame that has full force, such as that that we apply to bad apples, and the truly objective stance, which is not a sort of blame at all.

Reflecting on another set of examples might help to get our intuitions about formative circumstances clear. Consider the category of agents who are inexplicably in the grip of badly false moral views, agents who have no extenuating circumstances in their background. Call such people, 'moral outliers'. Despite normal upbringings, they grow up to do terrible things. Sometimes violent crime but, perhaps more commonly, their violence is indirect. Such people are often called 'sociopaths', but it can be hard to see where there is 'illness' other than in the perverted moral view.[16] Moral outliers can be highly functional, many of

---

[15] Watson (1987) quotes Harris's sister as saying that Harris claimed to know right from wrong. I discuss that issue more in Chapter 7.

[16] I come back to the question of how to define illness in Chapter 7.

them are very successful in business or politics. They ruthlessly promote their own interests at the expense of others, stealing, exploiting, and even killing through complex and indirect routes. They institute policies that will clearly hurt people, usually the already disadvantaged and disenfranchised. The actions of multinational corporations are hard to trace to individuals, but surely, somewhere, there are individuals who both understand the ramifications of the policies and have the power to change things. These people may be wracked by guilt, they may know that they are acting wrongly. But we should also consider the possibility that they are moral outliers: that they hold a moral view according to which their actions are justified.

Of course, it is hard to distinguish such people from people who grasp Morality and choose to ignore it, and there are unclear boundaries here. It is not always clear what someone knows, either morally or factually. So let's stipulate that we are talking about deep moral ignorance: not cases of self-deception, but cases where the agent knows what she is doing and genuinely believes that her appalling acts are permissible. Imagine, for example, that the chairman of a multinational corporation genuinely believes that the lives of others can permissibly be sacrificed in his pursuit of profit. (This seems unlikely, but notice that the alternative seems unlikely too, that the agent grasps Morality perfectly well and yet agrees to policies that will result in clearly unjust suffering and death.)

Moral outliers are deeply morally ignorant, but their terrible view comes from nowhere. As such they are the purest example of detached blameworthiness, and our detached blame is fierce. If there are no unfortunate formative circumstances, our blame is not undermined by considering the fact of their ignorance. Moral outliers are a candidate for the label 'evil' if anything is: there is no excusing factor. The point about moral outliers is that they are evil *de novo*.

This is not a supernatural account of evil. As Watson points out, there is always something that has gone wrong when an agent slips outside of our moral community, "if not in their socialization, then 'in them'—in their genes or brains" (1987, reprinted in 2004, 247). If we discovered a genetic mutation, or a reaction to a certain protein, that had caused the outliers to be as they are, our detached blame would be undermined just as it is by consideration of bad formative circumstances. So the zone of detached blameworthiness can shrink with a growing understanding of what makes people the way they are. That should not be surprising, and it is not a worry for this account. Ordinary blameworthiness is robust, it is not undermined by consideration of formative circumstances. It is only the realm of detached blame that is shrinking as we conceptualize more things as illness, and perhaps that is no bad thing: our talk of evil usually doesn't bring much of value to anything.

It is also worth noting that detached praiseworthiness, like detached blameworthiness, can be eroded towards something more objective, if we begin to see the agent as an artefact, created by her environment in an unusual way. Imagine an Aldous Huxley-esque scenario, where some people are created to be cheerful drone-like individuals, never complaining or envying others. Once we understand the unfortunate (or perhaps fortunate) formative circumstances, we move from detached praiseworthiness to the truly objective stance.

The relationship between ordinary blame, detached blame, and the truly objective stance should now be reasonably clear. Ordinary blame depends on shared moral community. Once we are in the realm of detached blame, we have already taken a step away from interpersonal engagement. Someone who is not in our moral community is not eligible for ordinary blame, our attitude to them can only be a sort of detached blame: it cannot involve normative expectations, or gratitude, or resentment in Strawson's sense. In detached blame we stand back and disapprove, disdain, despise, disavow, we do not engage, or at least, not with the aim of reciprocity. Detached blame can involve a modification of the relationship, but in a one-sided way: we avoid such people, and not just for prudential reasons, we do it for its own sake. Detached blame can be fierce, but it can also be undermined. Reflecting on the way that an agent was caused to be the way they are draws us towards the truly objective stance. When we see people from the truly objective stance we are ceasing to see them as agents at all, and the notion of blame becomes inapplicable.

4. Conclusion

In this chapter I have argued that there are different sorts of excuse that apply to different sorts of blameworthiness. The usual sort of excuse that applies in the case of ordinary blameworthiness is something that reveals that the agent did not act subjectively wrongly after all, that her will was not as it appeared. There cannot be a simple excuse for subjective wrongdoing: if you acted subjectively wrongly you were failing to try to do well by Morality, and that entails background knowledge and sufficiently conscious choice. However, there may be considerations that lessen that amount of blame that is appropriate, as when an agent is under great stress. An explanation for why the agent acted as she did does not count as a full excuse, though it may constitute mitigating circumstances.

I discussed cases where an agent is acting subjectively rightly and yet has bad motives that undermine her efforts. In such a case, I suggested, we should agree that the agent is acting subjectively rightly, and is praiseworthy in the ordinary sense. However, we can also acknowledge that the agent is detached blameworthy in a local way. I suggested that another approach is possible here: such agents should sometimes take responsibility for their inadvertent bad behaviour, and thus voluntarily re-enter the realm of ordinary blame. I return to that in Chapter 8.

Finally, I discussed the way in which detached blameworthiness can be undermined by consideration of formative circumstances. Excuses usually work by making a claim that the agent's will should be interpreted in an alternative way. This is true of both simple excuses and mitigating circumstances. Ultimately, the same is true of the way an excuse from detached blameworthiness works. In that case, formative circumstances are relevant, but what they do is make us think of the agent as less of an agent and more of an object, and we move along the scale from detached blame to the truly objective stance.

In the next chapter I go back to an issue that I have so far only discussed in very general terms: what determines the boundary between being in the realm of subjective obligation and being in the realm of detached praise and blame.

7

Exemptions

I have argued that there are broadly two kinds of blameworthiness and, correspondingly, two kinds of blame. The first kind of blameworthiness, which is essentially connected to subjective obligation, is ordinary blameworthiness. I argued that the best account of subjective obligation applies only to agents who have moral knowledge: an agent does what she subjectively ought when she tries to do well by Morality, where we take it that Morality is the broad value system we share. An agent is praiseworthy in the ordinary way when she tries to do well, and blameworthy when she fails to try. Failing to try, like trying, implies that the agent has a grasp of Morality: there is an important difference between failing to try to do well by Morality and simply not trying.

This means that agents who do not grasp Morality are exempt from ordinary blame. In this chapter I explore the complexities of who is in and who is out of our moral community. Some agents are clearly impaired, in that they are compulsive, deranged, or psychotic, or in some other way are unable to act on their moral knowledge. Such agents are exempt from ordinary blame in a very straightforward way, they lack the basic moral capacities required for moral responsibility. However, there are several more complex cases.[1]

I start with agents who are not impaired in any obvious way, but who are in the grip of a false moral view, and so lack knowledge of Morality. There is an implicit challenge here, which could be put as follows: given that such agents are not impaired in any way, that they do not lack any general moral capacities, they should be seen as blameworthy in the

---

[1] This chapter builds on (and sometimes repurposes) some arguments from my 2016. Copyright © 2016 from Mason E., 'Moral Incapacity and Moral Ignorance', in R. Peels (ed.), *Perspectives on Ignorance from Moral and Social Philosophy*, 30–51. Reproduced by permission of Taylor and Francis Group, LLC, a division of Informa plc.

ordinary way. Consider JoJo who, we can assume, would have been perfectly normal had he had my upbringing. JoJo has been epistemically isolated, and perhaps emotionally damaged to some extent, but there may well be a way back for him. JoJo's capacities are intact. Yet when we think about JoJo as he actually is, it is clear that he is not in our moral community. I argue that agents like JoJo are exempt from ordinary blame even if they could, in principle, be brought into our moral community. Furthermore, the potential culpability of deep moral ignorance is not relevant to the sort of blame that is applicable once the agent is ignorant. It would not make sense to blame a deeply morally ignorant agent in the ordinary way.

On the other hand, it is possible that there are agents who understand Morality, but have some sort of motivational incapacity. Such agents may be constitutionally very good or very bad and are, in a sense, unable to act badly or well. It is tempting to say that they do not have the right sort of capacities to be praise- or blameworthy. I reject that conclusion. My argument for this proceeds through a discussion of Susan Wolf's asymmetry thesis and Bernard Williams's account of moral incapacity. I argue that just as a psychological incapacity to do bad things does not undermine praiseworthiness, so a certain sort of incapacity to act well does not undermine blameworthiness. Rather, what undermines praise- or blameworthiness in the ambiguous cases is ignorance of Morality.

I go on to address a different sort of flaw in moral understanding. There is a spectrum of agents who can identify which actions are right and wrong, and who, despite having basic rational capacities and, without being deranged or acting compulsively, do seem to lack a relevant sort of moral capacity. (In the philosophy literature, these people are often referred to as psychopaths, but this is, of course, a term of art here.)[2] The question that I am interested in is whether psychopaths should be understood as lacking moral knowledge. I argue there is a way to understand psychopaths such that they do not have moral knowledge, and so are exempt from ordinary blame on that ground.

---

[2] I am relying on a chiefly stipulate definition of psychopaths, along with most philosophers who discuss psychopaths. For discussions of psychopathy and responsibility see Levy (2007), McGeer (2007), Nelkin (2015), Scanlon (2008), Talbert (2008; 2012b), Shoemaker (2011; 2015), Watson (2011). Shoemaker (2015) engages in an interesting and thorough examination of how the empirical facts affect what we should actually say about responsibility in marginal cases.

1. Deeply Morally Ignorant but Unimpaired Agents

If ordinary blame is paradigmatically communicative, we need to think about uptake: what sort of uptake is required for blame to be felicitous? Communications must assume some sort of uptake, and so there will be limits on when communicative blame is applicable. We cannot blame cars, or racoons, or filing cabinets. Defenders of communicative accounts of blame have argued for very different accounts of the boundaries on who can count as blameworthy. It is important to point out that simply appealing to communicative accounts of blame does not settle the issue of what sort of knowledge or capacity is required for an agent to be eligible for ordinary blame.[3]

I will start by considering JoJo. I am imagining JoJo as someone who has normal capacities, but has been brought up in an isolated community, and has deeply internalized the corrupt morality that he has been taught. JoJo, I suggest, cannot respond to ordinary blame. He cannot agree with our assessment, and recognize that he has acted wrongly by his own lights, and feel remorse for that, because his own lights are so badly oriented. Imagine an attempted blame conversation with JoJo. Our first question would be, 'do you understand that you should not be betraying your fellow students to your father, who will kill them?' JoJo will, perhaps calmly, perhaps angrily, perhaps manipulatively, perhaps naively, explain that his father's regime is justified, and that it is therefore justified to do whatever he can to protect it and keep it stable. We will see pretty quickly that the blame conversation is going nowhere.

---

[3] Gary Watson, who was one of the first to suggest that blame is communicative, says that the recipient of blame must be capable of "understanding the message" (1987, reprinted in 2004, 127). Scanlon argues that although a capacity to grasp practical reasons is a necessary condition for moral responsibility, there is no need for an agent to grasp moral reasons in particular. He argues that we can blame agents, who do not grasp moral reasons, just because of their bad will (1998, 288). Matthew Talbert argues along similar lines that, as blame is a form of protest, we don't need there to be uptake, and so capacities and so on are not relevant to the applicability of blame (2008, 2012a). Others have argued the opposite. Stephen Darwall argues that 'second-personal competence' (the ability to "take a second personal perspective on themselves and act on reasons they accept from that point of view") is essential for blame to be felicitous (2006, 75). Michael McKenna argues that someone who cannot grasp moral demands is not morally responsible for what she does (2012, 49). Similarly, Colleen Macnamara argues that a capacity for uptake is a necessary condition for blame to be felicitous (2015b).

It might be objected that JoJo is a perfectly normal agent, he is not impaired in any way. His problem, ignorance, is not deep enough or pathological enough for him to be exempted from ordinary blame. Gary Watson, for example, wants to make a distinction between those who are temporarily and those who are permanently unreachable. The latter category, which includes psychopaths, is the exempt category. Watson makes the distinction as follows:

Occasionally a Nazi or a Mafioso or white supremacist makes a genuine return to the moral point of view. I say "return" because the moral changes in question depend upon suppressed or partial or partitioned moral sensibilities that are somehow reengaged or extended—sensibilities involving an at least selective concern for some moral values, virtues and for some individuals . . . In contrast, I am supposing, there is nothing to which to return in psychopaths . . . The significance of this is not just that there is no chance that they will change but (again) that it makes no sense to address moral demands to them, as though these could be intelligible to them (or intelligible in the right kind of way) from their deliberative standpoints. It is partially in virtue of the competence embodied in the moral sentiments that it is possible for us to have relations of mutual accountability.   (2011, 318)[4]

Of course, it is not mere unlikelihood of uptake that mandates an exemption. We need to make room for refusal of blame.[5] But still, there is nothing in the uptake requirement that mandates that an exemption is only granted if uptake failure is permanent. Why wouldn't an agent for whom correction is very very unlikely be equally exempt? An agent might be very far gone indeed, and to all practical intents and purposes unreachable, and yet not permanently unreachable.

Watson is aware of this problem. He does not see the psychopath as being at one end of a spectrum of correctability. His view is that the psychopath is in a different category, in virtue of there being "nothing to return to". Watson's idea is not just that it is pointless, but that it

---

[4] Watson argues psychopaths cannot recognize the appeal to authority that is involved in moral address (this capacity is necessary for accountability, no such capacity is necessary for attributability).

[5] As Coleen Macnamara points out, not all uptake failures mean that the act of blaming has failed, the fault might be entirely in the blamee (2015b). Macnamara is objecting to Talbert's argument (2008), that blame doesn't always demand a response. Talbert points out that we blame very bad people even though they won't respond. I think I can capture the force of Talbert's point by talking about detached blame. I return to blame refusal below.

doesn't make sense to address demands to the psychopath. I am sceptical about the distinction between 'pointlessness' and 'not making sense' here. There is surely a scale, and at some point on that scale we start to say that it doesn't make sense, but is that really a difference of type rather than just of degree? I make moral demands of people who are paradigmatic moral agents, and of a range of people who are progressively further from the paradigm: moral responses get less and less reliable as we go down the scale. It is very hard to say when the lack of responsiveness in an agent is permanent. But even if we could say when that happens, why think it made sense to make demands of the person one step up the scale?

JoJo is deeply morally ignorant. He could perhaps be brought back to Morality, but not easily. It would take an intensive course of education and rehabilitation. So, right now, and in the short and mid-term future, there is no point is blaming him. It would be futile. It would not make sense. Even if it is true that JoJo could come to a different moral view, right now he is ignorant in a deep and important way. His ignorance is not temporary in the sense of 'temporary insanity'. He is himself. Compare someone who spends time in a cult, and becomes convinced that the cult leader is a genuine messiah and that we must obey and worship him. Such a person is temporarily insane, we knew what they were before, we hope to help them get back to being that. The person they are right now, in the cult, is not the real person. He is 'not himself', as Strawson says (1962, reprinted in Watson, 2003, 78). Of course, this sounds odd, but it is obviously true. If it turned out not to be possible to change them back to how they were, we would, eventually, accept the new person as the real person.

JoJo is a bad person, and we do not let JoJo 'off the hook': ordinary blame would be infelicitous, but we can still blame him in the detached way. Detached blame can be various things. It is a reaction to wrongdoing that goes beyond a mere judgment of wrongdoing. It is essentially directed at agents, and can be a reactive attitude that has emotional tone, and may involve a modification of the relevant relationship. But detached blame does not demand a response. It can be directed at agents who are deeply morally ignorant, who would not understand why we are blaming them, or what for.

Here is an analogy that helps to support my view that deep moral ignorance like JoJo's captures the sort of infelicity that makes an exemption appropriate. Just as we are part of a moral community, we are part of a philosophical community. What delineates membership in the community of analytic philosophy is not a general *capacity* to do analytic philosophy. Rather, it is just having a grasp on what analytic philosophy is, what it requires, what it takes for granted, what its methodology is and so on. Talking analytic philosophy to someone who is deeply ignorant of it—in the sense that they just don't get the basics—is infelicitous. There are lots of reasons someone might not have this knowledge. They might be pre-philosophical, a-philosophical, or alternatively-philosophical. These are all ways of being ignorant of analytic philosophy. And all suffice for philosophical address being infelicitous. If someone doesn't get what we are talking about, they are simply baffled by what we are up to when we engage in the familiar moves.

Sometimes of course, we bring people into the philosophical community by holding them to its standards even when we know they will not quite get it. The same is true of morality. We blame proleptically in order to bring people in. (Of course, if we are conscientious teachers, we should not make proleptic attitudes our only method of bringing people in, we should also simplify, explain, point out patterns, and so on.) And when someone is in the process of being brought into our community, there is a transitional stage, when blame moves from being proleptic to being paradigmatic.

The point is that it doesn't matter *why* someone is not in our philosophical community, or how easy it would be to bring them in. So long as it is not *too* easy—so long as their ignorance is not completely shallow, or fleeting, someone who doesn't get the basic picture is not apt for philosophical address. The same applies to the moral community. Given that ordinary blame is a communication, deep moral ignorance—being outside of our moral community—suffices for exemption. If someone does not have moral understanding, praise and blame are not felicitous. So someone like JoJo who has the general capacities required for moral thought may nonetheless be outside the realm of ordinary blame.

One issue that arises here is whether we can sometimes blame someone indirectly. Perhaps deep moral ignorance is culpably acquired, in which case we can blame them for whatever they did to acquire the ignorance and then blame them indirectly once they are ignorant. I turn to that issue now.

2. Culpable Ignorance

Most cases of deep moral ignorance are explained by the epistemic circumstances of the agent. It is thus not the agent's fault that she is deeply morally ignorant. That is true, but of course it does not imply that the agent has an excuse for not grasping Morality, and therefore 'deserves' to be in the realm of ordinary blame. The fact of her ignorance is what renders her exempt. That is the point of the analogy with the philosophical community: it doesn't matter why someone is outside of our community, but it makes a difference. We cannot sensibly blame such people in the communicative way.

However, it might be thought that there is an important distinction between those who are non-culpably deeply morally ignorant, and those who are culpably deeply morally ignorant. Perhaps in some cases the agent has voluntarily cultivated their outrageous moral view little by little. It is surely not the case they always thought like that and, surely, they did not swallow the view whole, all at once. Rather, it must be a series of small steps, by which they gradually came to a position that allows them to think that it is permissible to run a factory in Bangladesh on child labour with no safety standards. In that case, we might think, their ignorance is culpable. We could argue that if deep moral ignorance is culpable, ordinary blameworthiness transfers into the later acts.[6]

The question of culpable ignorance is not relevant to deep moral ignorance. To see that, consider a fictional example of voluntary moral degradation: Walter White, from AMC's *Breaking Bad*. Walter White is a middle-aged school teacher working a second job in a car wash under a sadistic manager to pay his mortgage and support his family. On finding he has lung cancer (having never smoked) something cracks, and he decides to start producing and selling methamphetamine. At first it

---

[6] Various questions arise about the difference between culpable and innocent moral ignorance. One question that is raised by Holly Smith (1983) is whether we should think of the will of the agent who acts out of culpable ignorance as including the bad motivations that were involved in the benighting act. One might do this simply by fiat, insisting that we should include past sins, even if they make no difference to current quality of will. But we might think that the will of an agent who is culpably ignorant is actually qualitatively different to the will of an agent who is innocently ignorant. If a culpably ignorant agent has no memory at any level of her past wrongdoing, and no inkling that her current acts are wrong, if she has forgotten everything, it seems less plausible that the motives for the benighting act should be included in what we count as her motivations for the downstream acts.

seems that he does it in order to pay for his medical treatment, and that he is a normal guy in abnormal circumstances. He does some bad things but, although they do not seem justifiable, they seem understandable: there are mitigating circumstances. But during the show's five seasons it becomes apparent that his moral compass is being progressively reset. Just as Aristotle's virtuous agent becomes virtuous by practising virtue, so Walter White becomes vicious by practising vice. The first few murders he commits all seem necessary, unavoidable, given the premise of the show. He finds it hard to do bad things, but he works at it, he persists. By the end of the show he is, apparently, wicked through and through.

Of course, it is not clear whether Walter White knows his actions are wrong and does them anyway, or whether he has changed his value system so that his acts now seem permissible to him. Let us assume that he has changed his value system. We need not think that he thinks his acts are *good* (that would be hard to imagine). All we need to imagine is that he thinks they are permissible: he is a nihilist, he thinks nothing matters. He thinks his own needs and desires trump the interest of others. As he finally says to his wife in the finale, "I did it for me". How should we judge Walter White? Is the fact that his deep moral ignorance was in some sense voluntarily acquired relevant to how we blame him now? I will argue that it is not.

The question to ask is, what difference would it make if Walter White's moral degradation was externally, rather than internally caused? Think again about Jo and JoJo. Both are ruthless dictators. JoJo was raised by his father Jo to be what he is, and (we can imagine) had no epistemic access to an alternative way of life. Wolf doesn't say much about Jo, but let's say that he chose his own path, and that he started within the ballpark of Morality. But now Jo has forgotten all he once knew about the True and the Good, and is, to all intents and purposes, just like JoJo. Both Jo and JoJo are now, we can imagine, thoroughly psychologically insulated from the correct moral view.

It is true that their histories are different. Perhaps JoJo has an excuse in the sense that excuses apply to detached blameworthiness: we think of JoJo as less of an agent, he had unfortunate formative circumstances. Neither Jo nor Walter White has that excuse (of course bad things may have happened to them, but that is true of almost everyone). But the fact that Jo and Walter White brought their ignorance upon themselves does not make them eligible for ordinary blame. If they are deeply morally ignorant, we cannot expect them to accept and understand ordinary blame. It would make no sense to blame them in that way, and we do not feel much temptation to blame in that way.[7]

3. Moral Motivation and Wolf's Asymmetry

Let us move on to cases of agents who are suffering some sort of motivational problem. I argue that, setting aside cases of compulsion and other clear impairments, there is a sort of motivational incapacity that does not exempt the agent from ordinary praise and blame. I will approach the question by looking at Susan Wolf's asymmetry thesis (1990, 79–88).[8] Wolf argues that agents who are incapable of bad acts can be praiseworthy, but that agents who are incapable of good acts are not blameworthy. So praiseworthiness and blameworthiness are asymmetrical with respect to motivational incapacity. I will argue that the relevant sort of incapacity does not rule out either praiseworthiness or blameworthiness, what really matters is moral understanding.

Wolf argues that for an agent to be blameworthy for a bad act, she must have been able to avoid it. This is not an appeal to metaphysical freedom: the idea is that the agent must have a psychological capacity, such that she could have opted for a better act. Wolf understands that capacity as follows: an agent must have the relevant "capacities, skills, talents, knowledge, and so on that are relevant to X-ing" (1990, 101). Wolf's basic thought here is intuitively compelling, that an agent (to put it in David Lewis's terms) must *have what it takes* (Lewis, 1976, 150).

By contrast, on Wolf's view, an agent can be praiseworthy, even if she is internally compelled to do good acts, and doesn't have what it takes to do bad acts. Mark Twain's well-known quip illustrates the point: "I am different from Washington; I have a higher, grander standard of principle. Washington could not lie. I can lie, but I won't."[9] Twain's remark is funny because, in fact, we think Washington *especially* praiseworthy because he lacks the capacity for lying. For some reason, we find this

---

[7] I do not wish to deny that there are cases of culpable ignorance and even culpable moral ignorance. My point is just that in deep ignorance, previous culpability is irrelevant.

[8] To be fair, Wolf's asymmetry thesis has few supporters. Perhaps only Dana Nelkin (2011) explicitly agrees that there is such a thing. My purpose here is to show that the way in which the asymmetry thesis is problematic reveals something interesting.

[9] Quoted in *Mark Twain*, Archibald Henderson.

thought much less intuitive when it applies to blameworthiness: we are inclined to agree with Wolf that someone who cannot help but act wrongly is not blameworthy.

Dana Nelkin (2011) defends and explains Wolf's asymmetry, arguing that you can be praiseworthy without having the ability to act badly, whereas to be blameworthy requires the ability to act well. Nelkin puts this in terms of rational ability, arguing that rational ability, *the ability to respond to the right reasons*, is essential to moral responsibility. Thus, whereas someone who acts well can respond to the right reasons (they do, therefore clearly they can), someone who acts badly may not be able to.

As Nelkin stresses, it is essential to define 'ability' clearly. Nelkin accepts Wolf's account, that the ability is a question of the agent's own talents, skills, and so on, as well as the absence of interference. In order for an agent to be responsible, she must have the here and now ability to perform the relevant act. There must be no external interference; the world must be cooperating. So, cases where an agent is interfered with, or where there is an insurmountable obstacle, are obviously cases where the agent is not responsible. And equally, if the agent's psychological make-up is such that they do not have what it takes to act well, the agent is not responsible.[10]

The crucial thing is to understand what exactly 'not having what it takes' means in this context. There are clearly cases where an agent has some sort of incapacity that completely undermines her agency and responsibility. For example, an agent may be entirely incapable of putting any of her resolutions to act into practice, or she may have a cognitive blind spot where she cannot understand anything related to normativity. But these are not the sort of cases I am interested in here. I am interested in cases where an agent is sufficiently unimpaired to count as an agent but is, as it were, committed to a certain track: a good one, or a bad one. Washington is on a good track, set on doing good things, his counterpart

---

[10] Nelkin argues that *counterfactual* intervention does not interfere with an agent's ability, so agents in Frankfurt style examples, where an evil neuroscientist is poised ready to intervene if the agent decides on the unfavoured course of action, do not count as cases where the agent lacks the ability. Ability in Nelkin's sense is focused on the agent (2011, 66–7). Thus an agent is responsible in a counterfactual intervener case *not* 'despite not being able to do otherwise', as many (e.g. Fischer and Ravizza) claim, but because so long as she has what it takes and there is no actual intervention, she *does* have the ability to do otherwise.

is on a bad track, set on doing bad things. We should understand their incapacities as psychological without being pathological, as very strong motivations.[11] They otherwise have normal agential capacities, capacities that we can all agree are a necessary condition for any sort of responsibility.

Bernard Williams makes this clear in his discussion of praiseworthiness in cases of moral incapacity (1995). Williams insists that there is an important difference between a 'moral' incapacity and a 'merely psychological' one. Clearly, if Washington could not lie because it gave him a panic attack, that would be a very different sort of thing. Crucial in backing up our intuition that Washington is praiseworthy is our background belief that Washington's incapacity is a sort of responsiveness to reasons. Washington is strongly committed to doing what is right. Washington does not have what it takes to act badly. The question, then, is whether a psychology that is genuinely equivalent, but oriented to the bad rather the good, counts as responsible. We need to think about an agent who cannot act well in the sense that Washington cannot act badly.

Let's see what happens if we reverse the story and imagine someone who cannot act rightly in a symmetrical sense to the sense in which Washington cannot act wrongly. If an agent who cannot act rightly is just like George Washington but bad, we are imagining someone who understands Morality (as Washington does), and acts akratically every time because of powerful motivations to do so. Take Milton's Satan. Satan is a fallen angel: he certainly had the capacity to act well at one point. However, he decides that he is done with that, and commits himself to bad action, saying, "So farewell Hope, and with Hope, farewell Fear, Farewell Remorse: all good to me is lost, Evil, be thou my good" (1664, book IV, 109–11). We can imagine Satan as a mirror image of Washington. Satan commits himself so strongly that acting well stops being a live option. But what is blameworthy in Satan is precisely his commitment to bad

---

[11] This is consistent with what both Wolf and Nelkin say. As Wolf puts it, an agent who acts well and is unable to act badly does so because "her moral commitment is so strong" (1990, 82). Nelkin's argument against Fischer and Ravizza's denial of asymmetry relies on this point. She argues that they try to show that agents are blameworthy in the absence of 'ability to do otherwise' by pointing to ways in which external circumstances make a certain act inevitable, whereas what Nelkin and Wolf are concerned with is cases where the internal state of the agent makes it the case that she lacks ability to do otherwise. I argue in more detail that we must be able to understand the relevant sort of incapacity as being a matter of strong motivations in my 2016.

action in the face of his understanding of Morality. Even if he can no longer find it in himself to act well, he seems blameworthy.

Imagine another, more mundane agent, call him Scrooge, who has little of the milk of human kindness, and has not tried to develop more. He is strongly motivated to misanthropy. Imagine that Scrooge grasps Morality. He knows that a certain level of respect and concern for others is morally required, and he sincerely believes that he *should* embody respect and concern in his actions. He believes that he could live up to the moral minimum if he tried.[12] However, every time he is faced with the option of being nice, he decides to be horrible. He doesn't even try to be nice and, plausibly, he feels no regret—he just refuses the moral call. His contempt for his fellow beings is much more powerful than moral considerations, so he defies Morality. Such a person does not have what it takes to act well, yet he seems blameworthy.

Scrooge's commitments may be less purely intellectual than Satan's. Scrooge might be a few steps along the way to being compulsive. But it is plausible that there is space here for an agent more ordinary than Satan who is not compulsive, not out of control, and yet who is so constituted that he does not have what it takes to act well. Scrooge understands Morality but refuses it. He is blameworthy in the ordinary way despite not having what it takes to act well.

If someone like Washington is praiseworthy, then someone like Satan, or Scrooge, is blameworthy. Why would we think there is any asymmetry? One possibility is that we are sometimes focusing on cases where responsibility is completely undermined. As Fischer and Ravizza argue in their discussion of Wolf's asymmetry, if there is a responsibility undermining factor in all the cases of bad action but not in the cases of good action, then no grounds for an asymmetry have been established (1998, 60–1).[13] In many of the bad action cases, there seems to be a

---

[12] I assume that moral incapacity can be unknowing. I also assume that it is at least *prima facie* plausible that one can act akratically without internal wrangling and without regret. One may just think, 'to hell with it'. (I suspect that thinking this possible implies accepting motivational externalism.)

[13] They argue that in all of Wolf's examples of unavoidable wrongdoing, and not in her examples of unavoidable right-doing, there is a responsibility undermining mechanism in play, such as kleptomania or some other form of compulsion. The same seems true of some of Nelkin's: for example, Lyddie England, the American soldier who engaged in torture at Abu Ghraib, who apparently suffered from multiple issues including cognitive impairment (2011, 11).

responsibility undermining mechanism: the bad agents are impaired in some way. Arguably, parallel cases of good actors—people who have something wrong with them such that they cannot respond to bad reasons—would also seem ineligible for ordinary praise.

The question, then, is how to mark the difference between the cases where an agent does not have what it takes and yet seems unimpaired, and subject to ordinary praise (or blame) and the cases where the agent's not having what it takes constitutes impairment, and puts her outside the realm of ordinary praise and blame. The problem is that it is very hard to draw the line between responsibility undermining mechanisms and merely fortunate or unfortunate mechanisms.

It seems that when we imagine positive cases, where agents are so good that they cannot act badly, we do not think of this as impairment. However, when we consider a case where an agent cannot act well, we take it to be a case of impairment, the kind of problem that undermines responsibility. Scrooge, it might be said, is ill, he is not just bad. There *must* be something wrong with him.

A couple of things need to be said about that. The first is that it might be true that, as a matter of fact, people who cannot act badly are, on some independent measure, mentally healthy, but people who cannot act well are, on some independent measure, mentally ill. In that case it is not that the conditions of praiseworthiness are different to the conditions of blameworthiness. Rather, all we would have is that the conditions for praiseworthiness are met by more people than the conditions for blame-worthiness. This does not support the asymmetry that Wolf and Nelkin want to defend. There would be an asymmetry, but it would be a purely statistical asymmetry.

What seems more likely is that the classifications are socially con-structed: we tend to classify those people who are very strongly commit-ted to acting act well as mentally healthy, and we tend to think of people who are committed to acting badly as mentally ill. In that case, the asymmetry is in our attitudes, and is not necessarily justified. Whether

---

The distinction between an impairment in the agent and an obstacle outside the agent can be blurry. For example, Nelkin discusses a case presented by Pereboom, where the agent has a brain tumour. Nelkin argues that either we should see this as something that removes the agent's capacities or we should see it as an obstacle/interference, like an actual intervener, and in both cases the agent is not responsible (2011, 69).

Scrooge is ill or bad is up to us to decide, and we should think about it in terms of our more general practice of responsibility attribution. How much badness do we want to countenance? I come back to that in the final section of this chapter.

It is hard to determine what counts as impairment in these cases. But there might be another way to distinguish between those who are exempt from ordinary praise and blame and those who are praise- or blame-worthy in the ordinary way. Bernard Williams (1995) makes a suggestion that points in the direction that I think we need to take here. He suggests that an incapacity does not undermine praiseworthiness if it is one that the agent identifies with. I think that this is on exactly the right lines: an agent has to have a certain attitude to her own actions. Washington is praiseworthy because he understands and values Morality: he does what is right because it is right. Satan is blameworthy because he pursues evil for its own sake.

This is another way of saying that what is important in these cases can be put in terms of the reflexivity requirement: the agent must have moral understanding and know what she is doing. An agent is praiseworthy if she understands Morality, and understands that what she is doing is right. This is true, even if in some sense she lacks a capacity to act badly. Conversely, an agent is blameworthy if she understands the badness, and 'ought-not-to-be-doneness' of her acts, and this is true even if, in some sense, she lacks the capacity to act well. Of course, general agential capacities are required, but we are imagining cases where the agent has all the general capacities, but lacks something very specifically moral. I shall argue that this approach makes sense of our various examples, and banishes the appearance of asymmetry.

Consider, first, praiseworthiness. Washington is praiseworthy in the ordinary way, and I have suggested that his grasp on Morality is essential to his praiseworthiness. By contrast, someone who is compelled to act well by their deep psychological states does not seem praiseworthy in the ordinary way if they do not understand Morality. Imagine an agent, Alethea, who has no understanding of morality, but is compelled to good actions, like a moth to the flame. She doesn't deliberate properly, doesn't really understand what she is doing, and does not take pride or satisfaction in her good actions in the ordinary way. This agent does not seem praiseworthy. Alethea is like Huck Finn, on one understanding of

Huck's psychology.[14] If we think of Huck as being deeply morally ignorant, as someone who really doesn't see at any level that in helping Jim to escape he is doing the morally right thing, then it is not at all clear that Huck is praiseworthy. People like Alethea and Huck are not praiseworthy in the ordinary sense. They are esteemworthy for their good motivations but that, as I argued in Chapter 4, is not the same as being praiseworthy in the ordinary way. Rather, they are praiseworthy in the detached way.

The Huck case illustrates another important point—that real life cases may be very hard to diagnose. Since Watson (1996), a popular strategy has been to say that we are pulled in two directions in many of the marginal cases—we think psychopaths, for example, are blameworthy insofar as they have a bad will, but at the same time we think they are not blameworthy because they are impaired. Watson argues that these are really two different sorts of blameworthiness, attributability and accountability (1996). Of course I agree with the basic pluralist strategy. Huck (assuming he is morally ignorant) is praiseworthy in the detached sense but not in the ordinary sense. But I think there is another source of explanation for our ambivalence about these cases—it is simply uncertainty—we do not know what people know. Take the much discussed case of the ancient slaveholders. Do they know, deep down, that slavery is wrong? Or is their ignorance, as Michele Moody-Adams (1994) suggests, motivated ignorance? What should we say in such cases about self-deception, lazy evidence gathering, and reluctance to complete inferences to undesired conclusions?[15] I leave these complexities aside here.

As I argued in Chapter 4, subjective rightness (and thus ordinary praiseworthiness) applies when an agent tries to do well by Morality. Trying requires that an agent understands her aim, and understands her own action as one she is morally permitted or required to do. Subjective wrongness (and thus ordinary blameworthiness) applies when an agent fails to try, and one counts as failing to try (as opposed to simply not trying) only when there is a good background grasp of Morality and its demands. Thus Washington counts as trying to do well, and he is

---

[14] I discussed Huck Finn in some detail in Chapter 4.

[15] See Calhoun (1989) for a discussion of the complexity of moral change and how we should assign responsibility in those contexts, and Mason and Wilson (2017) for a discussion of the sort of epistemic vice that might render moral ignorance culpable.

praiseworthy. Alethea, by contrast, is neither trying nor failing to try. She is not in the realm of ordinary praiseworthiness.

We can connect this with the communicative nature of praise and blame and the felicity conditions that apply. Washington cannot help but act rightly. However, it makes sense to praise him. He understands Morality, and so can accept ordinary praise on the terms that it is offered. He can agree that he has made the right sort of efforts in the context of the shared value system, Morality. The fact that Washington could not have done otherwise, in the sense that his motivations to do the right thing are very strong indeed, may mean that we are less impressed with particular instances of right-doing by him. We might notice that Washington did not have to try as hard as some people have to try, and we might take that as a mitigating his praiseworthiness somewhat.[16] But what is clear is that Washington is in the realm of ordinary praiseworthiness. His strong inclination to act rightly does not put him into a different category.

Alethea, by contrast, has no understanding of Morality at all. It would not make sense to praise her. Such praise would be infelicitous—it would not make sense to Alethea—she could not join you in approving of her efforts in following her conscience. She is not doing that. Her own acts do not appear to her in that way. She is not acting on conscience. Communicative praise, which, as I argued in Chapter 5, essentially involves an invitation to reflect on the efforts the agent has made in following her conscience towards Morality, is infelicitous when agents do not understand Morality.

Let's go back to Satan: Satan can understand blame. He knows exactly what he has done, and he knows that he deserves blame. However, he refuses it. Accepting ordinary blame, I argued in Chapter 5, involves accepting that one has acted wrongly by one's own lights, feeling remorse, being willing to make reparations and so on: it is engaging in a conversation with the blamer, and being willing to proceed as far down the sequence of conversational moves as is appropriate. Satan has explicitly disavowed remorse, he is training himself to be evil. But blame is not infelicitous: Satan can see that he has acted wrongly, and even wrongly by his own lights. He chooses evil as evil,

---

[16] See my discussion of mitigating circumstances in Chapter 6.

not as good. When he says, "Evil, be thou my good" he means only that he will pursue evil the way he used to pursue good. He does not think that evil *is* good.

Scrooge may be less clear in his assessment, but he is similar to Satan. Scrooge may go so far as accepting that he has acted wrongly by his own lights, but he is not willing to go further with that conversation, given that he fully intends to carry on acting badly. This is uptake failure in one sense: blame will not make him feel remorse or try to mend his ways. But the blame is not infelicitous. Scrooge counts as refusing because he knows that he acted wrongly. Scrooge is not baffled by the blame. In that sense, there is no infelicity in the Scrooge example, and Scrooge counts as blameworthy in the ordinary way. This is true, I think, even if Scrooge is motivationally so constituted that he will always refuse the moral call.

We might imagine a tortuous conversation with Scrooge, where he says, 'look, I understand that kindness is required, and I have considered being kind, but I find it beneath me. Other people are not my bag. I don't want to have anything to do with them. I am not made like that. So you should not blame me. Isn't it part of the deal that "ought implies can"? I don't have it in me to act well.' It is a slightly odd conversation, but Scrooge is an odd person. I think we would be inclined to press him on the question of whether he really does know that he ought to be kind— does he understand that other people *are* his business? And then we would want to establish that he is not suffering from some sort of compulsion—is he possessed by alien-seeming inclinations? Is he out of control? If he doesn't really understand Morality, or if he is in the grip of a compulsion, then his responsibility would be undermined. But if Scrooge does understand, and does intend to do the things he does, then our blame is intelligible to him. We would find ourselves saying to him, 'Sorry Scrooge, I do blame you. You should be more kind. You know that.'

With Scrooge, the door is open to continuing the blame conversation. Scrooge sees what the conversation involves and he understands why we want to have it. But he is refusing it. As I pointed out earlier, it is essential that we leave room for refusal. Scrooge is one picture of blame refusal. What makes it refusal rather than infelicity is that Scrooge understands what is going on, and an essential part of understanding what is going on is grasping Morality.

4. Psychopaths and Moral Knowledge

Psychopaths are much discussed in philosophy, but of course we are not using a clear medical definition. For my purposes here, a psychopath is someone who has normal agential capacities in most respects, but is morally abnormal, in that they appear to fail to see that morality matters, and are not guided by it. The case of psychopaths seems to challenge my suggestion that we can make sense of the examples where an agent seems exempt from ordinary blame by talking about lack of moral knowledge. The real problem with psychopaths, it might be said, is not that they lack moral knowledge. They may, or they may not. They may be able to parrot the rules, but what is really crucial, what really disqualifies them from ordinary blame, is something motivational: they do not see that morality is supposed to be action guiding, or they cannot care about moral reasons, or they cannot understand or care about reasons at all. It is unfair to describe this in terms of badness, as I described Scrooge.

I have not said much about whether grasping Morality entails being motivated by morality. This is now pressing: if we have someone who can recognize and repeat the rules, but is not motivated by them, do they grasp Morality? This, of course, is usually framed in terms of the debate between motivational internalists about morality, who claim that, as a conceptual matter, to grasp morality is automatically to be motivated by it, and motivational externalists, who claim that it is possible to properly grasp morality without being motivated by it.[17]

Let's assume that psychopaths are not motivated by morality. If we take the internalist route, they thus do not understand morality, and so are exempt on my view. If we take the externalist route, we can say that psychopaths do understand morality, and just lack motivation, but then they are fully blameworthy—we have no way to accommodate the intuition (which I share) that psychopaths are impaired in some crucial way.[18] As I said at the start, my discussion is purely hypothetical: if this is how an

---

[17] The literature on that debate is too voluminous to list here, for an overview see Rosati (2016). I argue for motivational externalism in Mason (2008).

[18] This is what is missing from Scanlon's view. Scanlon argues that basic rationality is enough to render psychopaths blameworthy. On Scanlon's view, ignoring the fact that someone will be hurt by your action is equivalent to judging that the fact that someone will be hurt is not a reason, and that constitutes a bad will (1998, 288). Talbert (2008) argues along the same lines. But as Watson (2011) points out, this conflates 'judging that x is not a reason' with 'not understanding that x is a reason'.

agent is, then this is what we should say. So, with that in mind, let me consider various possibilities.

Perhaps we should simply take at face value the (common) psychopath's claim to know right from wrong. At one point in Watson's description of Robert Harris, Watson quotes Harris's sister. She says, about her brother on death row, "He just doesn't see the point of talking... He told me he had his chance, he took the road to hell and there's nothing more to say" (1987, reprinted in 2004, 237). Harris claimed to know right from wrong. But there is something odd about this. It is hard to believe that Harris really did understand Morality. The question is, what is missing?

The motivational internalist says that someone like Harris is not really making that moral judgment, and we know this because he is not motivated by it. Motivational internalists would also disagree with my account of Scrooge, as someone who understands Morality, and makes moral judgments, but is very bad. Internalists will likely to want to categorize Scrooge as a psychopath. The motivational internalist cannot believe that someone like Scrooge really makes moral judgments, if he did, the internalist insists, he would be motivated. That argument, of course, ends up in deadlock very quickly, with the internalist insisting that lack of motivation means the agent must lack understanding, and the externalist insisting that it is conceptually possible that someone has a proper cognitive grasp of morality but fails to be motivated.

I have defended a position according to which it is possible to understand Morality and make moral judgments, and yet fail to be motivated by those judgments. Scrooge is one example, and I will discuss some others below. However, I will also argue that there is one sort of impairment, and we might as well call it psychopathy, which is not *just* a matter of being unmotivated by morality, that grounds an exemption from ordinary blame. Psychopaths may be able to point to the rules that they know constitute Morality, but they do not really understand the sense in which it is reason giving.

David Shoemaker (2011) uses the following example to try to make sense of something like the thought I am trying to express here. Shoemaker asks us to imagine that we encounter a group of aliens that we know to be more morally sensitive than us. The aliens tell us that it is bad for blades of grass to be walked on, because of what it is like to be a blade of grass. We are baffled, obviously. Shoemaker's point is that that is what it is like to be a psychopath: psychopaths do not really grasp moral reasons as reasons. The analogy is not perfect, the fact that there really is nothing that it is like to be a blade of grass gets in our way. It is hard to make sense of the idea that we are genuinely missing something. The problem with this way of explaining the idea is that if we cast ourselves in the role of the psychopath, the role where we do not understand the reasons, our very lack of understanding in that role will impede us from making sense of the example.[19]

Rather than trying to imagine an agent more morally aware than us, I will explicate the relevant impairment using Samuel Scheffler's (2010) discussion of the difference between believing valuable and valuing. Scheffler points out that it is possible to see that something is valuable without actually valuing it. We could see, in other words, that something is reason giving without actually being moved by the reason. I might think that opera is aesthetically valuable and yet not be moved by it myself.[20] To think that opera is 'reason giving' is, of course, a little obscure. The idea is that opera provides reasons for some emotional reactions and further, for some actions, and against others. The emotions or actions that we are given reasons for or against in aesthetic cases are very variable: we might have reasons to listen to opera, to protect and preserve it as an institution, to share it with others, and so on.

In both moral and aesthetic cases, the reasons that are given by the valuable thing may apply only to some people. Scheffler thinks of those people as being picked out by their position: he gives the example of relationships, which can be thought valuable by everyone but can only be valued by the participants.[21] We could put that point

---

[19] Matthew Talbert objects to Shoemaker that either we have no reason to believe the aliens, in which case we are not blameworthy at all, or we do have reason to believe the aliens, in which case we should be morally motivated and are blameworthy if we are not (2012b).

[20] Scheffler's example, in his useful discussion of what valuing is (2010). Thanks to Tori McGeer for pointing me to that. In his discussion of the prudential capacities of psychopaths, Watson (2013) considers Cleckley's claim that psychopaths do in fact lack a sense of aesthetic value as well as moral value.

[21] As Scheffler puts it, "So not only is it the case that nobody can value all valuable things, but, in addition, some things whose value everyone can recognize can, nevertheless, only be valued by certain people. In this sense, at least some valuing is *positional* in a way that believing valuable is not" (2010, 37).

about valuing in more general terms: we could say that to believe something is valuable is to believe that there are conditions under which one ought to be motivated by the reasons it provides. There are relevant conditions other than position, there are also time and place and so on, and in the aesthetic case there might also be conditions relating to desire. Aesthetic cases differ from moral cases in that it seems to be part of the concept of aesthetic value that the reasons it provides can be hypothetical, they can depend on our proclivities. We do not have a reason to go to the opera unless we would enjoy it. Perhaps we all have a reason to preserve opera (other things being equal) but we do not all have a reason to go to the opera. Take another aesthetic case: we can imagine someone who understands that music is reason giving, and prefers manufactured pop music to Aretha Franklin. In the aesthetic case, given that the conditions for appropriate valuing can be conditional on enjoyment, that might not count as a mistake, and insofar as we can stretch this analogy and talk about aesthetic blameworthiness, it is not blameworthy.

However, we can imagine that there are some aesthetic values that require valuing from everyone, regardless of their position or propensities. Sometimes we should protect, preserve, or respect something just because it is aesthetically valuable. Perhaps we all have a reason to go to the opera at least once. Perhaps we all have a reason to listen to Aretha Franklin. We might recognize that we have that reason and not be motivated by it. This seems a fairly normal state of affairs: we can believe valuable without valuing, either because we are not called on to value, or because we are not motivated as we accept we should be.

The important point is that to see that something is valuable is to see that it purports to give reasons, and to accept that it genuinely does, conditional on whatever conditions are applicable. However, an agent who could not see that it was reason giving at all has failed to understand something important, and does not understand value. The 'aesthetic psychopath' is baffled when I say that opera is valuable, and ought to be preserved, even though I don't go in for it myself. Perhaps this is what is going on with psychopaths: they fail to understand Morality in failing to see that it is reason giving at all. The idea that there are conditions under which you *should* be motivated just doesn't make sense to them. As the psychopath sees things, either you are motivated, or you are not.

If someone doesn't understand *any* reasons, they are not an agent at all, they are a wanton.[22] What I am trying to imagine here is a failure to understand reason giving force in a limited domain: an agent who has the minimal capacities required for agency, but who does not recognize some set of reasons. We can imagine someone, and perhaps it is easier in the aesthetic case than the moral case, who just doesn't see that values are reason giving at all. Such a person might be able to point to the greatest singers of all time, but be baffled when you try to explain that the fact that the Queen of Soul is singing gives them some reasons. 'But I am not interested', says the aesthetic psychopath, thinking that that closes the matter. This person is not a member of our aesthetic community, because they do not understand what aesthetic value is, they do not understand that it essentially gives reasons. By contrast, it would be aesthetically blameworthy for someone who recognizes that Aretha Franklin's music rightfully commands respect to needlessly destroy her records, or even to talk through her concerts. Such a person would fall into an aesthetic version of subjective wrongdoing and ordinary blameworthiness: they understand that they ought to respect something, and they would not be trying hard enough to do that.

In sum, one way to understand psychopathy is as a failure to understand the nature of moral reasons. This may not be the right way to characterize psychopaths. My point is that if there was such an impairment, it would count as lacking moral understanding on my view, and so psychopaths would be exempt from ordinary blame.

It is not entirely clear to me whether detached blame applies to psychopaths defined in this way.[23] As I argued in Chapter 6, detached blame is

---

[22] Frankfurt (1971). Psychopaths may be like that—see Kennett (2002) for discussion of the view that psychopaths equally fail to see their own self-interest as reason giving, also McGeer (2007) and Watson (2013). If that is the case, I would say that psychopaths lack the capacities necessary for agenthood, and thus are subject only to the truly objective stance.

[23] Another reason that we might resist even detached blameworthiness for psychopaths is given by Nelkin (2015). Nelkin argues that psychopaths do not exhibit moral vices on the grounds that they lack moral understanding. Nelkin points out (368) that we should distinguish between three different kinds of insensitivity that the psychopath might have: not being able to categorize the relevant moral features at all, being able to categorize them but not seeing that they are reason giving, and seeing that they are reason giving but not caring. Nelkin argues via a comparison with moral virtue (kindness) that only the last suffices for moral vice. This is in the same spirit as my general picture here, that moral understanding is necessary for ordinary blameworthiness. But Nelkin's point is that we may not be able to blame the psychopath at all, not even in the detached way, because we cannot

easily undermined by considerations about formative circumstances. In cases like Robert Harris's, we are strongly inclined to move to the truly objective stance. A parallel reason to move to the truly objective stance is the knowledge that there is something different about the agent's brain, and when we gain knowledge like that, we tend to think of the fault as an illness rather than an aspect of bad character. Thus even detached blame might be too much for the psychopath.

5. Psychopaths, Moral Outliers, and Morality Defiers

One thing that any discussion of blameworthiness ought to take seriously is that there are many extremely bad actors, and an account of blameworthiness should have something to say, not just about psychopaths, but about more quotidian cases of morally awful action. Of course, some morally awful action is done by people who are barely agents or clearly not agents: people whose mental capacities are, through nature or nurture, horribly damaged. These bad actors are not eligible for either ordinary blame or detached blame, instead we should take the truly objective stance, and we should be humane in our dealings with them. But many bad actors are definitely agents: they live amongst us, they hold down jobs, they may even run our corporations, our cities, our countries. As I said above in my discussion of Scrooge, we may decide that all of these people are ill, exempt in some way. But I think we should be willing to countenance a category of very bad people who are sane.

My map of the possibilities points to three possible ways to understand extremely bad agents. The first category consists of people who do not understand Morality at all, usually because they have a false view of morality. Sometimes these people are historically or otherwise distant, and their ignorance is explained by bad epistemic circumstances. But sometimes, such ignorance is apparently inexplicable. I called such people, 'moral outliers'. They may be perfectly normal on the outside,

---

even see the psychopath as cruel, given that cruelty requires moral understanding. For other discussions of whether psychopaths have morally vicious attitudes see Levy (2007), Scanlon (1998; 2008), Smith (2008), Talbert (2008), Watson (2011). My own response to Nelkin's worry is that moral vice such as cruelty is not necessary for detached blame, all that is required is that the agent act objectively wrongly or exhibit objectively problematic attitudes.

they do not suffer any of the pathological symptoms of mental illness or unfortunate formative circumstances. They are people who, without any apparent explanation, have a corrupted moral view. Such people act appallingly, and genuinely believe that their own actions are justified. Jo and his son JoJo accept a corrupt value system. In Jo's case we do not know why. In JoJo's case the explanation is clear: he was raised in a very limiting way, and unsurprisingly accepts the views he was indoctrinated with. We are more likely to think of JoJo as being damaged by his environment than Jo.

There are real versions of Jo and JoJo. There are also more mundane cases, like the ones that I referred to in Chapter 5: the president who supports a campaign of terror bombing, or supports a brutal regime elsewhere, the CEO who oversees a system of exploitation and corruption. It is possible that these people are deeply morally ignorant, that they genuinely believe that their acts are permissible. Moral outliers do not lack capacities, and there is no obvious explanation for their bad moral view. In such cases we blame them in the detached way with full force.

Moral outliers can be contrasted with a superficially similar category, the agents who understand Morality but act very badly anyway. We might call these people, 'Morality defiers'. Morality defiers are different from moral outliers in that they know or should have known (in the sense that I defended in Chapter 4) that their acts are morally reprehensible. Such agents may have made their peace with being morally reprehensible. They defy morality and may even luxuriate in their own badness. Milton's Satan is the apotheosis of Morality defying. Perhaps Morality defiers wrestle with their consciences from time to time, they care somewhat about the badness of their acts, and even try a little to do better, but do not try hard enough to count as trying to do well by Morality. Or perhaps, and this seems most likely, they live in a fog of self-deception. They have given up trying to do well by Morality, but they do not face that fact head on. They know at some level that their acts are terrible, but they pretend to themselves that that is not the case. It is a familiar point that power enables such self-deception. Morality defiers are subject to ordinary blame. They are just like us, but worse. They may refuse blame, but it makes sense to try and start the blame conversation.

Third, are psychopaths (as I have defined them), who do not understand the basic reason giving force of Morality and so are subject only to detached blame, if even that. They are often, probably usually, 'excused' in the sense relevant to detached blame in virtue of formative circumstances or pathology. That is to say, we retreat from detached blame to the truly objective stance.

There are several factors that make it easy to confuse or conflate these three categories. One is that we cannot tell, from observing one of these bad actors, or even from talking to them, which category they fall into. People do not tell the truth about themselves readily and, further, people's self-knowledge is often limited. Worse, the boundaries between the categories may not be clear. Psychopathy may come in degrees. Moral knowledge certainly comes in degrees, and as I admitted in my initial discussion of ordinary blameworthiness in Chapter 2, it is not always clear whether we should think of someone as having a blind spot, or as being outside our moral community. Is thinking that gay sex is a sin a moral blind spot, or does it place someone outside our moral community? Relatedly, moral disagreement may often seem to boil down to factual disagreement, but of course factual disagreement can be fuelled by morally infused motivations. Those who defend the view that gay sex is a sin tend to present this view as grounded in some sort of biological fact. But obviously in this case and many others, the so-called facts are not facts at all, but ideologically maintained fictions. It may, in the end, be indeterminate whether someone has a false moral view or whether they have the true view but have not bothered to think through how to try to do well. We often settle on lazy or convenient standards to live by, despite a dim awareness that such standards may not reflect Morality very well.

Another problem is that both moral outliers and Morality defiers seem psychologically unrealistic. How can people not see that killing innocent people for profit is wrong? But equally, how can people see that it is wrong and do it anyway? Whatever is going on in the actual psychologies of people who do terrible things, it is bound to be obscure to people who do not do terrible things. But something is going on, because there are lots of people doing terrible things. In thinking about such people we may be unclear whether they are moral outliers, or Morality defiers, or psychopaths. But I think it is helpful to think about the various options, and to think about the various different ways to be blameworthy. In thinking through the options we are learning morally, and of course, this is why we are so interested in these cases.

To some extent, it is up to us to decide how we categorize people, and when the facts themselves are ambiguous, it seems permissible to do it according to our interests. By that I mean our interests in the broad sense, what we are interested in, what sustains our responsibility practices in general. We do see cases where the classification of bad action is done according to the particular interests of those in power, and that is not defensible. But it is defensible to think in general terms about how useful it is to talk of badness. Clearly it is not useful in cases of clear pathology. But what about cases like the expensively educated and massively privileged CEO whose policies kill people? Perhaps this person is in the grip of deep ignorance, perhaps we cannot think of them as 'just like us'. Nonetheless, my inclination is to think that we should not shy away from labelling such a person as being a lot like us, as being in our moral community but being a defier, eligible for ordinary blame.

6. Conclusion

In this chapter I have argued that the best way to make sense of the difference between the realm of ordinary blame and the realm of detached blame is by appealing to a grasp of Morality. Agents who grasp Morality are eligible for ordinary blame. So long as they have the general capacities that qualify them as agents, it does not matter if they lack a capacity to choose 'freely' between acting well and acting badly. We should not say that we cannot praise them in the ordinary way. We can communicate our praise or blame, and we expect uptake.

I argued that not understanding the reason giving force of Morality is one way to be deeply morally ignorant, and so if we understand psychopaths as people who do not understand the way in which Morality gives reasons, we should see psychopaths as exempt from ordinary blame. They may be able to parrot the rules, and correctly identify right and wrong actions. But if they do not see that they should be motivated by Morality, they do not understand it. Psychopaths may be subject to detached blame, but perhaps they are not even to be subject to that. Usually, we see psychopaths as damaged by their circumstances, either by nature or nurture, and as such we are usually inclined to move towards the truly objective stance.

So far in this book I have argued that there are two sorts of blameworthiness. Ordinary blameworthiness involves background knowledge and understanding of Morality: in some sense, the agent knows what she is doing in acting wrongly. There is also detached blameworthiness, which applies to those who lack moral knowledge. In the next chapter I move on to a third sort of blameworthiness. Sometimes, perfectly ordinary agents act without knowing what they are doing. Such agents are not outside the realm of ordinary blame, they have a good grasp of Morality. Usually, for ordinary agents, acting without knowledge of what they are doing functions as a simple excuse. But there are some cases where things seem more complex that than. I turn to such cases now.

8

Taking Responsibility

I have argued for two different sorts of blameworthiness and, correspondingly, blame. Ordinary blame is communicative, and is applicable when the agent is a member of our moral community. By contrast, when someone is not in our moral community, when subjective obligation is not accessible to them, they are eligible only for detached blame. Detached blame is not communicative. It consists of certain attitudes that we take to *agents*, but we do not expect or demand a response.

In this chapter I will discuss a third sort of blameworthiness, extended blameworthiness.[1] I argue that sometimes we should take responsibility. I touched on one sort of case in Chapter 6: sometimes agents try hard, but because of their own bad motivations, do badly. In this chapter I will say more about that sort of case, and I will consider two other challenges: cases where an agent's act or omission is bad but entirely inadvertent,[2] and cases where an agent acts through implicit biases. In these cases, there is some pull to find the agent blameworthy. In what follows

---

[1] There is substantial overlap between this chapter and my 2018, Mason E., 'Respecting Each Other and Taking Responsibility for our Biases' in M. Oshana, K. Hutchison, and C. Mackenzie (eds.), *Social Dimensions of Moral Responsibility*, 163–84. Copyright © 2018, reprinted by permission of Oxford University Press: https://global.oup.com/academic/product/social-dimensions-of-moral-responsibility-9780190609610.

[2] I will not get too far into the question of what makes an omission an omission. Randolph Clarke, whose account of responsibility for inadvertence I discuss in this chapter, argues that although some omissions can be recast as actions—a child's 'not moving' can be redescribed as her 'staying still' (2014, 22)—not all can. Clarke claims that we need a normative account of omissions, something that is essentially an absence counts as an omission if there is some norm or standard requiring the agent to perform the act they failed to perform (2014, 29). Raz, whose account I also discuss, argues that something counts as an omission if the agent had something like an intention to perform the action she does not perform. There was some 'failure to connect' (2011, 249). The cases of omission that I am interested in here meet both conditions: there is a duty to do the things that are relevantly not done, and in the sense that the agent grasps Morality and accepts it, she intends to do what she ought.

I suggest that in some of these cases, agents should take responsibility for their failures.[3] In taking responsibility, I suggest, they become properly blameworthy in the extended way.

Bernard Williams makes essentially this point in his discussion of Homer's Telemachus. Telemachus and his father, Odysseus, are fighting the suitors, and suddenly Odysseus notices that the suitors are putting on armour and handing out spears. Unfortunately, someone has left the door to the weapons storeroom open. Telemachus immediately owns up to having inadvertently left the door open, and takes responsibility, saying that "no-one else is to blame" (1993, 50). Telemachus acted inadvertently, there is no hidden bad will behind his act. But his response, to take the blame, seems apt. As Williams says, there is an important element of responsibility that can be separated from the nature of the actions, and that is the response of the actor. What Williams is drawing attention to in the case of Telemachus is that it is *apt* for him to 'take the blame', and not because of any special circumstance or role or legal situation. It is just that Telemachus left the door open.

Williams contrasts Telemachus's mistake with Agamemnon's bad behaviour in his quarrel with Achilles:

In the case of Telemachus, his being *aitios* [responsible][4] contained two ideas: that he was, through normal action, the cause of what happened and that he might have to make up for it. Agamemnon agrees in his own case that he must

---

[3] The idea that we should take responsibility for things that are not under our control is not new. Robert Adams suggests in passing, in his 'Involuntary Sins', that we should take responsibility for traits that are not under our control, though he is talking about acts that reveal bad will (1985, 15). Susan Wolf suggests that there is a virtue of taking responsibility (2001, 10), and David Enoch (2012) argues that we sometimes have a moral duty to take responsibility: I discuss his view below. Fischer and Ravizza (1998, 208–10) talk about taking responsibility, but it is clear that they intend it to be appropriate only when the agent's act is under her control. As Fischer and Ravizza put it, "when an agent takes responsibility . . . he obviously is *not* accepting responsibility for all his actions *whatever their source*; rather, he is accepting responsibility for only those actions which flow from a certain source" (1998, 215). Thus Fischer and Ravizza's view is really a view about *accepting* responsibility. Their picture might be described as follows: there are conditions under which one is responsible in virtue of the way one's agency is exercised, and so long as one is able to accept that one is responsible, one genuinely is responsible.

[4] Williams explains 'aitios' as follows: "first, he was the cause of what happened . . . and second, that if anyone is to receive unfavourable comments about what happened, it is he. He may also, in one way or another, have to make up for his mistake" (1993, 52). This in itself is not clearly distinguishable from mere liability, but I think that remarks that Williams makes elsewhere in the chapter (ch. 3 'Recognising Responsibility'), e.g. on p. 57, make clear that he intends to be talking about something richer than liability.

make up for it. Moreover, he was immediately the cause of what happened; that is why he must pay. The one sense in which he is not *aitios* is that when he brought those things about, and indeed did so intentionally, he was not in a normal state of mind: he was, if we are prepared to let in that treacherous phrase, not his usual self. He is not dissociating himself from his action; he is, so to speak, dissociating the action from himself.

This reminds us of two further things about Telemachus. One is how normal Telemachus's state of mind was when he made his mistake; he was his usual self. You do not need Zeus and Fate and the mist-treading Erinys and their *ate* [delusion] to make you do things unintentionally. Everyone does that all the time. The other thing, related and just as familiar, is that the fact that you acted unintentionally does not, in itself, dissociate that action from yourself. Telemachus can be held responsible for things he did unintentionally, and so, of course, can we.   (1993: 53–4)

The 'familiar' thing here—that we can be held responsible for things we do unintentionally—is familiar in one sense. In presenting these examples I aim to remind us of that. We do hold people responsible for inadvertent fault. But the familiar thing is also controversial: it is very controversial indeed in the context of responsibility theory. Along with Williams, I want to urge that we should not let our theorizing take us too far from our actual practices.

1. Ambiguous Agency

There are various sorts of case where we might think that an agent is plausibly blameworthy, even though their act was not intentional. Consider again Kleinbart, who I discussed at length towards the end of Chapter 6. Kleinbart's problem is that he exercised his agency as well as could. He tried his best to be sensitive to his wife, not to do anything that would hurt her. But he went ahead and told a story at a party that did hurt her and quite possibly very predictably hurt her from an outsider's point of view. But Kleinbart didn't see that: from his point of view, after careful consideration, the story was fine. So Kleinbart acted subjectively rightly. The puzzle arises because Kleinbart's act was caused by a problematic part of his own character. How Kleinbart should see his own agency here is not clear.

A different sort of case where it might be appropriate to take responsibility is where failure is due to something purely inadvertent. Here is an example from Randolph Clarke: imagine that I have promised my spouse that I will get milk on the way home. Imagine that there is nothing that I have failed to do that I should have done in order to remember: as Clarke puts it, I could have set reminders, but it would have been 'borderline compulsive' behaviour to do so. I could have stopped myself from thinking about my work on the way home, but I often think about my work with no bad effects (2014, 165).[5] Thus it seems that I am not blameworthy for forgetting. Nor need we think that there is some hidden bad will in forgetting the milk—it does not reveal some suppressed loathing of family life. I just forgot, it was a glitch, or a blip. However, as Clarke suggests, and as seems very plausible to me, it might be that the agent is blameworthy in some sense for there being no milk.

Finally, consider action through unconscious bias. It seems very likely that people sometimes behave in biased ways without intending to do so. We might think that this always reveals a hidden bad will, but it might not. It might be that we act on automated processes, whose inputs we do not endorse on any level. Yet it seems that we are blameworthy when we act on biases, when we treat people unfairly.

The crucial point is that although these acts are not deliberate, do not involve the controlled exercise of our agency, and even undermine our primary agential efforts, such acts (or omissions) are plausibly *our* acts. They spring from our psychology, our agency is not obviously blocked. This is true for both acts and omissions. To see that, contrast the case of outcome luck, where a careful driver hits a deer. In that case, an identical act (or omission) might have turned out differently. The agent need not wish that she had behaved differently, she should wish that the deer had not been there. But when her act is problematic, if she was inadvertently speeding, for example, or if she had forgotten to check the brake fluid, or check her mirror, then she must wish that *she* had behaved differently.

George Sher (2009) argues that it is simply that the problem comes from us that makes blame appropriate. As Sher puts it, some features that an agent has are ones that *impede* her rationality rather than explain it. Sher compares agents to cars whose spark plugs do not always fire correctly, or computers that freeze occasionally. In one of his examples, a mother gets distracted whilst dropping her children off at school, and

---

[5] Clarke is interested in responsibility for omissions, but for the sake of my argument here nothing hangs on this being a case of omission.

leaves the dog in the hot car for too long. In this case, Sher says, the very features that normally help her respond to reasons hinder her: "her concern for her children, for example, or her tendency to focus intensely on whatever issue is at hand" (2009, 123). On Sher's view, the agent is blameworthy for an act that she was not aware of doing because the act comes from her constitutive features.

There are two problems with Sher's account. First, Sher's account of the scope of agency is not obviously correct. As Angela Smith points out, in her review of Sher's book, it is not clear that Sher has pointed to the right kind of connection between the agent and the act. As Smith stresses, when a fault is traceable to purely physical glitches we are not inclined to think the agent is responsible. A causal connection between the agent and her act is not enough, we need a rational connection (2010: 524). Smith's worry is that merely being a side effect of an agent's rational processes is not enough for the connection to count as rational.

The second problem is that even if we accept that Sher's account explains the difference between the acts that we can properly say the agent does, and mere events, it doesn't settle the question of whether inadvertent acts are *blameworthy*.[6] Pointing out that the act stems from the agent's agential features is just pointing out the puzzle: it seems that this sort of act could be blameworthy, but it also seems that there is no way to make sense of blameworthiness.[7] We seem to have the hallmarks of a simple excuse—ignorance, or lack of control, or both—so why is the agent not excused in this sort of case?

In this chapter I am chiefly concerned with dealing with the second problem, the question about how these bad acts might be blameworthy. On the first issue, I am content to say that these acts are ambiguous. It is not completely clear that they are connected to the agent in the right way. On the other hand, it is not completely clear that they are not connected

---

[6] The same problem applies to Julie Tannenbaum's account of 'mere moral failure' (2015). Gunnar Björnsson (2017b) suggests that there is a special sort of 'skill blame' that attaches to cases like the forgotten milk. I am aiming to establish something more ambitious—that the blame that we can engage in in such cases is close to ordinary blame.

[7] We might divide those who do not think we are responsible for inadvertent acts into those who worry that the acts are not properly acts, and so not the sort of thing that agents are responsible for at all, e.g. Wallace (1994, 138–9), Zimmerman (1997 and elsewhere), Rosen (2002 and elsewhere), Husak (2011); and those who worry that even if they are, properly speaking, acts, the fact that there is no bad will means that there is no way for them to be blameworthy, e.g. Vargas (2005), King (2009).

to the agent. It is this *ambiguous agency*[8] that is puzzling. We have acts that are plausibly the agent's acts, and yet the badness of them does not seems traceable to the agent in any meaningful way.[9]

Joseph Raz, like Bernard Williams, thinks that it is a philosophical prejudice to assume that there can be no luck in responsibility. Sometimes we can be blameworthy for acts and omissions that are unintentional. Raz argues, in a similar vein to Sher, that "Conduct for which we are (non-derivatively) responsible is conduct that is the result of the functioning, successful or failed, of our powers of rational agency, provided those powers were not suspended in a way affecting the action" (2011, 231). Raz says that there is a 'domain of secure competence', a domain where we can reasonably expect our efforts to issue in successful action. He argues that, unless there is a clear excuse, an excuse that shows that our competence was undermined, we are responsible for actions and omissions that fall within the domain of secure competence. The question is, why is inadvertence not itself an excuse? Unlike Sher, Raz offers an account of why we would think that we are responsible even in the absence of knowledge and control.

Raz's answer is that we need to hold ourselves responsible in order to maintain our self-respect, our sense of ourselves as agents. "Failure to control conduct within our domain of secure competence threatens to undermine our self-esteem and sense of who we are, what we are capable of, etc. We must react to it. We may conclude that we are no longer able securely to perform that kind of action. We have grown frail, our competence is diminishing. We come to recognize our limitations. Commonly that is not the case, and we do not allow it to be. We assert our competence by holding ourselves [responsible] for it" (2011: 245).

I agree that we can sometimes take responsibility, but I disagree with Raz about the reasons for taking responsibility. Raz thinks that holding ourselves responsible for failures within the domain of secure competence is required by self-respect. However, this is not entirely convincing. The fact that lots of people argue that we are not responsible for

[8] David Enoch talks about 'penumbral agency' in a much broader sense than the sense in which I am using the phrase 'ambiguous agency'. Enoch means to include acts that one's child has done, or one's dog, or perhaps even one's country (2012).
[9] For other discussions of inadvertent actions, see Amaya (2011), Bjornsson (2017b), Reis-Dennis (2018).

negligence (understood as pure inadvertence), while not being generally sceptical about responsibility, is indicative of that.[10] It seems to many that it would be possible to respect ourselves while thinking that we are not responsible for the glitches. Add that many cases of negligence are cases that can be traced back to a prior culpable act,[11] then it is even more likely that we don't have to worry too much about admitting that we are sometimes glitchy, and accepting that we are not responsible in those cases.

More importantly, Raz's picture is inward looking in an inappropriate way. On my account, the rationale for extending the zone of responsibility is outward looking: it is not to do with self-respect, but to do with respecting others in the right way. We voluntarily extend our responsibility zone in order to secure the respect and trust of others, and as a way of showing commitment and investment in our relationships.

2. Liability

Before I proceed with my argument for taking responsibility, I need to distinguish taking responsibility from taking on liability. Clearly, we can be liable in some cases where there is no personal fault, no blameworthiness or responsibility in the 'deep sense', the sense that moral philosophers and responsibility theorists are interested in. It might be objected that although there are cases where it is apt for us to be held liable, and indeed, where we should voluntarily take on liability, it is not possible to take on responsibility.

Enoch has suggested that, in cases of 'penumbral agency', we should sometimes take on responsibility, but his argument illustrates the difficulty of showing that what we should take on is responsibility rather than mere liability. His focus on the *moral* duty to take responsibility makes it sound as if what he is really talking about is liability, not responsibility. He argues, for example, that the fault in the lorry driver who does not take on anything after (through no personal fault) having killed a

---

[10] See e.g. Wallace (1990, 138–9), Zimmerman (1997 and elsewhere), Rosen (2002 and elsewhere), Neil Levy (2011 and elsewhere). The issue is not always framed in terms of 'negligence' but often, rather, in terms of non-culpable ignorance. See also Vargas (2005), King (2009). In philosophy of law see Alexander and Ferzan (2009), Moore and Hurd (2011).

[11] Moore and Hurd (2011) argue that point.

pedestrian is that he has violated his moral duty to take responsibility (2011, 110–11). It is easy to see that one can have a duty, legal or moral, to take on liability—to make reparations—but it is not at all easy to see how there could be a moral duty to take on responsibility, to engage in the blame conversation, and feel remorse.

Enoch himself insists that taking responsibility is taking on a sort of accountability, and that when you take on responsibility, you become accountable: "A is responsible (in this sense) for X to P if and only if, if X is wrong or otherwise morally problematic, A owes it to P to justify X (or the relevant X-related thing), or to offer an excuse for it, or to apologize for it, or to explain it, or something of this sort" (2011, 118).[12] This draws attention to an ambiguity in the notions of apology, justification, excuse, and so on. A sincere apology normally involves acknowledging responsibility. But there is a different sense of apology, in which apology merely involves acknowledging liability. When my dog digs into someone else's garden, it is appropriate for me to apologize. In doing so I am not necessarily accepting that it is my fault (it might be, it might not be). Rather, I am accepting and acknowledging liability. Similarly, it would be natural to say, 'I have no excuse for my dog's behaviour'. Again, if I say that, I do not mean that the dog's actions are really my actions, actions that issue from my agency and my bad will. Rather, I mean, 'I am not denying liability'.

Enoch is right that we have a moral duty to take on liability in many cases of penumbral agency. But he has not established that there is a moral duty to take on responsibility for inadvertent acts. I shall argue for a different account of the justification for taking on responsibility. My argument is that we should sometimes take on responsibility, where that is more than liability. But the 'should' is not a moral 'should', it is derived from requirements of our relationships. We should take responsibility in the sense that it is required for our relationships. The 'should' here is the very same 'should' that I used in discussing engagement in blame conversation in Chapter 5. It is a broadly hypothetical 'should', not a first order moral 'should'. We should engage in the blame conversation because it is part of being in the moral community.

---

[12] He references Marina Oshana's account (1997) of responsibility as his model.

3. Remorse and Agent Regret

Taking responsibility is taking on something deeper than liability. It is engaging in the blame conversation in a sincere way. Someone who genuinely takes responsibility is willing to engage in the blame conversation. They understand and are willing to acknowledge blame, and to move through the steps of acceptance, apology, reparations, and so on. But of course, someone might do this in a merely polite and superficial way, without taking on anything more than liability. What marks the difference between engaging in the blame conversation merely for politeness, and genuinely taking responsibility, is the agent's tendency to feel remorse. Remorse is evidence of sincere engagement in the blame conversation by the blamee. This is why we want remorse when we blame people. We want to know that the agent we are blaming has really internalized what we are saying, that they care. I will argue that genuine remorse is possible even for inadvertent acts. Remorse requires taking ownership of the relevant act.

It might be objected that the agents in my examples need not feel remorse, they should only feel what Bernard Williams calls 'agent regret' (1981). Agent regret is the feeling of regret that attaches specifically to one's own actions. Williams says "[agent-regret] can extend far beyond what one intentionally did to almost anything for which one was causally responsible in virtue of something one intentionally did" (1981, 28).[13] Feeling agent regret does not amount to taking responsibility. On a very thin understanding, agent regret is merely recognition of *causal* involvement, and is very different to remorse. Williams's central example in 'Moral Luck' is a lorry driver who kills a child through no fault of his own. The moral luck here is outcome luck: the lorry driver acted exactly as he should have done, he drove carefully and did not do anything wrong, but nonetheless is the cause of a death. On the thin understanding of agent regret, it applies when an agent does everything right and the external world does not cooperate and things turn out badly. But richer understandings of agent regret are also possible. Williams himself says

---

[13] Williams gives various examples over several decades. He introduces the idea of agent regret in his 1979 article, 'Moral Luck'. He returns to the topic in *Shame and Necessity* (1993) and in *Making Sense of Humanity* (1995).

that the distinction between agent regret and remorse cannot be clearly drawn (1981, 30).

Let's accept that there are shades of agent regret, and that it can shade into remorse. We nonetheless need an account of remorse, since, as I say, the tendency to feel something at the remorse end of the scale is what marks the blamee as sincerely accepting blame. An account of remorse will help us to see what is essential in taking responsibility.

Remorse is not easy to define. It has both a cognitive aspect, a belief about what has happened, and non-cognitive aspect, a feeling. I shall not focus on the feeling here. It is usually unpleasant, but beyond that I will not attempt to describe it. I will concentrate on the cognitive aspect, the belief, or belief-like commitment that is definitive of remorse. I will argue that taking ownership of the action is what is important. It is this commitment that is essential in taking responsibility.

We must be careful about how we define the cognitive aspect of remorse if it is to be useful for my purposes. There are ways to define it that would of course rule out the sort of case I am interested in defending here. If we say that remorse involves something like the thought, 'I have knowingly acted wrongly and should try harder in future', there would be no room for remorse for inadvertent actions.[14] On the other hand, if we restrict the cognitive component to a claim that there was some agential involvement, we are left with what looks like the thinnest sense of agent regret, which does not entail responsibility at all. I am looking for space between full blown remorse for a wrong act knowingly done, and mere causal agent regret. But we seem to have a dilemma. The cognitive commitment in full blown remorse seems to be the thought that I acted wrongly and should not have done so, and cognitive commitment in agent regret seems to be the thought that I was the causal agent of a harm. What is there between the two?

The crucial issue here is the extent to which the agent sees the action as her own action. Gabrielle Taylor makes this point in distinguishing between regret and remorse. "Remorse is always felt about an event which the agent sees as an action of hers. It is therefore not surprising that the person who feels remorse and the person who feels regret should

---

[14] This is how Marcia Baron defines remorse in her discussion (1988). Baron is concerned to argue that agent regret is truly distinct from remorse, and that both are needed to make sense of good moral character.

view differently the relevant past event. If she feels remorse then she wants to undo the relevant action and its consequences which cause the remorse, but when feeling regret she need not think that she would undo the relevant action if she could" (1996, 66).

Unfortunately, it is not always clear whether an action is one of ours, one it would be appropriate to wish to undo. One way for an action to be the agent's own action is for it to have been done knowingly and in a self-controlled way. This is why remorse might seem to paradigmatically involve the thought, 'I did something wrong and I should have done better'. Being in control of an act, knowing what you are doing, choosing to do it, these are obviously correlated with an action's being one's own. But it seems possible to feel remorse and not just agent regret for things that one has done through un-self-aware bad will. If an agent forgets her friend's birthday, or carelessly insults someone, she should feel remorse, not because she knew what she was doing at the time, but because she should think of the action as her action. The crucial issue is not the manner in which the action is one's own, but *that it is one's own*.

This is basically how the argument for attributionism works.[15] Opponents of attributionism, including Searchlight theorists, are effectively arguing that the agent need not think of involuntary states as hers. But attributionists argue that the non-voluntary aspects of our selves are importantly ours, and within the realm of what we should be seen as responsible for. Robert Adams (1985), for example, famously argues that we are responsible for our involuntary sins: "Our desires and emotions, though not voluntary, are responses of ours, and affect the moral significance of our lives, not only by influencing our voluntary actions, but also just by being what they are, and by manifesting themselves involuntarily. Who we are morally depends on a complex and incompletely integrated fabric that includes desires and feelings as well as deliberations and choices" (1985, 11). Adams's point here is that our involuntary motivations are part of us in an important way. We should thus acknowledge that. As he says, "To refuse to take responsibility for one's emotions

---

[15] I discussed attributionism in Chapter 4. Traditionally, attributionism is contrasted with volitionalism, where volitionalists think that voluntary control is necessary for responsibility. The taxonomy here is disputed, but I take it that the Searchlight View is a version of volitionalism, where Searchlight theorists focus on awareness as a necessary condition for responsibility.

and motives is to be inappropriately alienated from one's own emotional and appetitive faculties" (1985, 16). I am arguing for a further step: we should sometimes take responsibility for our purely inadvertent acts too.

It might be useful to make a distinction between guilt, which we could say requires voluntary action in some sense, and remorse, which attaches to less voluntary, or to involuntary, sins.[16] Taking responsibility in the sorts of case I am concerned with does not make guilt fitting. But, it does entail feeling remorse rather than mere agent regret. It is conceptually possible to feel remorse even for acts that were not under our control—in order to feel remorse, we just have to feel ownership of the act. So the question about the sort of action that I am interested in, purely inadvertent action, becomes a question about whether we should see the action as our own action—whether we should be prepared to own it. I shall argue that we should, not because of properties of the actions themselves, which I agree do not clearly suggest ownership by the actor. Rather, I argue, our relationships require that we take on ownership and hence responsibility.

This is not to deny that both remorse and regret come in several shades. The guilt that I feel for something that I did in full knowledge of its wrongness is different, and not just in intensity, to remorse that I feel for something I did with a glimmer of understanding, or something that I did through being overcome by hidden motives, or something that I did entirely inadvertently. The agent regret that I feel when my action directly has a bad result is different to the agent regret that I feel when my action has bad results much more indirectly, or when I am part of a bad chain of events without any action at all. Helen of Troy might feel something in the agent regret family when the Trojan War begins, but it is very different to what the lorry driver would feel on killing a pedestrian. The scale here is not just intensity, as I say. Agent regret can be more intense than remorse: Williams's lorry driver might feel very intense agent regret, whereas I feel only minor remorse, but it is surely remorse, for the grumpy remark I made to my spouse this morning. The different shades of remorse and agent regret involve different levels of ownership of the action and, also, extrinsic features, such as who else is involved, and how they are affected. The agent regret of a lorry driver

---

[16] Thanks to Michael McKenna for this suggestion.

who kills someone he knows is likely to be different, not just in intensity, to the agent regret of the lorry driver who kills a stranger.

4. Taking Responsibility in Relationships

Let's return to Clarke's case of the forgotten milk. The case is very trivial as Clarke has it, so consider another example with the same structure. Let's imagine that Perdita borrows a friend's sentimentally valuable necklace, and loses it. Clearly, when we fail in our duties to our loved ones we should think carefully about our motives. Perdita examines her own conscience: was she careless? Did she knowingly do something silly? Did she take the duty to look after the necklace insufficiently seriously? Let's imagine that she finds her conscience clear: there was no bad will: Perdita simply forgot where she put the necklace. In such a case it seems plausible that Perdita should feel really bad about what she did, *even though* there was no bad will. She should apologize, she should try to make amends, but more than that, it is plausible that she should feel something in the region of remorse.

Imagine two versions of the conversation where she tells her friend she has lost the necklace:

PERDITA: I'm very sorry, but I lost your necklace. It was a pure glitch, no bad will. I'll buy you another one. I know that won't make up for it of course, but clearly it is all I can do.

FRIEND: Oh no! Um, What do you mean, no bad will?

PERDITA: I just mean you don't have to blame me for carelessness or not taking the duty to look after your necklace seriously enough. I know how much it meant to you. I was perfectly careful, I didn't do anything reckless, I just forgot where I put it.

FRIEND: You are saying it was not your fault?

PERDITA: I am saying I was not *at* fault, it was just one of those things.

In that conversation, Perdita is right, strictly speaking—she had no bad will. But the conversation reveals something lacking. I will argue that it reveals that she is not sufficiently invested in her duty to her friend. The problem is that she focuses on her own conscience, rather than on the other person. She takes a very strict approach to her own responsibility— she had no bad will, so she is not at fault. But when we think about the loss to her friend, the fact that the necklace is now gone forever, *that* seems like the thing to focus on here, not the bad will or lack thereof. Compare this version of Perdita, who takes responsibility:

> PERDITA: I'm very sorry, but I lost your necklace. I'm so sorry, I feel really terrible. I'll buy you another one. I know that won't make up for it of course, but clearly it is all I can do.
>
> FRIEND: Oh no!
>
> PERDITA: I am really, really, sorry. I know how much it meant to you. I am so angry with myself about this. If there is anything I can do to make up for it, please tell me.
>
> FRIEND: What happened?
>
> PERDITA: I just forgot where I put it. I have no excuse. I wish I could undo it.

The Perdita who takes responsibility is acting as her relationship requires. In order to make that convincing, I need to defend the background assumptions about what relationships require. Let's take a step back and look at the various things we expect in relationships. First of all, although the exact nature and extent of the duties varies, we accept that there are special duties that apply in personal relationships. Some of these duties are practical, and are usually formally or informally negotiated within a relationship: who will do what in terms of house cleaning, childcare, earning money, and so on. Some duties are more general, for example the duties to protect, to nurture, duties of companionship, of loyalty, of solidarity, and so on. There can be legitimate variation, that is to say, variation within basically good and valuable relationships about how these duties work. Some couples insist on monogamy, others don't, and there may be differences in what counts as monogamy. The exact details of what sort of duties are required by the emotional commitment can vary. One couple may have a strict rule that when one of them is ready to leave a party, they will both leave. Another couple may be more flexible.

But just talking about duties will not capture all that characterizes personal relationships. There are also, crucially, attitudes and feelings. Feelings, notoriously, cannot be commanded. But they are usually thought of as essential to personal relationships. A wife who dutifully leaves the party when her husband wants to might be fulfilling her duty of companionship and solidarity. However, if she doesn't feel any empathy, and doesn't have a desire to be with her husband—if she lacks a sense that being without him at the party would be less good anyway—then leaving with him is not worth much. A father who takes his child to the football every Saturday may be doing his best to fulfil his duty of care, but without the attendant paternal feelings it is rather pointless. It is clear that many duties in personal relationships are not just mechanical duties, one has to be *invested* in them in the right way.[17]

We can contrast duties that require attitudinal back up with the purely legalistic duties we have in many impersonal settings. I have a duty to park my car in such a way that it does not block anyone else in, I have a duty to pay my taxes, I have a duty to put my garbage out on the right day in the right container. It doesn't matter how I feel about these duties, it only matters that I do them. If I rent a car and accidentally scratch it, I am most likely liable for the damage, but there is no reason to feel or to express remorse. I do not have to take ownership of my inadvertent failure to do my duty. In taking on duties to the rental car company I am only taking on a legalistic duty, to return the car in the condition I found it, or failing that, to pay the penalty. I may be entirely indifferent to the choice between fulfilling the duty and paying the penalty. Whereas, with the special duties that come with and demarcate my personal relationships, attitudinal back up is required. I need to do my duty, but I also need to be invested in doing my duty in the right way. Thus a certain kind of emotional work may be needed, work to align one's emotions with what is required.

When thinking about the duties of personal relationships, and what it is to be invested in them, we usually focus on how we feel about *having* the duty, and about *doing* it. I will take for granted that we have a good sense of how investment in duties works with regard to how we feel about having and doing our duties within relationships. My interest is in a different aspect of investment. I will argue that investment in our duties has implications for how we should react to failure to do our duties to our loved ones.

Clearly, when failure in our duties to our loved ones results from some sort of bad will, guilt or remorse is fitting. But failure can be inadvertent too. I will try to show that, in certain circumstances within personal

---

[17] Marcia Baron (1984) makes this point in arguing that there are emotional duties.

relationships, remorse is the right response to our inadvertent failings too. It is part of being invested in the duties that we have, and the duties and investment in those duties are together what makes a relationship a personal relationship of the particular sort that it is. Or, to put it another way, being invested in the duties of personal relationships in the right way requires taking on extended responsibility. It requires owning our failures, feeling remorse, and not just regret when we fail, even when that failure is inadvertent.

At this point we need to return to the question of what blame is. As I argued in Chapter 4, ordinary blame is communicative. Imagine the conversation between Perdita and her friend. When the friend asks, 'what happened?', we can take that as her asking whether Perdita has an excuse—that is the standard move before engaging in blame.

> PERDITA: I am so sorry, I lost your necklace.
> FRIEND: Oh no! What happened?
> PERDITA: I spaced out. Not because I did anything careless—it was just a glitch.

How should the friend respond at this point? She would probably be slightly baffled. In this sort of case it is not at all clear that she should take 'spacing out' as an excuse. In fact, in a normal conversation, the onus is clearly on Perdita to indicate how she thinks the loss of the necklace should be taken. The situation itself is just a bit ambiguous. And as I indicated earlier, Perdita has a choice: she can either take responsibility, or she can argue that spacing out should be taken as an excusing condition.

In my presentation of the earlier conversations, I tried to elicit the intuition that Perdita would be being a better friend if she takes responsibility. I can now say more about why that is. Duties in relationships require a sort of investment. In not taking responsibility in this case, Perdita would be showing that she is more concerned with herself than with her friend. The act is caused by a glitch, so it is not independently clear that the act is Perdita's. But what Perdita needs to focus on is that from her friend's point of view, Perdita is the one that lost the necklace. Perdita should care more about her friend's loss. The thought that her friend has been hurt by Perdita's (inadvertent) action should be enough for Perdita to set aside quibbles about the exact causal origin of her act, and own it. Thus, she should accept responsibility, allow herself to feel remorse, and express that remorse.

Imagine a different case, where Perdita rents a necklace from a jewellery rental company, and loses it in the same sort of way, through simply spacing out, suffering a glitch. In that case, Perdita should certainly take on liability (pay for the necklace), and may feel angry and frustrated with herself that she wasted money. But there is no requirement that she take on responsibility, no one needs her to do that. Furthermore, going back to Raz's view, which says that we should take responsibility for the sake of our own self-respect, we can now see that self-respect is not what is chiefly at issue here. In fact, the most psychologically healthy and self-respectful thing to do in this sort of case is often not to dwell on it, but rather to shrug it off and move on.

The difference between the two cases is that in the case where Perdita's glitch has hurt her friend, there is someone there to whom she must answer. The friend has been injured, and not by something inanimate, but by Perdita. When the friend asks Perdita, 'what happened?', she is making a legitimate move in the conversation: and to reach resolution, she needs either a satisfactory excuse or some appropriate remorse. Blame in personal relationships is a plea for recognition and acceptance of a wrong done, a plea for remorse. In the absence of a clear excuse (and spacing out is certainly not a clear excuse), Perdita shows her respect and love for her friend by accepting that the action is her own, and feeling remorse. Perdita need not feel full blown guilt. After all, it is clear that she did not do something *knowingly* wrong. Likewise, Perdita's friend need not engage in deep and lasting resentment. The point is that the friend needs to see that Perdita is engaging with her, responding to her being hurt, and to the fact that Perdita hurt her. Agent regret, at least in the thinnest sense, would not be enough. Thin agent regret does not fully answer the call of the injured party. A blame conversation is appropriate, though it is not the same as the sort of blame conversation that is appropriate in cases of ordinary blameworthiness.

In an ordinary blame conversation, the fierceness of the blamer's blame should be more or less proportional to the injury and the extent to which the agent failed to try. The blamee should feel remorse and, similarly, that amount of remorse should depend on how bad the offence was as well as how flawed the offender's quality of will was. Various other factors affect what the further steps are: apology, reparations, forgiveness, and so on. In an extended blame conversation, by contrast, the right move for the blamee is remorse, but it would not usually be appropriate for the blamer to indulge in fierce blame, even if the injury is severe. Rather, the appropriate move is to accept the blamee's remorse as sufficient, and to move on. Similarly, the blamee should be willing to feel some remorse, but it need not be directly proportional to the injury. Of course, they may feel a great deal of agent regret mingled with remorse in cases of severe injury, and these things are hard to disentangle. My point is not to lay down the exact rubric for appropriate reaction. My point is just that some remorse is apt, but it works differently to the way that remorse works in ordinary blameworthiness.

5. Impersonal Relationships and Implicit Bias

A worry that might arise here is that there is no firm dividing line between the relationships that demand that we take on extended responsibility and those that require liability alone, just as there is no firm dividing line between personal relationships and more formal trust or duty involving relationships. What do we want from a doctor who is performing surgery on us? Or a teacher who looks after and teaches our children all day?

First and foremost we want them to do a good job, of course: we want them *not* to space out and make a fatal error. That is the big difference with personal relationships, where the most important requirement is that the loved one has the right sort of loving and committed attitude. The first and foremost requirement of doctors and other professionals is they do not make mistakes, that they take the right level of precautions and that the system is designed so that a glitch does not result in a bad outcome. So what attitude do we hope for if the doctor or the teacher *does* suffer a glitch, and does something harmful? Does it matter to us that they take on responsibility as opposed to mere liability? As I say, I bring these cases up precisely because they are not easy. But I would venture that, particularly in the case of the surgeon, we do not need remorse. We just need her to be professional.

Let's think through how we think the surgeon should feel if she, despite having taken all possible measures to do everything right, and having no evidence that she is out of sorts, forgets to reattach some crucial part of the patient. There are lots of reactions she should have that are not remorse. First, she should search her conscience carefully: did she do anything reckless? Did she ignore any signs that she was out of sorts?

In many, if not most cases of medical negligence it is likely that the doctor *did* knowingly, or through carelessness, cut a corner. The standard for reasonable care is so high in these life or death cases—you must double check and triple check and then check again that everything is correct—that it is hard for pure negligence to translate into a bad outcome. Second, clearly, she should think about how the patient and the patient's family feels, and react to that with sympathy and empathy. Third, possibly she should feel a form of agent regret, something milder than remorse, but something that reflects awareness that she was the one who forgot the crucial step.

But I do not think that we need more than that. Imagine that a hospital staff member comes in and delivers the news that an operation has been botched, and let us stipulate that there was no bad will, and that the patient's family knows that there was no bad will. Imagine that the staff member informs the family that the doctor would like to apologize. That might be acceptable, as I said, apology is sometimes just acceptance of liability or expression of regret. But what would not be acceptable at all would be the doctor wringing her hands and expressing her remorse, signalling her desire to go through the blame conversation with the family. What the doctor owed was to do her best, and if that failed, to accept liability, to make reparations in whatever way possible.

It is worth stressing that liability is a serious matter. One conclusion to draw from my arguments sounds slightly absurd—that the person who forgets the milk is blameworthy for forgetting the milk, but the doctor who inadvertently kills someone is not. That is a misleading way to put things: first, the doctor may be subject to very serious sanctions as a result of her liability. She may lose her licence, for example. The thought is not that she is 'off the hook'. The thought is rather that remorse is not the appropriate reaction, so long as her failure was truly independent of a flawed will. Agent regret, rather than remorse is appropriate. Second, the appropriate remorse in the milk forgetter's case can be mild, while the appropriate agent regret in the doctor's case could be very intense. Finally, the blameworthiness of the milk forgetter is a special sort of blameworthiness, extended blameworthiness. In the final section I argue that it is real blameworthiness, but we need not see it as exactly the same as other sorts of blameworthiness.

There is one place that the need to take responsibility might go beyond our personal relationships, and that is where a morally faulty act is due to implicit bias. Implicit bias may involve problematic motivations at a deep level, or it may somehow bypass the will altogether. Either way, it is in the category I am interested in in this chapter: ambiguous agency. What should an agent do when faced with a complaint that she has acted in a biased way? Sometimes our biases reveal themselves in personal relationships, as when a father refuses to give his daughter the freedom, or the education, or simply the respect, that his sons take for granted. But more often, and very commonly, our biases reveal themselves in the context of professional and other impersonal relationships.[18]

An implicit bias is not usually acquired deliberately or through carelessness, and so the agent is not usually blameworthy for acquiring the bias. However, the mere fact that a bias is caused by external forces does not mean that it does not implicate the agent's will, and there is good reason to think that implicit biases often implicate the agent's will. People who test positive for implicit racist biases also tend to exhibit avoidance behaviour, suggesting that there is something visceral going on, something that it would be hard to characterize without referring to the agent's deep motivations.[19] In other words, we could think of implicit bias as working a bit like Kleinbart's insensitivity. An agent might be trying very hard to do well, to act in an egalitarian way, and yet end up being swayed by deep sexist or racist motivations.

Alternatively, it is possible that we should see biases more on the model of glitches. Returning to the point that implicit biases seem to come from outside us, there is another way to understand this so that it makes more sense as a potential excuse. It might be that the operation of biases *bypasses* our will. We might just absorb information about stereotypes and reproduce it in our behaviour without any attitude being involved at all. On this picture we are, as animals, as machines, partly automated.[20]

---

[18] I discuss taking responsibility for implicit bias in more detail in my 2018.

[19] Research by R. Fazio et al. (1995) shows a correlation between implicit racism and sitting further away from people of that race. G. R. Bessenof and J. W. Sherman (2000) demonstrate a similar correlation between bias against fat people and avoidance behavior. These and other results are discussed in N. Dasgupta (2004). My general point here is independent of any particular empirical results: the idea is just that our unconscious biases may be related to reactions like dislike and disgust, and therefore implicate our deep attitudes to others.

[20] This view is suggested by the psychologist John Bargh (2005). I owe the reference to Holly Smith's discussion (2011b, 135). Smith concedes that if there are indeed fully automatic processes then we are not blameworthy for them, and her overall view is that we are blameworthy only if a sufficient proportion of our attitudes are involved in our behavior.

If our biases operate by bypassing our wills, then it cannot be said that we have a bad will in exhibiting bias. Even if implicit biases are automated, and do not engage the agent's motivations, and so do not reflect bad will, they nonetheless seem to issue from agency. They do not seem to be in the category of mere events. If I unknowingly discriminate against the women on the shortlist, this is something *I have done*. It seems too quick to say that I am not responsible in any way.

Implicit bias seems to me to be a case of ambiguous agency. So the agent has a choice: what should she do, when faced with an injured party, someone that she has acted in a biased way towards? Is taking on liability enough? Imagine a case where a white doctor fails to prescribe sufficient pain relief to a black patient. Later, the doctor reads the evidence that shows that the medical profession is often biased in ways that result in differential pain relief prescriptions according to race.[21] She comes to see that, through racial bias, she allowed this patient to suffer much more pain than was necessary. Let's take for granted that the doctor really was trying her best in this case. Let's assume also that she is willing to take on liability as applicable. Is that enough?

The issue here is about how respect works in this sort of relationship. The doctor has done something disrespectful as well as harmful. That is not exactly like the case when she inadvertently fails to reattach an important part of the patient during surgery. There, her inadvertent fault is certainly harmful, but it is not disrespectful. I argued that she need not feel remorse when her inadvertent action is harmful, so long as she takes on liability. But this case is different. Her action expresses disrespect whether she likes it or not, and the person that she has harmed and disrespected is entitled to react with resentment. In other words, a blame conversation makes sense.

In arguing that a blame conversation makes sense in the case of personal relationships, I argued that taking responsibility for inadvertent fault is an essential part of investment in the duties of relationships. Here the role of investment is the same. Insofar as we owe respect to our fellows, it is something that requires investment. It is not mechanical, or legalistic. We cannot respect our fellow people without attitudinal back up. Taking responsibility for inadvertent disrespect is part of the

---

[21] See Campbell and Edwards (2012) for a review of the evidence that this is the case.

required attitudinal back up. It is a way to show the person who has been slighted that they are respected, and a way to demonstrate investment in a shared community.

One thing to note here is that the extended blame conversation is not obligatory. As always, the blamer has some discretion in how to proceed. In the scenario described, the patient probably deals with this sort of bias all the time, and it would be understandable for her to recuse herself from the blame conversation, and even to move towards the objective stance.[22] But let's suppose that the patient is willing to engage. At that point, it is up to the doctor to either brush it off as a random error, or to take ownership of her fault, even if she does not express that to the patient in clear terms.[23] In taking ownership, in being willing to feel remorse, the doctor is doing what is necessary to show that she does respect her patient, that she wants to be respected in turn, that she sees the social meaning of her offence. In focusing on the social meaning, rather than what she herself intended, the doctor is prioritizing the patient's status as respectworthy, and going some way to undoing what she did.

In sum, in cases where an agent acts in a biased way through ambiguous agency, it is very plausible that she should take responsibility. As members of the same community, the community of people, we should respect each other. Respect, like personal relationships, requires investment. It sometimes means focusing more on the harm done to the other person than on the limits of one's own responsibility. In taking responsibility, we accept extended blameworthiness.

6. Avoiding Blameworthiness

This leads to a worry: it seems that you can avoid blameworthiness in this sort of case by refusing to take it on.[24] But, it might be objected, surely that makes you *more* blameworthy, not less so. The first thing to point

---

[22] As Strawson suggests, it sometimes makes sense to move to the objective stance even when we see the offending agent as an agent, because the strains of communicative engagement are too much.

[23] Part of the problem is about *expressing* remorse: in impersonal relationships, it is very hard to judge what moves are appropriate in an actual conversation. There are firm boundaries for impersonal relationships and expressions of emotion are usually out of bounds.

[24] Fischer and Ravizza consider this objection to their account of accepting responsibility, and give basically the same response that I give here (1998, 220).

out is that agents who treat other agents badly can be held liable, and that can be a weighty matter. Liability cannot be avoided by refusing to take it on. Second, it is worth remembering that in real life cases of inadvertent action, the agent is often blameworthy in the ordinary way, for not having taken the indirect measures that would have prevented her harmful action. Given all we know about unconscious bias, for example, and how much work has been done to raise awareness and suggest ways to ameliorate it or avoid it, people who nonetheless exhibit bias in harmful ways are very often blameworthy for not taking it seriously enough, for not trying hard enough to do well by Morality, which requires fair treatment for everyone. So we should remind ourselves that we are talking about stipulative cases, cases where the agent genuinely did try hard enough.

In those cases it is true that, in a sense, you can avoid blameworthiness by refusing to take it on. My response to that worry is that in this context, we should see blameworthiness as a privilege, not a burden.[25] Think of a romantic relationship in which one person gradually stops seeing their partner as a proper interlocutor, stops holding them accountable. That is a sign that the relationship has dissolved. Although being blameworthy, and being blamed, sting in the moment, over the long term it is the better way to be. Taking responsibility is part of being in relationships, part of being a member of a community. We can let go of all that, but estrangement and alienation are a high price to pay for avoiding blameworthiness.

It is worth stressing that, on my view, taking responsibility is not a duty, and nor is it a virtue.[26] It is not something we ought to do for first order moral reasons, and so I avoid being committed to the strange sounding conclusion that if one does take responsibility one is blameworthy, and if one does not, one is blameworthy for not taking responsibility. Rather, taking extended responsibility is sometimes fitting, but it is morally optional. Whether it is a good idea depends on the social context. Sometimes our relationships require it, sometimes they do not. Sometimes our relationships are worth preserving, sometimes they are not. As I shall argue in the next section, not all relationships are equal,

---

[25] James Lenman makes this point in his account of a contractualist basis for responsibility (2006, 20). See also Christopher Bennett (2008), and Duff (2001).

[26] As I pointed out above, Enoch thinks of taking responsibility as a duty (2012). Susan Wolf suggests that it is a virtue (2001).

and not all the requirements that we are presented with should be taken as given.

A related point here is that we might think that it is virtuous or noble for the injured party to step back from the blame conversation, to say, 'No need to apologize! I see that it was just a glitch.' Sometimes that might be appropriate, but it is not always so. Sometimes to step back is to disengage more than the blamee would want. As I pointed out above, a victim of a racially biased injury may decide to move towards the objective stance. That is perfectly legitimate in the face of that sort of injury. But it is certainly a way of withdrawing from a social relationship, of giving up on the other person. It is not what we usually want from our friends, loved ones, or even our fellow community members. We want to be taken seriously, to be seen as agents. We want our actions to matter as actions.

7. The Psychology of Taking Responsibility

An important question that arises about this account is whether it is psychologically possible to take responsibility. It seems to me obvious that it is, in fact we do it all the time, as Williams points out. Telemachus takes responsibility immediately, automatically. He doesn't have to think it through. This is important: taking responsibility for our inadvertent harms to loved ones is not something that we should do on a case by case basis. Rather, it is a standing disposition we should have, to own our failures. Our friends and loved ones need to feel that we are solid, that we are committed in certain ways. We agree to limit what we will count as an excuse, we extend responsibility in the realm of our relationships.

However, we do not always take on the right amount of responsibility. We are familiar with cases where people take on too little or too much responsibility due to individual character quirks. Some agents are just like the first version of Perdita, the necklace loser: denying responsibility, shrugging off blame, focusing on explaining the lack of bad will instead of focusing on the slight. Some people take a very strict approach to their own responsibility. Such people are hard to be with. They may be at the edge of our friendship circles, but we tend not to get too close to them, we tend not to marry them. On the other hand there are people who take on too much, who feel bad to too large a degree about too many things. 'Give yourself a break!' we want to say, 'it's not your fault'. Such people can also be hard to be with, though taking on too much responsibility seems a less serious flaw than taking on too little.

Of course, that raises the question, 'how much responsibility is the right amount?' We negotiate the terms of our own relationships, both what duties we take on, and how much extended responsibility we take on. We can demand and accept more or less from our friends and loved ones, depending on what we need and want. Our needs and wants can legitimately vary, and relationships vary accordingly. However, we should be aware of the fact that what we expect from ourselves and from others in personal relationships can be socially influenced, for example along gender lines, as well as being individual quirks.

It is a common observation, and much discussed by sociologists, that women tend to take on more *responsibilities*, in the sense of feeling that they have more duties, than men. For example, women in a heterosexual relationship are very likely to do most of the 'kin work'.[27] They do it as part of the deal of being a family, and they are invested in these special duties, to send cards, to keep track of ages, to remember distant cousins, to make room for and organize family visits. (The claim is not that women are essentially or by nature invested in kin work. Rather it is that this is 'women's work' in the anthropological sense—the work that has traditionally been assigned to women in a hierarchically structured society.)

It is fairly obvious that women take on more of the special duties in relationships than men do, and that is expected in our society. It is less obvious, but it is important, that part of what we expect is that women take the duties to heart more. It is not a huge leap to suggest that we expect women to invest more in their special duties. Here is a simple way to put the point: the duties that require investment are the special duties of relationships. If we recognize that we expect women to take on more of those duties, then we should recognize that we are asking women to

---

[27] See for example Di Leonardo (1987). Kin work and emotional work are closely connected, and both are gendered. The issue has not been discussed much by philosophers, but Iris Marion Young mentions it in the context of a critique of Marxist Feminism, and the idea of the exploitation of women's labour: "The gender socialization of women makes us tend to be more attentive to interactive dynamics than men, and makes women good at providing empathy and support for people's feelings and at smoothing over interactive tensions. Both men and women look to women as nurturers of their personal lives, and women frequently complain that when they look to men for emotional support they do not receive it" (1990, 50–1). See also Calhoun (2016), chapter 8, 'Emotional Work'.

take more responsibility. And it is easy to see how that bleeds into other areas—that even when men and women take on equal duties, it is plausible that women are socialized to take on more responsibility, and are more likely to take it to heart when they fail, even inadvertently.

This is not the place to assess the empirical facts about socialized gender differences in tendencies to take on responsibility. I am merely addressing the possibility that there are social influences on our tendencies, and it seems obvious that it is possible that there are such differences. Seeing taking on responsibility as a legitimate move in relationships might help us to understand better the social forces that result in some groups taking on too much and some too little. If we thought that the only way to be genuinely responsible, blameworthy in particular, is to have a bad will, we are simply dismissing the experience of large groups of people who feel terrible about missing Aunty Ginnie off the invitation list, even when missing her was just a glitch. My account vindicates the experience of all those, mostly women, who feel remorse in those circumstances. But my account should also give us resources to critique the system that encourages such remorse only in one gender.

A different issue about the psychology of taking on responsibility arises when we think about tragic cases. In the cases that I have focused on, agents fail in duties to their loved ones, but in mundane ways. There are, of course, tragic cases, where people inadvertently cause the death of their own children, for example, and these, I think, should be dealt with differently. Our relationships do not require us to take on responsibility in those cases, and this is because the psychological strain is already too much. Agent regret in such cases is unavoidable, but more than that is not healthy.

8. Extended Blameworthiness and the Shape of Remorse

I have argued that taking on responsibility for inadvertent faults makes good sense in the context of personal relationships. It is part of the requisite investing in the duties of a personal relationship. It is part of demonstrating that the other person is being taken seriously as a person. Similarly, taking responsibility can make good sense in the context of some impersonal relationships. In cases where an inadvertent act expresses disrespect, an agent who cares about the broad social relationship she has with her peers has a reason to take on extended blameworthiness, to show her fellow people that she does, after all, respect them, and to ask for respect in return. The practice of taking responsibility is justified by its role in our interpersonal relationships.

This raises a 'wrong kind of reason worry'. I seem to be trying to justify taking responsibility by its consequences. But surely, it will be objected, we ought to take responsibility when we are responsible. If we are not responsible in the first place we cannot take responsibility for the reason that it would be helpful, or good for our relationships to do so. That is the wrong sort of reason to take responsibility. To put it another way, the shape of remorse dictates that it is only fitting to feel remorse when you have acted subjectively wrongly.[28]

The suggestion I am making here, that we should sometimes take responsibility, aims to disrupt the standard view of what would count as the wrong sort of reason in this context. It can be fitting to take responsibility even when there is no pre-existing blameworthiness in the ordinary sense. The phenomenon of ambiguous agency opens a space where it is not unfitting to take responsibility, to feel remorse.

It might be objected that remorse has a narrower profile than that, that ambiguous agency does not license remorse. But that is just to flatly deny the claim I have been arguing for, that we can take ownership of our acts when our agency is ambiguous. Here is an analogy: sometimes happiness is fitting, sometimes it is not. Sometimes, it is not clear whether an occurrence makes happiness fitting. Happiness is obviously a complex emotion, and so, I am arguing, is remorse. When it is not clear whether happiness is fitting, for example, as a response to a rainbow, it is not unfitting to feel happiness. And one good reason to respond with happiness in this sort of circumstance is that one lives a better life overall by being happy at the sight of a rainbow. If we can become the sorts of people who are cheered by everyday beauty, we should. Similarly, reacting with remorse in a case of ambiguous agency is not unfitting. And sometimes, it makes sense overall to react with remorse.

---

[28] D'Arms and Jacobson (2000) argue that the fittingness of emotional reactions should be distinguished from extraneous reasons to feel emotions, such as moral reasons. Fittingness is determined by the 'shape' of the emotion, which is a way of saying that the emotion presents the world as being a certain way. If it is that way, the emotion is fitting. The 'shape' of remorse is exactly what I am questioning.

Furthermore, as social beings, we cannot help ourselves from taking on responsibility when we have injured others. This is the point Williams is making in his account of agent regret, when he says: "To insist on such a conception [one that rules out all luck], moreover, would, apart from other kinds of absurdity, suggest a large falsehood: that we might, if we conducted ourselves clear-headedly enough, entirely detach ourselves from the unintentional aspects of our actions" (1981, 125). We cannot detach ourselves from the unintentional aspects of our action. Nor should we. We should accept that blameworthiness sometimes extends beyond subjective wrongdoing.

Extended blameworthiness, that which comes from taking responsibility, does not amount to a paradigm case of ordinary blameworthiness. Extended blameworthiness is like ordinary blameworthiness in that it invites communicative blame, and assumes the shared understanding that makes that possible. However, the blame conversation may be truncated, in that the injured party should not expect the blamee to go through all the steps of the ordinary blame conversation. But there are lots of variations in how a blame conversation should go, and there are various conditions that affect what is apt.

9. Conclusion

In this chapter, I have argued that there is a third way to be blameworthy. Sometimes, when we generally are in the realm of ordinary blame, but our problematic action is not subjectively wrong, we should take responsibility, and accept extended blameworthiness.

I started with Kleinbart, whose blunder occurred despite his trying as hard as he should have. The problem with Kleinbart is that his blunder was caused by his deep motivations, so it is not at all clear that his acting subjectively rightly is the full story about his praise- or blameworthiness. The traditional answers in responsibility theory ask us to choose between two mutually exclusive approaches: either Kleinbart is blameworthy because he had bad motives, or he is praiseworthy because he tried hard and was doing as well as he could by his own lights. But a pluralist approach can say something more subtle. First, as I suggest in Chapter 6, a pluralist can say that Kleinbart is praiseworthy in the ordinary way but locally blameworthy in the detached way.

Although I think that that is a satisfactory answer, I think that another approach is also possible, and important to recognize. Cases like Kleinbart's, where there is a relationship at stake, draw our attention to the personal relationship, and the norms of a blame conversation in that context. I have argued that sometimes, the most important thing in a blame conversation is not the quality of will of the person whose act was problematic. Rather, the most important thing is the fact that somebody hurt someone, even if they did it inadvertently. Kleinbart's wife has been injured by Kleinbart, but Kleinbart's agency in this case is ambiguous. So Kleinbart has a choice. He can either insist that his conscience is clear, he did his best; or, he can take responsibility.

The same applies in cases where there is no bad will at all. We often act in ways that are entirely inadvertent, we suffer glitches, memory lapses, momentary fugues. These causes of action are not at all the sort of thing that responsibility theorists usually think of as constituting relevant quality of will, the right sort of thing to hold people responsible for. But they are not totally outside agency either. It is not the case that a glitch is an external cause of a bodily movement, or that the bad effects of these inadvertent actions are equivalent to outcome luck. There is an important sense in which some inadvertent actions are actions of agents.

So agents who have inadvertently injured someone have a choice. They can either focus on explaining to the person they have hurt or disrespected that they had no bad will, that despite appearances they were trying their hardest. Or, they can take responsibility. They can take ownership of the agentially ambiguous action and accept extended blameworthiness. This is not to say that agents should consider whether to take responsibility on a case by case basis. Instead, they should cultivate a standing disposition to take responsibility in cases of ambiguous agency in the context of personal relationships. They should be willing to feel remorse, and to accept the blame of the person they have hurt. The blame conversation that ensues is governed by different norms to an ordinary blame conversation. It is not usually appropriate for the blamer to go in for full blooded blaming. Rather she should accept that the blamee has taken responsibility, and is feeling some remorse, and then let it go.

9

Conclusion

My aim in this book has been to illuminate the relationship between our normative concepts, rightness and wrongness, and our normative responsibility concepts, praise- and blameworthiness, and to give an account of the various ways that we can be blameworthy.

I started by drawing a distinction between different accounts of rightness and wrongness. Clearly, deontic concepts like rightness and wrongness are constrained by a need to be relevant to actual agents: to be connected to what actual agents can do, and what they can know. In other words, there is some sort of responsibility constraint on accounts of rightness and wrongness. Deontic notions are not independent of responsibility notions. We can think of accounts of rightness and wrongness as meeting weaker or stronger versions of a responsibility constraint. I argued that although we often use a moderately objective account of obligation, one that meets only a moderate version of the responsibility constraint, and makes rightness and wrongness independent of the point of view of particular agents, we also need an account of subjective rightness. The moderately objective account of rightness is very useful as a standard to aim for, and to teach people about moral ideals. However, we also need an account of rightness that meets a stronger version of the responsibility constraint. The concept of subjective obligation has two ideas associated with it: first that subjective obligation would be action guiding, and second, that it would correlate with praiseworthiness and blameworthiness.

It turns out that action guidance, at least in the sense generally understood, is not the main raison d'être of subjective obligation. The point of a subjective account of obligation is to make sense of praise- and blameworthiness. To focus only on blameworthiness for a moment: there must be some sense in which an agent is acting wrongly, something she is doing wrong. The idea of subjective wrongness is the obvious candidate, and so I have developed an account of subjective obligation that works as an explanation of praise- and blameworthiness.

I argued that acting subjectively rightly is a matter of trying to do well by Morality. There are several features of this account of subjective obligation that might be unexpected. First, this account of subjective obligation applies only to those who understand Morality, where by 'Morality' I mean something like what Susan Wolf means by 'The True and the Good'. This is not just common sense morality, but the best we can do, collectively, at understanding morality. I use a capital letter to indicate that I am talking about a particular value system. Someone is in our moral community so long as they have a good enough grasp of Morality. This may not be a perfect grasp, it is possible to make mistakes, and one can have a good enough grasp of Morality without knowing what to do on a particular occasion.

I argued that this does not undermine the accessibility of subjective obligation. It might seem that if we judge whether an agent has acted subjectively rightly by reference to an external standard, one they may or may not have access to, we are not talking about the agent's subjective point of view at all. But this is to misunderstand the scope of my account of subjective obligation. Of course there are agents for whom Morality is not accessible, but those agents are in a different category. Agents who grasp Morality are the ones with whom we can communicate, and blame in the ordinary way. For these agents, subjective obligation in my sense is always accessible. Given what we are interested in, an account of subjective obligation that correlates with praise- and blameworthiness, it makes sense to limit an account of subjective obligation to those in our moral community.

I argue that acting subjectively rightly is a matter of *trying*, trying to do well by Morality, rather than doing what one believes is morally required. This captures the complexity of subjective obligation, which is not just to do what one believes best at a particular moment, but to cultivate general dispositions and attitudes that will be responsive to changing circumstances. Part of that is trying to balance complex value choices, thinking about how to deal with uncertainty, and how to move on from past mistakes. I illustrated the point with an analogy: trying to do well by Morality is a bit like trying to be a good parent. We don't always know what to do, but we know enough to have something to go on in making hard decisions. So long as we are sincerely trying, we are acting well by our own lights. We are acting subjectively rightly.

In Chapter 4 I argued that my account of subjective obligation does indeed yield a plausible account of ordinary praise- and blameworthiness. First, I pointed out that all plausible accounts of praise- and blameworthiness are consistent with something like a 'reflexivity requirement'. In order for an agent to be praiseworthy in the ordinary way, she must know what she is doing in some sense. Being drawn to the good like a moth to the flame would not be praiseworthy. The question then is how *much* awareness is required. I argued that the common sense account of trying that I defended in Chapter 3 gives us the right level: the agent must have the right sort of background knowledge of her aim, and accept it as an aim. If she tries to do well by Morality she is praiseworthy, if she does not try hard enough, or fails to try altogether, she is blameworthy.

This picture of blameworthiness naturally corresponds to a communicative account of praise and blame. When we praise or blame someone we are communicating with them, which means that we are relying on their understanding us: it is essential that they can see what we are disapproving of and why. When we blame someone in the ordinary way, we are asking them to accept that they acted wrongly. The fact that they acted wrongly by their own lights makes this reasonable. We then move through a blame conversation, which can vary according to context, but at the very least involves a call for acknowledgement of fault, and then, ideally, acceptance of the blame and remorse. It might further involve apology, reparations, forgiveness, and so on.

Ordinary blame applies only to those who grasp Morality. Agents who are outside our moral community are excluded from the realm of ordinary praise- and blameworthiness. But agents outside our moral community are not exempt. Rather, I argue, we blame them in the detached way. Detached blame is not communicative. The methodology for understanding detached blame is very different to the methodology for understanding ordinary blame. My analysis of ordinary praise- and blameworthiness takes the agent's quality of will, in particular her mental activity in acting subjectively rightly or wrongly, as the starting point. It is because the agent has a certain quality of will that communicative praise and blame make sense. By contrast, my analysis of detached praise and blame is the other way around. We react to wrongdoing by an agent with a species of blame. But we are not necessarily diagnosing the agent's quality of will. We are reacting to what they have *done*, and our reaction is more about us, and more aimed at other members of our moral community than at the perpetrator. Thus my account of detached blameworthiness is not a quality of will account.

I go on to look at the various sorts of excuse that apply to the different species of blameworthiness. It is important to see that a simple excuse from someone in our moral community is a plea that although an action was objectively wrong, it was not subjectively wrong—the agent was not acting wrongly by her own lights. Perhaps she was ignorant, or not in control. This raises the question of whether there can be excuses for acting subjectively wrongly. I argue that so long as the conditions of responsible agency are met, an agent who acts subjectively wrongly is blameworthy.

Having said that, there are complications. First, there may be mitigating circumstances, and partial excuses, which I understand as working the same way as simple excuses. The plea is a request to take more into account than is immediately visible, and see that there are factors that have made the situation more difficult. It is possible that the agent is not acting as badly as she seemed to be acting at first glance. However, insofar as she is acting subjectively wrongly, she is blameworthy.

Another complicated case concerns agents who are acting subjectively rightly—trying to do well by Morality—who fail because of their own bad motives. In that case the person is praiseworthy in the ordinary way. However, we can blame the person in a local way in the detached mode. Someone who tries hard, but is fundamentally aggressive, or adulterous, or unloving, deserves some credit for trying hard, but in the end, our attitudes to them will be strongly influenced by our perception of who they are, of what they are like. We move away from full interpersonal engagement, at least in that sphere, and take one step towards the fully objective stance. Such patchy blame reflects the complexity of our experience: when we blame people for things they have done we are often blaming them in different ways for difference aspects of their action. Just as we might think someone is respectworthy for acting on conscience, but blameworthy (in the detached way) for acting on a corrupt morality, so we might think that someone is praiseworthy (in the ordinary way) for trying to do well by Morality, but blameworthy (in the detached way, locally) for being too selfish and mean to achieve much.

I considered what kind of excuse bad formative circumstances might be. I argued that for subjective wrongdoing, this is no excuse. So long as an agent is a competent agent and understands Morality, she can be held to the standards of subjective obligation. However, formative circumstances are relevant to detached blameworthiness. Our detached blame applies to agents. When we reflect on unfortunate circumstances, we come to see the agent as less of an agent, and we move towards the truly objective stance. From that perspective, we are less inclined to detached blame.

In Chapter 7 I explored the conditions that render some agents outside our moral community. I argued that being deeply morally ignorant is sufficient for being outside the realm of subjective obligation and ordinary blameworthiness. Agents who do not grasp Morality may not be impaired, but impairment is not necessary for exemption. On the other hand, there may be agents who are so strongly motivated to the good or the bad that they lack a moral capacity. But I argue that so long as such agents understand Morality, they are in the realm of ordinary praise- and blameworthiness.

Finally, I considered what we might say about 'psychopaths'. One way to imagine the psychology of such an agent is that she is impaired in being unable to see that Morality gives us categorical reasons for action. In that case, the agent does not grasp Morality properly and so, on my view, is not in the realm of subjective obligation and ordinary praise- and blameworthiness.

The final part of my picture was my story about extended blameworthiness. This sort of blameworthiness does not depend on quality of will at all. Rather, I argued, we can take on responsibility in situations where we have done a bad act without any bad will. We do this by cultivating a disposition to see ourselves as responsible for agentially ambiguous acts when our relationships require it.

In the end, our responsibility practices are deeply entwined with our relationships. In doing normative responsibility theory, we need to keep that in mind, to pay attention to how our relationships actually work. As Strawson puts it:

> We should think of the many different kinds of relationship which we can have with other people . . . Then we should think, in each of these connections in turn, and in others, of the kind of importance we attach to the attitudes and intentions towards us of those who stand in these relationships to us, and of the kinds of reactive attitudes and feelings to which we ourselves are prone. . . .
> The object of these commonplaces is to try to keep before our minds something it is easy to forget when we are engaged in philosophy, especially in our cool, contemporary style, viz. what it is actually like to be involved in ordinary interpersonal relationships, ranging from the most intimate to the most casual.
>
> (1962, reprinted in Watson 2003, 76–7)

Moving away from worrying about free will and working on normative responsibility theory enables us to think clearly about what our responsibility practices are actually like, and what we want from our responsibility practices. For ordinary people in our moral community, the way to judge blameworthiness is to focus on the agent's subjective wrongdoing. However, not all cases are so neat. Sometimes people are not in our moral community. Sometimes people have motives that are problematic, but are not suitable for blaming in the ordinary way. Sometimes people act badly in ways that are inadvertent. In all those cases there is a pull to some sort of blame reaction. My account gives us the resources to explain blame in these cases. We should accept that judgments of blameworthiness and blame itself are complex. We should accept that there are many ways to be blameworthy.

Bibliography

Adams, Robert Merrihew (1976). 'Motive Utilitarianism'. *Journal of Philosophy* 73: 467–81.

Adams, Robert Merrihew (1985). 'Involuntary Sins'. *Philosophical Review* 94: 3–31.

Alexander, Larry and Ferzan, Kimberley K. (2009). 'Against Negligence Liability'. In P. H. Robinson, S. P. Garvey, and K. K. Ferzan (eds.), *Criminal Law Conversations*. New York: Oxford University Press: 273–80.

Amaya, Santiago (2011). 'Slips'. *Noûs* 47 (3): 559–76.

Anderson, Elizabeth (2016). 'The Social Epistemology of Morality: Learning from the Forgotten History of the Abolition of Slavery'. In Michael Brady and Miranda Fricker (eds.), *The Epistemic Life of Groups: Essays in the Epistemology of Collectives*. Oxford: Oxford University Press: 75–94.

Anscombe, G. E. M. (1957). *Intention*. Ithaca, NY: Cornell University Press.

Aristotle (2000). *Nicomachean Ethics*. Trans. Roger Crisp. Cambridge: Cambridge University Press.

Arpaly, Nomy (2003). *Unprincipled Virtue: An Inquiry Into Moral Agency*. Oxford: Oxford University Press.

Arpaly, Nomy and Schroeder, Timothy (1999). 'Praise, Blame and the Whole Self'. *Philosophical Studies* 93 (2): 161–88.

Arpaly, Nomy and Schroeder, Timothy (2014). *In Praise of Desire*. New York: Oxford University Press.

Austin, J. L. (1956). 'A Plea for Excuses'. *Proceedings of the Aristotelian Society* 57: 1–30.

Austin, J. L. (1975). *How to Do Things With Words*. Cambridge, MA: Harvard University Press.

Bargh, J. A. (2005). 'Bypassing the Will: Toward Demystifying the Nonconscious Control of Social Behavior'. In R. R. Hassin, J. S. Uleman, and J. A. Bargh (eds.), *The New Unconscious*. Oxford: Oxford University Press: 37–60.

Baron, Marcia (1984). 'The Alleged Moral Repugnance of Acting from Duty'. *Journal of Philosophy* 81 (4): 197–220.

Baron, Marcia (1988). 'Remorse and Agent-Regret'. *Midwest Studies in Philosophy* 13 (1): 259–81.

Baron, Marcia (1995). *Kantian Ethics Almost Without Apology*. Ithaca, NY: Cornell University Press.

Baron, Marcia (2007). 'Excuses, Excuses'. *Criminal Law and Philosophy* 1 (1): 21–39.

Bell, Macalester (2013a). *Hard Feelings: The Moral Psychology of Contempt*. New York: Oxford University Press.

Bell, Macalester (2013b). 'The Standing to Blame: A Critique'. In D. Justin Coates and Neal A. Tognazzini (eds.), *Blame: Its Nature and Norms*. Oxford: Oxford University Press: 263–81.

Bennett, Christopher (2002). 'The Varieties of Retributive Experience'. *Philosophical Quarterly* 52 (207): 145–63.

Bennett, Christopher (2008). *The Apology Ritual: A Philosophical Theory of Punishment*. Cambridge: Cambridge University Press.

Bennett, Jonathan (1974). 'The Conscience of Huckleberry Finn'. *Philosophy* 49 (188): 123–34.

Bennett, Jonathan (1980). 'Accountability'. In Z. van Stratten (ed.), *Philosophical Subjects: Essays Presented to P. F. Strawson*. New York: Oxford University Press.

Bentham, Jeremy (1789). *An Introduction to the Principles of Morals and Legislation*. London: T. Payne.

Bergstrom, Lars (1996). 'Reflections on Consequentialism'. *Theoria*, 62 (1–2): 74–94.

Bessenoff, G. R. and Sherman, J. W. (2000). 'Automatic and Controlled Components of Prejudice toward Fat People: Evaluation versus Stereotype Activation'. *Social Cognition* 18: 329–53.

Björnsson, Gunnar (2017a). 'Explaining (Away) the Epistemic Condition on Moral Responsibility'. In Philip Robichaud and Jan Willem Wieland (eds.), *Responsibility: The Epistemic Condition*. New York: Oxford University Press: 146–62.

Björnsson, Gunnar (2017b). 'Explaining Away Epistemic Skepticism about Culpability'. In David Shoemaker (ed.), *Oxford Studies in Agency and Responsibility*, vol. 4. Oxford: Oxford University Press: 141–64.

Bok, Hilary (1998). *Freedom and Responsibility*. Princeton, NJ: Princeton University Press.

Brown, Campbell (2011). 'Consequentialize This'. *Ethics* 121 (4): 749–71.

Calhoun, Cheshire (1989). 'Responsibility and Reproach'. *Ethics* 99: 389–406.

Calhoun, Cheshire (2016). *Moral Aims: Essays on the Importance of Getting It Right and Practicing Morality with Others*. New York: Oxford University Press.

Campbell, C. M. and Edwards, R. R. (2012). 'Ethnic Differences in Pain and Pain Management'. *Pain Management* 2 (3): 219–30.

Chang, Ruth (1997). 'Introduction'. In Ruth Chang (ed.), *Incommensurability, Incomparability and Practical Reason*. Cambridge, MA: Harvard University Press: 1–34.

Chang, Ruth (2012). 'Are Hard Choices Cases of Incomparability?' *Philosophical Issues* 22 (1): 106–26.

Clarke, Randolph (2014). *Omissions: Agency, Metaphysics, and Responsibility*. Oxford: Oxford University Press.

Coates, D. Justin and Tognazzini, Neal A. (eds.) (2013). *Blame: Its Nature and Norms*. Oxford: Oxford University Press.

Cohen, G. A. (2006). 'Casting the First Stone: Who Can, and Who Can't, Condemn the Terrorists?' *Royal Institute of Philosophy Supplement* 58: 113–36.

D'Arms, Justin and Jacobson, Daniel (2000). 'The Moralistic Fallacy: On the "Appropriateness" of Emotions'. *Philosophical and Phenomenological Research* 61 (1): 65–90.

Darwall, Stephen (2006). *The Second-Person Standpoint: Morality, Respect, and Accountability*. Cambridge, MA: Harvard University Press.

Dasgupta, Nilanjana (2004). 'Implicit Ingroup Favoritism, Outgroup Favoritism, and Their Behavioral Manifestations'. *Social Justice Research* 17: 143–69.

Dennett, Daniel (1978). *Brainstorms*. Cambridge, MA: MIT Press.

Di Leonardo, M. (1987). 'The Female World of Cards and Holidays: Women, Families, and the Work of Kinship'. *Signs* 12 (3): 440–53.

Driver, Julia (1992). 'The Suberogatory'. *Australasian Journal of Philosophy* 70 (3): 286–95.

Driver, Julia (2001). *Uneasy Virtue*. New York: Cambridge University Press.

Driver, Julia (2011). *Consequentialism*. New York: Routledge.

Duff, R. A. (1990). *Intention, Agency and Criminal Liability*. Oxford: Blackwell.

Duff, R. A. (1996). *Criminal Attempts*. Oxford: Oxford University Press.

Duff, R. A. (2001). *Punishment, Communication, and Community*. Oxford: Oxford University Press.

Enoch, David (2012). Being Responsible, Taking Responsibility, and Penumbral Agency. In Ulrike Heuer & Gerald Lang (eds.), '*Luck, Value, and Commitment: Themes From the Ethics of Bernard Williams*'. Oxford University Press, USA.

Faraci, David and Shoemaker, David (2014). 'Huck vs. Jojo: Moral Ignorance and the (A)symmetry of Praise and Blame'. In Joshua Knobe, Tania Lombrozo, and Shaun Nichols (eds.), *Oxford Studies in Experimental Philosophy*, vol. 1. Oxford: Oxford University Press: 7–27.

Fazio, R. H., Jackson, J. R., Dunton, B. C., and Williams, C. J. (1995). 'Variability in Automatic Activation as an Unobtrusive Measure of Racial Attitudes: A Bona Fide Pipeline?' *Journal of Personal and Social Psychology* 69: 1013–27.

Feinberg, Joel (1970). 'Justice and Personal Desert'. In Feinberg, *Doing and Deserving*. Princeton, NJ: Princeton University Press: 55–94.

Feinberg, Joel (1975). 'Some Conjectures on the Concept of Respect'. *Journal of Social Philosophy* 4: 1–3.

Feldman, Fred (1986). *Doing the Best We Can*. Dordrecht: Reidel.

Feldman, Fred (1993). 'On the Consistency of Act- and Motive-Utilitarianism: A Reply to Robert Adams'. *Philosophical Studies* 70 (2): 201–12.

Feldman, Fred (2004). *Pleasure and the Good Life: Concerning the Nature, Varieties and Plausibility of Hedonism*. Oxford: Clarendon Press.

Feldman, Fred (2006). 'Actual Utility, the Objection from Impracticality, and the Move to Expected Utility'. *Philosophical Studies* 129: 49–79.

Feldman, Fred (2012). 'True and Useful: On the Structure of a Two Level Normative Theory'. *Utilitas* 24 (2): 151–71.

Fischer, John Martin and Ravizza, Mark (1998). *Responsibility and Control: An Essay on Moral Responsibility*. Cambridge: Cambridge University Press.

Fischer, John Martin and Tognazzini, Neal A. (2011). 'The Physiognomy of Responsibility'. *Philosophy and Phenomenological Research* 82 (2): 381–417.

FitzPatrick, William J. (2008). 'Moral Responsibility and Normative Ignorance: Answering a New Skeptical Challenge'. *Ethics* 118 (4): 589–613.

Frankena, William (1950). 'Obligation and Ability'. In Max Black (ed.), *Philosophical Analysis: A Collection of Essays*. London: Prentice-Hall: 148–65.

Frankfurt, H. (1969). 'Alternate Possibilities and Moral Responsibility'. *Journal of Philosophy* 66 (23): 829–39.

Frankfurt, H. (1971). 'Freedom of the Will and the Concept of a Person'. *Journal of Philosophy* 68: 5–20.

Frankfurt, H. (1988). *The Importance of What We Care About*. Cambridge: Cambridge University Press.

Frankfurt, H. (1999). *Necessity, Volition and Love*. Cambridge: Cambridge University Press.

Fricker, Miranda (2016a). 'What's the Point of Blame? A Paradigm Based Explanation'. *Noûs* 50 (1): 165–83.

Fricker, Miranda (2016b). 'Fault and No-Fault Responsibility for Implicit Prejudice: A Space for Epistemic Agent-Regret'. In Michael Brady and Miranda Fricker (eds.), *The Epistemic Life of Groups: Essays in the Epistemology of Collectives*. Oxford: Oxford University Press: 33–50.

Gensler, Harry J. (1987). 'Paradoxes of Subjective Obligation'. *Metaphilosophy* 18 (3–4): 208–13.

Goldberg, John C. P. and Zipursky, Benjamin C. (2007). 'Tort Law and Moral Luck'. 92 *Cornell L. Rev.* 1123.

Goldberg, Sanford C. (2017). 'Should Have Known'. *Synthese* 194 (8): 2863–2894.

Graham, Peter A. (2010). 'In Defense of Objectivism about Moral Obligation'. *Ethics* 121: 88–115.

Gruzalski, Bart (1981). 'Foreseeable Consequence Utilitarianism'. *Australasian Journal of Philosophy* 59: 163–76.

Guerrero, Alexander A. (2007). 'Don't Know, Don't Kill: Moral Ignorance, Culpability, and Caution'. *Philosophical Studies* 136 (1): 59–97.

Haji, Ishtiyaque (1998). *Moral Appraisability: Puzzles, Proposals, and Perplexities*. Oxford: Oxford University Press.

Hare, R. M. (1963). *Freedom and Reason*. Oxford: Clarendon Press.

Harman, Elizabeth (2011). 'Does Moral Ignorance Exculpate?' *Ratio* 24 (4): 443–68.

Hart, H. L. A. (1968). *Punishment and Responsibility*. Oxford: Oxford University Press.

Herman, Barbara (1981). 'On the Value of Acting from the Motive of Duty'. *Philosophical Review* 90 (3): 359–82.

Hieronymi, Pamela (2004). 'The Force and Fairness of Blame'. *Philosophical Perspectives* 18 (1): 115–48.

Hills, Alison (2009). 'Moral Testimony and Moral Epistemology'. *Ethics* 120 (1): 94–127.

Hooker, Brad (2000). *Ideal Code, Real World*. Oxford: Oxford University Press.

Hornsby, Jennifer (1981). 'Which Physical Events are Mental Events?' *Proceedings of the Aristotelian Society* 55: 73–92.

Howard-Snyder, Frances (1997). 'The Rejection of Objective Consequentialism'. *Utilitas* 9 (2): 241–8.

Howard-Snyder, Frances (2005). 'It's the Thought that Counts'. *Utilitas* 17 (3): 265–81.

Hudson, James L. (1989). 'Subjectivization in Ethics'. *American Philosophical Quarterly* 26 (3): 221–9.

Husak, Douglas (2011). 'Negligence, Belief, Blame and Criminal Liability: The Special Case of Forgetting'. *Criminal Law and Philosophy* 5 (2): 199–218.

Jackson, Frank (1986). 'A Probabilistic Approach to Moral Responsibility'. *Studies in Logic and the Foundations of Mathematics* 114: 351–65.

Jackson, Frank (1991). 'Decision-Theoretic Consequentialism and the Nearest and Dearest Objection'. *Ethics* 101 (3): 461–82.

Jackson, Frank (2001). 'How Decision Theory Illuminates Assignments of Moral Responsibility'. In Ngaire Naffine, Rosemary J. Owens, and John Williams (eds.), *Intention in Law and Philosophy*. Aldershot: Ashgate: 19–36.

Jackson, Frank and Smith, Michael (2006). 'Absolutist Moral Theories and Uncertainty'. *Journal of Philosophy*, 103 (6): 267–83.

Kahneman, D. and Tversky, A. (1972). 'Subjective Probability: A Judgment of Representativeness'. *Cognitive Psychology* 3 (3): 430–54.

Kavka, Gregory S. (1983). 'The Toxin Puzzle'. *Analysis* 43 (1): 33–6.

Kennett, Jeanette (2002). 'Autism, Empathy and Moral Agency'. *Philosophical Quarterly* 52 (208): 340–57.

King, Matt (2009). 'The Problem with Negligence'. *Social Theory and Practice* 35 (4): 577–95.

Kolodny, Niko and MacFarlane, John (2010). 'Ifs and Oughts'. *Journal of Philosophy* 107 (3): 115–43.

Lenman, James (2006). 'Compatibilism and Contractualism: The Possibility of Moral Responsibility'. *Ethics* 117 (1): 7–31.

Levy, Neil (2005). 'The Good, the Bad, and the Blameworthy'. *Journal of Ethics and Social Philosophy* 1 (2): 1–16.

Levy, Neil (2007). 'The Responsibility of the Psychopath Revisited'. *Philosophy, Psychiatry, and Psychology* 14 (2): 129–38.

Levy, Neil (2011). *Hard Luck: How Luck Undermines Free Will and Moral Responsibility.* Oxford: Oxford University Press.

Levy, Neil (2013). 'The Importance of Awareness'. *Australasian Journal of Philosophy* 91 (2): 221–9.

Lewis, David (1976). 'The Paradoxes of Time Travel'. *American Philosophical Quarterly* 13 (2): 145–52.

Lockhart, Ted (2000). *Moral Uncertainty and Its Consequences.* Oxford: Oxford University Press.

Lord, Errol (2015). 'Acting for the Right Reasons, Abilities, and Obligation'. In Russ Shafer-Landau (ed.), *Oxford Studies in Metaethics*, vol. 10. Oxford: Oxford University Press: 26–52.

Lord, Errol (2017). 'On The Intellectual Conditions for Responsibility: Acting for the Right Reasons, Conceptualization, and Credit'. *Philosophy and Phenomenological Research* 95 (2): 436–64.

Lyons, David (1965). *Forms and Limits of Utilitarianism.* Oxford: Clarendon Press.

McConnell, Terrance (1989). '"Ought" Implies "Can" and the Scope of Moral Requirements'. *Philosophia* 19: 437–54.

McGeer, Victoria (2007). 'Varieties of Moral Agency: Lessons from Autism (and Psychopathy)'. in Walter Sinnott-Armstrong (ed.), *Moral Psychology, Vol. 3: The Neuroscience of Morality: Emotion, Disease and Development.* Cambridge, MA: MIT Press: 227–57.

McGeer, Victoria and Pettit, Philip (2015). 'The Hard Problem of Responsibility'. In David Shoemaker (ed.), *Oxford Studies in Agency and Responsibility*, vol. 3. Oxford: Oxford University Press: 160–88.

McGrath, Sarah (2009). 'The Puzzle of Pure Moral Deference'. *Philosophical Perspectives* 23 (1): 321–44.

McKenna, Michael (2005). 'Where Frankfurt and Strawson Meet'. *Midwest Studies in Philosophy* 29 (1): 163–80.

McKenna, Michael (2008). 'Putting the Lie on the Control Condition for Moral Responsibility'. *Philosophical Studies* 139: 29–37.

McKenna, Michael (2012). *Conversation and Responsibility.* Oxford: Oxford University Press.

Macnamara, Coleen (2015a). 'Reactive Attitudes as Communicative Entities'. *Philosophy and Phenomenological Research* 90 (3): 546–69.

Macnamara, Coleen (2015b). 'Blame, Communication and Morally Responsible Agency'. In Randolph Clarke, Michael McKenna, and Angela Smith (eds.), *The Nature of Moral Responsibility.* New York: Oxford University Press: 211–36.

Markovits, Julia (2010). 'Acting for the Right Reasons'. *Philosophical Review* 119 (2): 201–42.

Mason, Elinor (2002). 'Against Blameless Wrongdoing'. *Ethical Theory and Moral Practice* 5: 287–303.

Mason, Elinor (2003). 'Consequentialism and the "Ought Implies Can" Principle'. *American Philosophical Quarterly* 40: 319–31.

Mason, Elinor (2008). 'An Argument against Motivational Internalism'. *Proceedings of the Aristotelian Society* 108: 135–56.

Mason, Elinor (2012). 'Coercion and Integrity'. In Mark Timmons (ed.), *Oxford Studies in Normative Ethics*, vol. 2. Oxford: Oxford University Press: 180–205.

Mason, Elinor (2013). 'Objectivism and Prospectivism about Rightness'. *Journal of Ethics and Social Philosophy*, 7 (2): 1–22.

Mason, Elinor (2015). 'Moral Ignorance and Blameworthiness'. *Philosophical Studies* 172: 3037–57.

Mason, Elinor (2016). 'Moral Incapacity and Moral Ignorance'. In Rik Peels (ed.), *Perspectives on Ignorance from Moral and Social Philosophy*. New York: Routledge: 30–52.

Mason, Elinor (2017). 'Do the Right Thing: An Account of Subjective Obligation'. In Mark Timmons (ed.), *Oxford Studies in Normative Ethics*, vol. 7. Oxford: Oxford University Press: 117–37.

Mason, Elinor (2018). 'Respecting Each Other and Taking Responsibility for our Biases'. In Marina Oshana, Katrina Hutchison, and Catriona Mackenzie (eds.), *Social Dimensions of Moral Responsibility*. Oxford: Oxford University Press: 163–84.

Mason, Elinor (2019a). 'Consequentialism and Moral Responsibility'. In Christian Seidel (ed.), *Consequentialism: New Directions, New Problems?* Oxford: Oxford University Press: 219–34.

Mason, Elinor (2019b). 'Between Strict Liability and Blameworthy Quality of Will: Taking Responsibility'. In David Shoemaker (ed.), *Oxford Studies in Agency and Responsibility*, vol. 6. Oxford: Oxford University Press.

Mason, Elinor and Wilson, Alan T. (2017). 'Vice, Blameworthiness, and Cultural Ignorance'. In Philip Robichaud and Jan Willem Wieland (eds.), *Responsibility: The Epistemic Condition*. Oxford: Oxford University Press: 82–100.

Mason, Michelle (2003). 'Contempt as a Moral Attitude'. *Ethics* 113: 234–72.

Mason, Michelle (2011). 'Blame: Taking it Seriously'. *Philosophy and Phenomenological Research*, 83: 473–81.

Mele, Alfred (2003). 'Agent's Abilities'. *Noûs* 37: 447–70.

Mill, John Stuart (1863). *Utilitarianism*. London: Parker, Son & Bourne.

Miller, D. E. (2003). 'Actual-Consequence Act Utilitarianism and the Best Possible Humans'. *Ratio* 16: 49–62.

Mills, Charles (2007). 'White Ignorance'. In Shannon Sullivan Nancy Tuana (ed.), *Race and Epistemologies of Ignorance*. Albany: State University of New York Press: 11–38.

Milton, John (1664). *Paradise Lost*.

Montmarquet, James (1999). 'Zimmerman on Culpable Ignorance'. *Ethics* 109 (4): 842–5.

Moody-Adams, M. (1994). 'Culture, Responsibility, and Affected Ignorance'. *Ethics* 104: 291–309.

Moore, G. E. (1903). *Principia Ethica* (Revised edition with 'Preface to the second edition' and other papers, ed. T. Baldwin, Cambridge: Cambridge University Press, 1993).

Moore, G. E. (1912). *Ethics*. London: Williams and Norgate.

Moore, M. S. and Hurd, H. M. (2011). 'Blaming the Stupid, Clumsy, Selfish and Weak: The Culpability of Negligence'. *Criminal Law and Philosophy* 5 (2): 147–98.

Nelkin, Dana Kay (2011). *Making Sense of Freedom and Responsibility*. Oxford: Oxford University Press.

Nelkin, Dana Kay (2015). 'Psychopaths, Incorrigible Racists, and the Faces of Responsibility'. *Ethics* 125: 357–90.

Nelkin, Dana Kay (2016). 'Difficulty and Degrees of Moral Praiseworthiness and Blameworthiness'. *Noûs* 50 (2): 356–78.

Norcross, Alastair (2006). 'The Scalar Approach to Utilitarianism'. In Henry West (ed.), *Blackwell Guide to Mill's Utilitarianism*. Oxford: Oxford University Press: 217–32.

Norcross, Alastair (forthcoming). *Morality by Degrees: Reasons Without Demands*. Oxford: Oxford University Press.

Nucci, L. and Turiel, E. (1978). 'Social Interactions and the Development of Social Concepts in Preschool Children'. *Child Development* 49 (2): 400–7.

Oddie, Graham and Menzies, Peter (1992). 'An Objectivist's Guide to Subjective Value'. *Ethics* 102: 512–33.

Oshana, Marina (1997). 'Ascriptions of Responsibility'. *American Philosophical Quarterly* 34 (1): 71–83.

Oshana, Marina (2004). 'Moral Accountability'. *Philosophical Topics* 32 (1/2): 255–74.

Oshana, Marina (2006). 'Moral Taint'. *Metaphilosophy* 37: 353–75.

O'Shaughnessy, Brian (1980). *The Will: A Dual Aspect Theory*. Cambridge: Cambridge University Press.

Owens, David (2012). *Shaping the Normative Landscape*. Oxford: Oxford University Press.

Parfit, Derek (2011). *On What Matters*, vol. 1. Oxford: Oxford University Press.

Peels, Rik (2010). 'What Is Ignorance?' *Philosophia* 38 (1): 57–67.

Pereboom, Derk (2001). *Living without Free Will*. Cambridge: Cambridge University Press.

Pereboom, Derk (2014). *Free Will, Agency, and Meaning in Life*. Oxford: Oxford University Press.

Persson, Ingmar (2008). 'A Consequentialist Distinction between What We Ought to Do and Ought to Try'. *Utilitas* 20: 348–55.

Portmore, Douglas (2011). *Commonsense Consequentialism*. Oxford: Oxford University Press.

Prichard, H. A. (1932). 'Duty and Ignorance of Fact'. Reprinted in Prichard, *Moral Writings*. Oxford: Clarendon Press, 2002: 84–101.

Railton, Peter (1984). 'Alienation, Consequentialism, and the Demands of Morality'. *Philosophy & Public Affairs* 13 (2): 134–71.

Raz, J. (2010). 'Responsibility and the Negligence Standard'. *Oxford Journal of Legal Studies* 30 (1): 1–18.

Raz, J. (2011). *From Normativity to Responsibility*. Oxford: Oxford University Press.

Regan, Donald (1980). *Utilitarianism and Co-operation*. Oxford: Clarendon Press.

Reis-Dennis, S. (2018). 'Responsibility and the Shallow Self'. *Philosophical Studies* 175 (2): 483–501.

Rosati, Connie S. (2016). 'Moral Motivation'. In *The Stanford Encyclopedia of Philosophy* (Winter 2016 Edition), ed. Edward N. Zalta. <https://plato.stan ford.edu/archives/win2016/entries/moral-motivation/>.

Rosen, Gideon (2002). 'Culpability and Ignorance'. *Proceedings of the Aristotelian Society* 103 (1): 61–84.

Rosen, Gideon (2004). 'Skepticism about Moral Responsibility'. *Philosophical Perspectives* 18 (1): 295–313.

Rosen, Gideon (2008). 'Kleinbart the Oblivious and Other Tales of Ignorance and Responsibility'. *Journal of Philosophy* 105 (10): 591–610.

Ross, W. D. (1930). *The Right and the Good*. Oxford: Oxford University Press.

Ross, W. D. (1939). *Foundations of Ethics*. Oxford: Clarendon Press, reprint 1968.

Sartorio, Carolina (2015). 'Sensitivity to Reasons and Actual Sequences'. In David Shoemaker (ed.), *Oxford Studies in Agency and Responsibility*, vol. 3. Oxford: Oxford University Press: 104–19.

Scanlon, T. M. (1998). *What We Owe to Each Other*. Cambridge, MA: Harvard University Press.

Scanlon, T. M. (2008). *Moral Dimensions: Permissibility, Meaning, Blame*. Cambridge, MA: Belknap Press.

Scanlon, T. M. (2013). 'Interpreting Blame'. In D. Justin Coates and Neal A. Tognazzini (eds.), *Blame: Its Nature and Norms*. Oxford: Oxford University Press: 84–99.

Scheffler, Samuel (2010). 'Valuing'. In Scheffler, *Equality and Tradition: Questions of Value in Moral and Political Theory*. Oxford: Oxford University Press: 15–40.

Schoeman, F. (ed.) (1987). *Responsibility, Character, and the Emotions: New Essays in Moral Psychology*. Cambridge: Cambridge University Press.

Sepielli, Andrew (2009). 'What to Do When You Don't Know What to Do'. In Russ Shafer-Landau (ed.), *Oxford Studies in Metaethics*, vol. 4. Oxford: Oxford University Press: 5–28.

Sepielli, Andrew (2012). 'Subjective Normativity and Action Guidance'. In Mark Timmons (ed.), *Oxford Studies in Normative Ethics*, vol. 2. Oxford: Oxford University Press: 45–72.

Shabo, Seth (2012). 'Where Love and Resentment Meet: Strawson's Intrapersonal Defense of Compatibilism'. *Philosophical Review* 121 (1): 95–124.

Sher, George (2006). *In Praise of Blame*. Oxford: Oxford University Press.

Sher, George (2009). *Who Knew?: Responsibility Without Awareness*. Oxford: Oxford University Press.

Shoemaker, David (2011). 'Attributability, Answerability, and Accountability: Toward a Wider Theory of Moral Responsibility'. *Ethics* 121 (3): 602–32.

Shoemaker, David (2015). *Responsibility from the Margins*. Oxford: Oxford University Press.

Sidgwick, H. (1874). *The Methods of Ethics*. Reprinted: Indianapolis, IN: Hackett, 1981.

Sliwa, Paulina (2016). 'Moral Worth and Moral Knowledge'. *Philosophy and Phenomenological Research* 93 (2): 393–418.

Smart, J. J. C. (1961). 'Free Will, Praise and Blame'. *Mind* 70 (279): 291–306.

Smart, J. J. C. (1973). 'An Outline of a System of Utilitarian Ethics'. In J. J. C. Smart and Bernard Williams, *Utilitarianism: For and Against*. Cambridge: Cambridge University Press: 3–74.

Smith, Angela M. (2005). 'Responsibility for Attitudes: Activity and Passivity in Mental Life'. *Ethics* 115: 236–71.

Smith, Angela M. (2008). 'Control, Responsibility, and Moral Assessment'. *Philosophical Studies* 138: 367–92.

Smith, Angela M. (2010). 'Who Knew? Responsibility Without Awareness'. *Social Theory and Practice* 36 (3): 515–24.

Smith, Angela M. (2012). 'Attributability, Answerability, and Accountability: In Defense of a Unified Account'. *Ethics* 122 (3): 575–89.

Smith, Angela M. (2013). 'Moral Blame and Moral Protest'. In D. Justin Coates and Neal A. Tognazzini (eds.), *Blame: Its Nature and Norms*. Oxford: Oxford University Press: 27–48.

Smith, Holly (1983). 'Culpable Ignorance'. *Philosophical Review* 92 (4): 543–71.

Smith, Holly (1988). 'Making Moral Decisions'. *Noûs* 22: 89–108.

Smith, Holly (1989). 'Two-Tier Moral Codes'. *Social Philosophy and Policy* 7: 112–32.

Smith, Holly (1991a). 'Varieties of Moral Worth and Moral Credit'. *Ethics* 101: 279–303.

Smith, Holly (1991b). 'Deciding How To Decide: Is There a Regress Problem?' In Michael Bacharach and Susan Hurley (eds.), *Essays in the Foundations of Decision Theory*. Oxford: Basil Blackwell: 194–219.

Smith, Holly (2010). 'Subjective Rightness'. *Social Philosophy and Policy* 27 (2): 64–110.

Smith, Holly (2011a). 'The "Prospective View" of Obligation'. *Journal of Ethics and Social Philosophy* 5 (1) (online): 1–9.

Smith, Holly (2011b). 'Non-Tracing Cases of Culpable Ignorance'. *Criminal Law and Philosophy* 5 (2): 115–46.

Smith, Holly (2012). 'Using Moral Principles to Guide Decisions'. *Philosophical Issues* 22: 369–86.

Smith, Holly (2014). 'The Subjective Moral Duty to Inform Oneself before Acting'. *Ethics* 125: 1–28.

Smith, Holly (2018). *Making Morality Work*. Oxford: Oxford University Press.

Sorensen, Roy (1995). 'Unknowable Obligations'. *Utilitas* 7 (2): 247–71.

Strawson, P. F. (1962). 'Freedom and Resentment'. *Proceedings of the British Academy* 48: 187–211.

Tadros, Victor (2007). *Criminal Responsibility*. Oxford: Oxford University Press.

Talbert, Matthew (2008). 'Blame and Responsiveness to Moral Reasons: Are Psychopaths Blameworthy?' *Pacific Philosophical Quarterly* 89: 516–35.

Talbert, Matthew (2012a). 'Moral Competence, Moral Blame, and Protest'. *Journal of Ethics* 16 (1): 89–109.

Talbert, Matthew (2012b). 'Accountability, Aliens, and Psychopaths: A Reply to Shoemaker'. *Ethics* 122 (3): 562–74.

Tannenbaum, Julie (2015). 'Mere Moral Failure'. *Canadian Journal of Philosophy* 45 (1): 58–84.

Taylor, Gabrielle (1996). 'Guilt and Remorse'. In Rom Harré and W. Gerrod Parrot (eds.), *The Emotions*. London: Sage: 57–73.

Timmons, Mark (2012). *Moral Theory: An Introduction*, 2nd edition. Lanham, MD: Rowman & Littlefield.

Tooley, Michael (1972). 'Abortion and Infanticide'. *Philosophy & Public Affairs* 2 (1): 37–65.

Vargas, Manuel (2005). 'The Trouble with Tracing'. *Midwest Studies in Philosophy* 29 (1): 269–91.

Vargas, Manuel (2013). *Building Better Beings: A Theory of Moral Responsibility*. Oxford: Oxford University Press.

Wallace, R. Jay (1994). *Responsibility and the Moral Sentiments*. Cambridge, MA: Harvard University Press.

Wallace, R. Jay (2011). 'Dispassionate Opprobrium: On Blame and the Reactive Sentiments'. In R. Jay Wallace, Rahul Kumar, and Samuel Freeman (eds.), *Reasons and Recognition: Essays on the Philosophy of T. M. Scanlon*. New York: Oxford University Press: 348–72.

Watson, Gary (1987). 'Responsibility and the Limits of Evil: Variations on a Strawsonian Theme'. In F. Schoeman (ed.), *Responsibility, Character, and the Emotions: Essays in Moral Psychology*. Cambridge: Cambridge University Press: 256-86 (reprinted in Watson 2004).

Watson, Gary (1996). 'Two Faces of Responsibility'. *Philosophical Topics* 24 (2): 227-48 (reprinted in Watson 2004).

Watson, Gary (ed.) (2003). *Free Will*, 2nd ed. Oxford: Oxford University Press.

Watson, Gary (2004). *Agency and Answerability*. Oxford: Clarendon Press.

Watson, Gary (2011). 'The Trouble with Psychopaths'. In R. Jay Wallace, Rahul Kumar, and Samuel Freeman (eds.), *Reasons and Recognition: Essays on the Philosophy of T. M. Scanlon*. New York: Oxford University Press: 307-31.

Watson, Gary (2013). 'Psychopathic Agency and Prudential Deficits'. *Proceedings of the Aristotelian Society* 113: 269-92.

Wiland, Eric (2005). 'Monkeys, Typewriters, and Objective Consequentialism'. *Ratio* 18 (3): 352-60.

Williams, Bernard (1973). *Problems of the Self*. Cambridge: Cambridge University Press.

Williams, Bernard (1981). *Moral Luck*. Cambridge: Cambridge University Press.

Williams, Bernard (1993). *Shame and Necessity*. Berkeley, CA: University of California Press.

Williams, Bernard (1995). *Making Sense of Humanity*. Cambridge: Cambridge University Press.

Wolf, Susan (1987). 'Sanity and the Metaphysics of Responsibility'. In F. Schoeman (ed.), *Responsibility, Character, and the Emotions: New Essays in Moral Psychology*. Cambridge: Cambridge University Press: 46-62.

Wolf, Susan (1990). *Freedom Within Reason*. Oxford: Oxford University Press.

Wolf, Susan (2001). 'The Moral of Moral Luck'. *Philosophic Exchange* 31 (1): 1-16.

Wolf, Susan (2011). 'Blame, Italian Style'. In R. Jay Wallace, Rahul Kumar, and Samuel Freeman (eds.), *Reasons and Recognition: Essays on the Philosophy of T. M. Scanlon*. New York: Oxford University Press: 332-47.

Young, Iris Marion (1990). *Justice and the Politics of Difference*. Princeton, NJ: Princeton University Press.

Zimmerman, Michael J. (1986). 'Negligence and Moral Responsibility'. *Noûs* 20: 199-218.

Zimmerman, Michael J. (1988). *An Essay on Moral Responsibility*. Lanham, MD: Rowman & Littlefield.

Zimmerman, Michael J. (1997). 'Moral Responsibility and Ignorance'. *Ethics* 107 (3): 410-26.

Zimmerman, Michael J. (2006). 'Is Moral Obligation Objective or Subjective?'
    Utilitas 18 (4): 329–61.
Zimmerman, Michael J. (2008). *Living with Uncertainty*. Cambridge: Cambridge
    University Press.
Zimmerman, Michael J. (2014). *Ignorance and Moral Obligation*. Oxford: Oxford
    University Press.

Name Index

Index

Printed and bound by CPI Group (UK) Ltd, Croydon, CR0 4YY